T0282930

Nonprofit Bookkeeping & Accounting

2nd Edition

by Maire Loughran, CPA
Sharon Farris, author of the first edition

A Wiley Brand

Nonprofit Bookkeeping & Accounting For Dummies®, 2nd Edition

Published by: **John Wiley & Sons, Inc.**, 111 River Street, Hoboken, NJ 07030-5774, www.wiley.com

Copyright © 2024 by John Wiley & Sons, Inc., Hoboken, New Jersey

Media and software compilation copyright © 2024 by John Wiley & Sons, Inc. All rights reserved.

Published simultaneously in Canada

For general information on our other products and services, please contact our Customer Care Department within the U.S. at 877-762-2974, outside the U.S. at 317-572-3993, or fax 317-572-4002. For technical support, please visit https://hub.wiley.com/community/support/dummies.

Wiley publishes in a variety of print and electronic formats and by print-on-demand. Some material included with standard print versions of this book may not be included in e-books or in print-on-demand. If this book refers to media such as a CD or DVD that is not included in the version you purchased, you may download this material at http://booksupport.wiley.com. For more information about Wiley products, visit www.wiley.com.

Library of Congress Control Number: 2023943486

ISBN 978-1-394-20601-8 (pbk); ISBN 978-1-394-20602-5 (ebk); ISBN 978-1-394-20607-0 (ebk)

SKY10081997_081424

Contents at a Glance

Table of Contents

Introduction

Counting the money in your wallet or purse is an act of accounting. And if you ever make a note of how much you have, you're performing a bookkeeping function. You count things all the time in everyday life without thinking twice about accounting. For example, you count the plates before setting the table at home. You count the number of emails you receive while you're out of the office. Even a gesture such as looking at your watch and thinking about how much time you have before your next appointment is a form of accounting.

Bookkeeping and accounting involve general accounting, cost accounting, budgeting, and internal auditing. Even though your organization is a nonprofit, these services are essential parts of your daily activities. Adjacent to bookkeeping and accounting tasks and important for most nonprofits are external auditing, tax return preparation, and management advisory services.

In the wake of increasing nonprofit accountability, understanding how to track and account for the everyday activities of your nonprofit is important. Keeping the books for a nonprofit is exciting. Getting federal grant money to fund your programs relieves financial stress. Getting a clean bill of health from your financial audit adds credibility.

About This Book

Bookkeeping and accounting for nonprofits involves several fundamental steps. Beginning with a simple transaction such as a donation and ending with financial statements, you go through a yearly accounting cycle of 12 months. The cycle repeats as long as your nonprofit continues to operate.

This book explains normal day-to-day transactions, preparing financial statements, and getting ready for audits. It also discusses keeping your books using a manual or automated system. Thus, this book is helpful for nonprofit directors, managers, bookkeepers, and accountants.

This book is designed to help you with everything you need to know to operate your nonprofit according to generally accepted accounting principles (GAAP). It covers information about the steps to file your own payroll taxes and federal tax Form 990. It also explains how to account for many different nonprofit situations.

This book is a reference tool you can pick up from time to time during your accounting cycle to brush up on the following nonprofit events:

>> Entering into a transaction with a second party

>> Preparing a business document, such as a sales invoice, that leaves a paper trail

>> Recording a transaction in a journal, which is the book of original entry

>> Posting journals to the general ledger

>> Reporting on financial statements

>> Paying taxes and getting ready for audits

This book serves as a reference tool, no matter where you are in the accounting process, by helping you reach your ultimate goal of accurate financial statements.

Within this book, you may note that some web addresses break across two lines of text. If you're reading this book in print and want to visit one of these web pages, simply key in the web address exactly as it's noted in the text, pretending as though the line break doesn't exist. If you're reading this as an e-book, you've got it easy — just click the web address to be taken directly to the web page.

Foolish Assumptions

I assume you don't have more than a rudimentary knowledge of nonprofit accounting, and I'm guessing you're one of the following people:

>> The executive director of a newly formed, small nonprofit, wanting to know how to manage your own books

>> The director or manager of a midsize nonprofit wanting to understand a little more about how to manage day-to-day accounting operations

>> Someone interested in seeking employment keeping the books of a nonprofit organization

>> Someone interested in bookkeeping and accounting as a profession

>> Someone who has already been performing the functions in this book who's not sure if they've been doing them correctly

>> Someone who's thinking about starting their own nonprofit and wanting to know how an effective nonprofit keeps track of its bookkeeping and accounting needs

Icons Used in This Book

Throughout the book, you see the following icons in the margins:

TIP

Text accompanied by the Tip icon contains useful hints you can apply to make handling your nonprofit a bit easier and more successful.

REMEMBER

When you see the Remember icon, warm up your brain cells, because this icon sits next to information you want to commit to memory.

WARNING

Looking for what not to do in the world of nonprofit accounting? Check out paragraphs next to the Warning icon, because they alert you to what can trip you up while working in the field.

TECHNICAL STUFF

The Technical Stuff icon includes information that enhances the topic under discussion but isn't necessary to understand the topic. If you're short on time, you can skip anything marked with this icon.

Beyond the Book

In addition to the material in the print or e-book you're reading right now, this product also comes with a free Cheat Sheet that covers the three key nonprofit financial statements, as well as important terms and definitions. To get this Cheat Sheet, simply go to www.dummies.com and type **Nonprofit Bookkeeping & Accounting For Dummies Cheat Sheet** in the Search box.

Where to Go from Here

If you're a nonprofit director wanting to find out how to start keeping your books, turn to Chapter 2 on basic bookkeeping, Chapter 7 on balancing your checkbook, or Chapter 5 on setting up your chart of accounts. If securing a federal grant is on your mind, head to Chapter 11. Check out the table of contents or index for a topic that interests you, or jump in anywhere to find the nonprofit accounting or bookkeeping information you're wondering about.

1

Accounting and Bookkeeping Nonprofit-Style

Brush up on basic accounting terminology and financial statements.

Account for your nonprofit's activities using either a manual recordkeeping system or a sophisticated computerized system.

Understand the difference between a debit and a credit.

Find out how to expense assets and which steps you should follow to keep your accounting books in order.

Get a basic understanding of the bookkeeping and accounting processing you need to master to get an approved audit.

IN THIS CHAPTER

» Getting an overview of bookkeeping and accounting

» Performing a balancing act with your books

» Hitting up Uncle Sam for some free money

» Paying payroll taxes to the IRS

» Closing the year with financial statements

Chapter **1**

Introducing Nonprofit Bookkeeping and Accounting

Your accounting period indicates the beginning and end of your reporting period. This period can be usually 6, 12, or 18 months depending on your company's needs. Let's assume you chose the most common reporting period of 12 months; this period can be a calendar year ending from January to December or a fiscal year ending using another 12-month period. If you use the calendar year, the first transaction on January 1 starts your accounting cycle, and your last transaction on December 31 ends the cycle. You compile your financial statements after the cycle ends, perhaps get your financial statements audited, and start the cycle all over again.

Being a good steward for your nonprofit requires that your books are materially correct. To make this happen, you need sound financial management by qualified employees, independent accountants, and other consultants. This chapter serves as a jumping-off point into the world of nonprofit bookkeeping and accounting and touches on the important concepts. Subsequent chapters dive deeper into these topics.

Getting Started with Your Nonprofit's Books

Before you start, keep in mind your goal, which most likely is the preparation of financial statements. The road to finalizing a set of financial statements begins with journalizing an event that happens in your nonprofit — for example, your nonprofit receives a donation or writes a check to pay the telephone bill. (See Chapter 8 for more information about journals and journal entries.)

TIP

Every financial transaction creates a record or document to support its occurrence/existence, accuracy, valuation, completeness, rights, and obligations (also known as *management assertions*). Adapting the habits of a pack rat isn't a bad idea when it comes to keeping up with your paperwork. For at least three years, hold on to every accounting document after you record it in the proper journal. Some nonprofits have a five-year record retention policy. For any asset you may purchase (such as a computer, a building, or a vehicle), you should keep all records related to the asset until you dispose of the asset and file the subsequent tax return reflecting the disposition.

REMEMBER

The central location of transactions can be your checking account, showing deposits from donors or checks written to pay the bills and can be an important key to tracking accounting transactions. (Check out Chapter 7 to find out how to manage and balance a checking account.)

Just as important is keeping in mind the users of your financial statements and their needs. Nonprofit users can fall into three categories:

>> Existing or potential donors

>> Individuals or businesses thinking about extending credit terms to your nonprofit

>> Governmental agencies, such as the Internal Revenue Service (IRS), which want to make sure your nonprofit is fairly presenting its financial position (See Chapter 13 for information about compliance and fair presentation.)

All users share a common need: They need assurance that the information on your nonprofit's statements (see Chapters 17 through 20) are both materially correct and useful. In a nutshell, to be *materially correct*, the financial statements can't contain any serious or significant errors that could impact the decisions of its users. In order to be *useful*, the information has to be understandable to anyone not closely related to the nonprofit's day-to-day activities.

Identifying the difference between bookkeeping and accounting

Before you determine your role in the accounting cycle, you need to have a firm understanding of bookkeeping and accounting. In the following sections, I cover the main differences.

Bookkeeping

Bookkeepers are paraprofessionals who work in accounting. No specific education, experience, or licensing is required for this designation. Many bookkeepers learn accounting by starting off in the accounts payable or accounts receivable department, filling in accounting knowledge as they go along.

They record day-to-day activities in the accounting cycle and carry out routine tasks (such as paying bills, making deposits at the bank, or reconciling bank statements). Bookkeepers may record transactions when cash changes hands, called the cash basis of accounting or maintain the books on the *accrual basis*. (The next section of this chapter and Chapter 2 provide more insight on cash versus accrual.) Usually bookkeepers pass the books to the accountant at the end of the accounting period to generate financial statements.

TIP

Depending on their knowledge, some bookkeepers prepare financial statements, which are then reviewed and adjusted by an in-house accountant or by an independent certified public accountant (CPA) hired by the nonprofit.

Accounting

Accountants handle an array of tasks, including managing cash receipts and payments, tracking assets, preparing financial statements and budgets, or governmental reporting. Accountants generally have a four-year university degree in accounting with a certain number of accounting-based credit hours (which varies depending on what that particular university requires).

Accounting isn't complicated mathematics; it's adding, subtracting, dividing, and multiplying, or grasping the nuances of entering information into accounting software. The accounting professionalism comes into play when applying generally accepted accounting principles (see the "Adhering to GAAP and GAAS" section, later in this chapter) to decide how to handle accounting transactions.

Many nonprofit accounting transactions are simple exchanges of cash or credit for a good or service, but there can be situations in which accountants have to dig a bit deeper into the right way to handle a particular transaction. Examples of this may be elimination of funds for reporting purposes, whether donor stipulations make the gift conditional, or how to handle customer revenue contracts. (Don't worry, I discuss all this and more in Chapters 6 and 8.) A bookkeeper may not be able to analyze accounts, but they can record the transaction after receiving guidance from the accountant.

Another important consideration is that accountants get paid more than bookkeepers. Your nonprofit may be better served by having a bookkeeper on your payroll to perform day-to-day functions and an accountant on retainer to put together reports on a quarterly or annual basis.

Some accountants opt to take the Uniform CPA Examination. This standardized examination is developed, maintained, and scored by the American Institute of Certified Public Accountants (AICPA). It contains four parts:

>> Auditing and Attestation

>> Business Environment and Concepts (business law)

>> Financial Accounting and Reporting (the main topic of this book)

>> Regulation (taxation)

Accountants who pass the test are called CPAs. CPAs are the only individuals who can audit your financial statements. To maintain this licensure, the CPA must take 80 hours of continuing education, including an ethics course, every two years.

REMEMBER

Don't be intimidated by CPAs because they have passed this tough exam. Use their knowledge and ask questions about your nonprofit issues. That's what you're paying them for!

Picking your accounting method

It's important to distinguish between the key accounting methods. Your *accounting method* determines when you record activities. For a nonprofit the key methods are either cash or accrual:

>> **Cash basis:** Records transactions only when cash is received or paid

>> **Accrual basis:** Records revenues when they're earned, expenses when they're used, and purchases when they take place

Using the cash method is quite easy. However, the ease of using the cash method is offset by two important facts:

>> If your nonprofit is required to have audited financial statements, cash-based books must be converted to accrual.

>> Because the cash method doesn't match donations or any other program income to expenses that the nonprofit incurs to earn that income, cash basis financial statements usually do not present as accurate a picture of how the nonprofit is carrying out its mission as accrual method statements do.

Let's say in March, your nonprofit has pledged donations of $50,000 and expenses totaling $35,000 associating with those donations. Donations for $40,000 were received in cash, and the entire $35,000 in expenses was paid. Using the cash method, your nonprofit shows $5,000 of net income.

Under the accrual method, you record income under the revenue recognition guidelines set forth in the Financial Accounting Standards Board (FASB) Accounting Standards Codification (ASC) Topic 958. (You find out more about FASB and ASC in Chapter 14.)

Unconditional contributions (donations for which the donor has placed no restrictions on their use), including the promise to give, are recorded as income as soon as you receive the cash or pledge. It gets slightly more complicated when the donor imposes conditions on the use of the donation (for example, if the donor states that a future and uncertain event has to occur in order for the nonprofit to be able to retain the donation). Conditional donations are usually only recognized as income when the conditions set by the donor are materially met.

The accrual method takes cash out of the equation, because money changing hands doesn't determine if you recognize a transaction. As a result, a nonprofit keeping accrual-based books will have an accounts receivable, which shows that donations and other program income are owed to the nonprofit, and an accounts payable, which shows all the money the nonprofit owes to its vendors.

Using the same example as shown earlier for the cash method, under the accrual method, your nonprofit shows $15,000 of income ($50,000 − $35,000). For this example, the difference is relatively small — $10,000 ($15,000 − $5,000) — but proportionately the difference is 67 percent, which is material.

Check out Chapter 2 for more in-depth discussion about these two methods and which one may be best for your nonprofit.

WARNING

KEEPING WATCH OVER YOUR NONPROFIT'S FINANCES

Sometimes nonprofit directors and managers feel they don't have the knowledge to do their own books, so they turn everything over to a CPA. This book gives you the help you need to do some of your nonprofit's basic bookkeeping and accounting. However, you may rightfully need a licensed professional to help with the more technical aspects of keeping your nonprofits books. Certainly, you will need an independent CPA if you need a set of audited financial statements. (See Chapter 14 for more information about financial statement audits.)

Understanding the basic terms

Before jumping into doing the bookkeeping and accounting, let's walk through some basic terminology, accounting procedures, and processes. This section introduces you to important concepts, all of which I discuss at length in subsequent chapters in this book.

To begin, it's important to understand that accounting is based on a double-entry system. That means that for every action, there must be an equal reaction. In other words, if you add $4,000 in assets by buying a new computer using store credit, there must be a corresponding $4,000 entry showing the nonprofit has an obligation to pay this debt. (Check out Chapter 2 for more info on double-entry accounting.)

In accounting lingo, these actions and reactions are called *debits* and *credits*. You find out more about them in the "Logging debits and credits" section, later in this chapter, as well as in Chapter 6.

Classifying your transactions

When classifying your transactions, all of them will generally fit into five different types of accounts:

>> Assets

>> Liabilities

>> Net assets

>> Revenue

>> Expenses

First, I walk you through assets, liabilities, and net assets, which show up on the statement of financial position. Then I walk you through revenue and expenses, which show up on the statement of activities.

ASSETS, LIABILITIES, AND NET ASSETS

Assets are accounts for items your nonprofit owns or that adds value. An asset adds value, whether it's monetary or not. Common examples of nonprofit assets are

» Accounts receivable

» Buildings

» Cash

» Equipment

» Furniture

» Inventory

» Pledges receivable

» Prepaid expenses

» Property (land)

» Vehicles

Liabilities are debt your nonprofit owes or other items that in some way reduce equity. A liability is something the nonprofit owes or has an obligation in terms of time, money, or resources. Anything that must be paid is considered a liability. Some common nonprofit liabilities are

» Accounts payables

» Accrued expenses

» Car notes

» Mortgages

» Notes payable

» Short-term payables

Net assets are the difference between assets and liabilities. In the for-profit world, net assets are called *retained earnings* or *owners' equity*, which is net earnings or loss over the years less dividends paid to shareholders. Nonprofits do not have owners, so the term *owner's equity* is replaced with *net assets*.

A nonprofit must also break net assets between those with donor restrictions and without donor restrictions.

Assets, liabilities, and net assets are listed on the *statement of financial position,* which is the equivalent of a for-profit business balance sheet. Going back to the double-entry accounting system discussion earlier in this chapter, total assets must equal total liabilities plus net assets. (See Chapter 18 for more information about assets, liabilities, net assets, and how to prepare the statement of financial position.)

TIP

Your statement of financial position summarizes how financially stable your organization is and how solvent it is. A quick eye can look at this statement and gain great insight into your future to determine whether your organization can sustain the forces of the market.

REMEMBER

If you've taken financial accounting classes or worked at a for-profit business, you're probably familiar with the fundamental accounting equation, which states "Assets = Liabilities + Owners' Equity." Truncating the equation results in "Assets – Liabilities = Net Assets." In general (like everything in accounting, there can be exceptions, which are outside the scope of this chapter), a nonprofit doesn't have any owners, so this truncated version is what nonprofits report via the statement of financial position.

REVENUE AND EXPENSES

In addition to assets, liabilities, and equity, two other important account categories are revenue and expenses. Nonprofit *revenue* is generally program income, such as grants, community support, and donor contributions. Nonprofits can also have income from investments and fees. *Expenses* are current-period costs needed to run the nonprofit, such as payroll, rent, and utilities. Operating income/loss, which is the difference between revenue and expenses, affect equity. If revenue is more than expenses, the operating income increases net assets (equity).

Find revenue and expense accounts on your statement of activities, which is the nonprofit term for what the for-profit world calls the *income statement.* On the statement of activities, operating income is the difference between income and expenses. Next comes any non-operating revenue and expenses, such as interest income or loss on sale of assets. The bottom-line figure shows up as either an increase or decrease to net assets.

TIP

Gains and losses also reflect on the statement of activities. Gains and losses show accounting events not reflected to program revenue expenses such as gain on the sale of a fixed asset or casualty loss from a fire or weather. (Keep this information in the back of your mind for now — I cover them completely in Chapter 17.)

Your goal at the end of the year is to have an increase in net assets and not a decrease in net assets. (See Chapter 17 for more information about operating and non-operating revenue and expense and how to prepare the statement of financial position.)

Considering the transaction methodology

Before you enter an event into your accounting system, you have to consider the *transaction methodology*, which is a five-step process to confirm the correctness of whatever entry you're preparing. Here are your five considerations:

- » **What's going on?** This question addresses the precipitating event causing the entry. For example, did your nonprofit receive a contribution or buy a new piece of office equipment?

- » **Which accounts does this event affect?** In the case of a cash contribution, it would affect both cash and an income account.

- » **How are the accounts affected?** You increase or decrease an account based on how the account is affected. Assets and expenses increase using a debit, and decrease using a credit. On the flip side, liabilities and revenue increase with a credit, and decrease with a debit. For example, to record paying $250 to buy merchandise at an office supply store using cash, you debit supplies expense (increase) for $250 and credit cash (decrease) for $250. Find out more about debiting and crediting by jumping ahead to the "Logging debits and credits" section of this chapter.

- » **Do all debits for an entry equal all credits for the same entry?** I talk about this more in Chapter 6. For now, just remember that for every debit there must be a credit.

- » **Does the entry make sense?** Does what you enter in the books match the facts and circumstances of the accounting event? For example, although the net effect on the books is the same, you can't credit an expense to book income such as a cash contribution.

Keeping a journal

Accounting journals are the day-to-day recording of events affecting your nonprofit. Accountants call journals the *books of original entry* because no transaction gets into the accounting records without being entered into a journal first. Your nonprofit can have many different types of journals. (See Chapter 8 for more information about cash, income, purchases, and the general journal.)

Logging debits and credits

Accounting reflects what happens financially by increasing and decreasing accounts in the form of debits and credits. You also need to know the normal balance of each account. The *normal balance* of asset, net asset, and expense accounts is a debit. The normal balance of liability and revenue accounts is a credit.

Accountants use the following methodology to report debits and credits in the journals:

» The date of the entry is offset in the left-hand column.

» The account debited or credited is in the middle column.

» The left side is the *debit* side of an account.

» The right side is the *credit* side of an account.

» The amounts are shown in the right-hand column.

» Proper journal entries always list debits first and credits afterward.

Figure 1-1 shows the general format of a journal entry.

FIGURE 1-1:
The standard
journal entry
format.

Date	Debited account	XX,XXX	
	Credited account		XX,XXX

For every debit, there must be a credit, but you can have more than one debit or credit in a single journal entry. For example, Figure 1-2 shows cash received on March 10 from two sources.

FIGURE 1-2:
Recording cash
received via
donors and
grants.

10-Mar	Cash	55,000	
	Campaign contribution		5,000
	Government grant		50,000

Throughout your accounting period, you make debits and credits not only to your statement of financial position accounts, but also to your statement of activities accounts. Understanding how to increase and decrease these accounts is also important.

Adhering to GAAP and GAAS

Before you can play a game, you read the instructions, right? Well, before you can fully understand bookkeeping and accounting for your nonprofit, you have to familiarize yourself with the accounting ground rules. The ground rules of the accounting profession — the standards that accountants follow when making decisions about how to handle accounting issues — are generally accepted accounting principles (GAAP).

GAAP defines for financial accountants the acceptable practices in the preparation of financial statements in the United States. Specifically, GAAP tells accountants exactly how financial data has to show up on the nonprofit's statement of activities, statement of financial position, and statement of cash flow (see Chapters 17, 18, and 19 for more information about each of these statements). GAAP was put in place to help accountants put their clients' needs first, behave ethically, and make sure that all accountants are playing by the same rules. (See Chapter 13 for more on GAAP.)

Many nonprofits need a set of audited financial statements, which means your nonprofit has to secure a qualified independent CPA to conduct a financial statement audit and prepare an audit report giving an opinion on your financial statements. Auditing is gathering and reviewing evidence about your organization to report on the degree between the way your nonprofit's financial information is presented and the standards set by rule makers.

Generally accepted auditing standards (GAAS) are rules or standards your independent CPA uses in this process to perform and report audit findings. Statements on auditing standards for CPAs working with nonprofits are issued by the Auditing Standards Board (ASB), which is part of the AICPA.

TECHNICAL STUFF

AICPA is the U.S. national professional organization for all CPAs. The ASB is a senior technical committee of the AICPA. The ASB issues standards and procedures that financial accountants must follow when conducting audits. It also sets quality-control standards to use for peer reviews, which is when one CPA firm evaluates the operations of another CPA firm.

Auditors give opinions by writing a report about your operating procedures, compliance with specific laws, and whether your financial statements are stated according to GAAP. As a nonprofit director or manager, you need to be concerned with three types of audits (see Chapter 14 for more information about the auditing process):

>> **Audit of financial statements:** An audit of financial statements, sometimes called an accounting audit, verifies whether statements have been prepared according to GAAP.

>> **Compliance audit:** A compliance audit, sometimes referred to as a grant audit, reviews your financial records to determine whether your nonprofit is following specific procedures, rules, or regulations set down by some higher authority.

>> **Operational audit:** An operational audit, also called the *management audit* or *performance audit,* measures and evaluates how efficiently you're operating and how effectively you're managing your nonprofit's resources. Boards of directors often request this audit to evaluate organizational systems, computer operations, and marketing. The aim of an operational audit is ultimately to optimize efficiency.

Keeping a paper trail

Leaving tracks in the sand is essential to proper management of your nonprofit's books. You need documentation to support why you did what you did, which adds credibility to your management of funds. Good housekeeping starts by keeping your checkbook register balanced (see Chapter 7) and continues with maintaining organized records (see Chapter 4) using either a manual bookkeeping system (see Chapter 8) or an accounting software program (see Chapter 9).

TIP

Keep original source documents of where every donation comes from and how each dollar is spent. Part of being a good steward is leaving a clear audit trail to account for your nonprofit activities and support how you treat transactions.

Additionally, your auditor will want to backtrack in your steps to find the initial record that began a single transaction. Auditing can be like looking for a needle in a haystack. Sometimes only your auditor knows what they're looking for and why, but you'll have to provide the records in order to complete the financial statement audit. Depending on your nonprofit circumstances, getting an audit of your financial statements may be a necessary part of keeping your nonprofit status. (Chapter 14 tells you what to expect during an audit.)

Making Sure Your Books Are Balanced

Staying on top of your nonprofit's financial activities is important because, as the director or accountant, you can be held accountable. The way to start is making sure you have balanced books. Balanced books are up-to-date, current information about your accounts, in which debits equal credits. Every transaction that takes place affects two or more items in accounting, and you have to make sure everything stays in balance. Whether you create your own manual system or take advantage of the software on the market, you need to keep your books in order.

This section walks you through some basics to help you ensure your books are balanced. Follow the chapters in Part 2 for tools to assist you in maintaining balanced books.

Establishing a chart of accounts

Your chart of accounts is your blueprint for assigning numbers to specify accounts and having a method to track all accounts. Using a chart of accounts, you can recognize what type of account it is based on the beginning number. For example, accounts beginning with 1 are usually assets accounts. After you get used to using the chart of accounts, you'll enjoy the benefits of coding transactions according to their classification. (Chapter 5 has more on setting up your chart of accounts.)

Tracking transactions

To have a firm grasp on your nonprofit's financial status, your records have to be accurate. The best way to have accurate records is to record transactions when they take place, when the event is still fresh in your mind.

Tracking your income and costs and keeping your checking account balance up to date lets you know when you're short on cash and when you've got plenty of money to pay the bills. Without a good tracking device or accounting system, you can easily lose track of your true checking account balance.

TIP

So, how can you keep track of transactions? Don't feel overwhelmed. You don't need a PhD in aeronautical engineering. The following are a couple of easy ways to track them. Check out Chapters 6 and 7 for more on recording transactions and using a checkbook.

>> **Use online banking.** Online banking gives up-to-date, current balances any time, day or night.

>> **Itemize your transactions when they happen.** When you swipe your credit card or bank debit card, write it down right away in your checkbook register.

REMEMBER

One of the most important things you need to keep track of is your donors list. A donors list includes contributors' names, addresses, and phone numbers, as well as the donation dates. Your auditor will use this list to verify where the money came from and when.

Developing a budget

Your budget is your financial plan. It shows your expected sources of income and how much you expect to spend. When you create a budget, you develop a formal plan for paying for your organization's future activities.

You need not only an operating budget for your organization, but also a separate budget for each and every program. (Chapter 10 explains how to create a budget.)

REMEMBER

Always know how much money is needed to operate your nonprofit. If a private donor asks, you should know the exact amount needed to break even (the amount of money it takes to cover all expenses).

Being compliant

After all your hard work setting up your nonprofit, you don't want to inadvertently have your nonprofit status revoked. Make sure you file your paperwork with the IRS, abide by any state and local regulatory guidelines, and keep your non-program income in line (see Chapter 16 for more on unrelated business income). Additionally, operate according to your bylaws, be mindful of your mission statement and steer clear of any perceived conflict of interest.

In addition, you have to mind some accounting standards: GAAP, rules set by FASB, and laws established by the Sarbanes–Oxley Act (SOX). (I explain the ins and outs of these guidelines in Chapter 13.)

Finding Out about Federal Grants

Finding donations and revenue for your nonprofit may be frustrating at times. The good news: The federal government provides free money in the form of grants that you can apply for and not have to pay back. Grants come in all sizes, from tiny ones of $10,000 to supersizes of $1 million and more.

Positioning your organization to receive grants requires four important things:

>> **Organization:** You need to keep up with the paperwork involved to make the application and management process easier.

>> **Reading:** In order to understand the dos and don'ts of how to put together your grant application, you need to carefully read all the grant application guidelines.

>> **Writing:** You need to put your plan on paper. Federal proposal writing is different from other writing you may do on a regular basis.

>> **Accountability:** To fulfill reporting requirements, you need to be accountable. You successfully receive the grant; now you have to tell the government how you're spending the grant money and how folks are benefiting from the funds.

This section gives you a snapshot of the federal grant process. (Chapters 11 and 12 provide more information about federal grants and accounting for them.)

Gleaning some grant basics

Federal grants are award instruments given by the federal government to implement programs that benefit people. You don't have to pay grants back — they're not loans. It's free money! With some work, figuring out the grant application process is easy, and the benefits of receiving a grant are phenomenal.

Although many sources other than the federal government offer grants, Chapter 11 of this book focuses on federal grant. Hundreds of federal agencies provide grants to:

>> Help nonprofits implement programs to benefit communities

>> Do work that government can't do

>> Carry out a public purpose

TIP

Go to www.federalgrants.com/agency to browse through grants by federal agency.

Following the rules

When your nonprofit gets federal grant money, you're not free to spend it however you want. Like any grant you may be awarded, federal grant money has red tape and paperwork. For the grant novice, managing a grant can be a bit tricky, but after you get your first one behind you, managing subsequent ones should be easier. (Chapter 12 provides more insight to managing grant money.)

REMEMBER

The main challenge of managing a federal grant is submitting two reports in a timely manner. These reports tell the federal agency from whom you secured the grant:

>> What progress you've made toward your program goals to date

>> How you've spent the federal money and how much is left

After you master the rules, you can play the grant game like a pro and become a grant guru.

Going through a grant audit

For many people, the word audit brings to mind the freezing of assets and the endless search for paper trails that may lead to the discovery of something that wasn't handled properly. For the record, an audit verifies and confirms the accuracy of your financial records and your compliance with the grant requirements.

The grant audit is usually conducted by someone from the granting agency and is done to ensure grant funds have been used as per your agreement with the funding agency. Your grant auditor checks out the federal government's investment by seeing if you're a good steward of grant dollars. The auditor will view your accounting system to see how you separate your grant money from the rest of your funds. Your auditor also looks at other areas, such as your organization's travel, personnel, and purchasing policies and procedures. (Chapter 14 discusses what to expect during a grant audit.)

Paying Federal Taxes

Although your organization is a nonprofit and is exempt from paying federal taxes, you're still responsible for collecting and remitting federal payroll taxes for all of your employees, which includes FICA and federal withholding tax. The Federal Insurance Contributions Act (FICA) is a federal payroll tax that both employees and employers have to pay. The funds collected from FICA are used to fund Social Security and Medicare retirement benefits and to provide for disabled workers and children of deceased workers.

As of the publication date of this book, the FICA rate is 15.3 percent. Of the 15.3 percent, you withhold 7.65 percent of each employee's gross wage (subject to threshold limits) for FICA. As the employer, you must match this amount by paying 7.65 percent of the employee's gross wage. Federal withholding amounts are a function of how the employee filled out Form W-4.

Chapter 15 has more information about calculating payroll and payroll taxes, as well as figuring any thresholds. It also provides a guide on when and how to remit payroll taxes to the IRS.

WARNING

Nonprofits generally pay no federal income tax, but your nonprofit may be subject to federal income taxes if you engage in for-profit business enterprises in which you gain unrelated business income. Unrelated business income is any income generated by a business that is regularly carried on and unrelated to the exempt function of your nonprofit.

Getting a Grasp on Financial Statements

Financial statements are records of where your income comes from, where it goes, and in some instances, accumulated balances. (Check out the chapters in Part 4 for more in-depth explanations on these statements and how to create and use them to keep track of your organization's finances.)

Your financial statements include the following:

>> **Statement of activities:** The equivalent of a for-profit income statement, the statement of activities lists all program revenues earned and all expenses paid for a specific time period. It also reports other income and expenses, such as interest income or loss on the sale of an asset. The difference between revenue, expenses, other income, and other expenses increases or decreases net assets. (Refer to Chapter 17 for more info.)

>> **Statement of financial position:** Similar to the for-profit business balance sheet, this statement reveals your organization's solvency and stability by summarizing its assets (things it owns) and liabilities (things it owes) and calculates its net assets (the difference between what the organization owns and what it owes). Your statement of financial position reports your organization's assets, liabilities, and net assets as of a certain date. The difference between assets and liabilities equals your net assets. (Check out Chapter 18 for more.)

>> **Cash flow statement:** This statement evaluates all inflows and outflows of cash for the accounting period according to the activity. The cash flow statement breaks activities into three categories: operating, financing, and investing. (See Chapter 19 for more on the cash flow statement.)

>> **Statement of functional expense:** Your statement of functional expense reveals by line item and category how much you've spent for the different categories of expenses reported on the statement of activities — program costs, management and general expenses, and fundraising expenses. As such, this statement is an itemized list providing detailed information about the expenses reported on the statement of activities. After you've completed the statement of activities, the statement of functional expense allocates your total expenses among activities. (See Chapter 18 for functional expense classifications.)

>> **Notes to the financial statements:** The notes section tells the story behind the numbers. The notes describe your organization, explain your accounting methods, and explain any changes in those methods, potential lawsuits, or contingencies that threaten the livelihood of your existence. Plus, they provide detailed information for some of the amounts in the financial statements.

In addition, the notes clarify all restricted assets. In the notes you find pertinent information about bonds and notes payable. Anything that can have a material impact on your organization should be disclosed in the notes to the financial statements. (See Chapter 21 to understand the importance of completing the notes to your financial statements.)

ANSWERING FIVE IMPORTANT QUESTIONS

Don't be a nonprofit director or manager staying up nights worrying that you've missed an important deadline or done something to jeopardize your nonprofit status. Manage that worry by staying organized. Here are five questions and answers to make your life a little easier:

- **Why do I need a system to track and record revenues and expenses?** You need to do so because you're a good steward of the funds you manage, and you want to keep your supporters happy. A good steward is wise and prudent in the way they handle money. You want to establish and then maintain a good reputation as being a good charitable investment. You need a bookkeeping system that tracks and accounts for the funds you manage and the expenditure made. This makes you accountable and gives your nonprofit credibility.

- **How do I go about finding more stable sources of income to fund my programs?** Explore all relevant grants (see Chapters 11 and 12 for more information). One of the most stable sources of income are government grants. First, do a little research on applicable grants. Carefully read the criteria and go over the grant application. Gather necessary paperwork and prepare your application. One last thing: Be mindful of the grant application submission deadline.

- **What do I need to do with my records so I'm ready if I'm ever audited by the IRS?** Record and store for safekeeping all backup documents for any transactions you make. In other words, keep copies of everything pertaining to income received, expenses paid, and assets purchased. Leave a paper trail that leads to every purchase. In real estate, it's all about location, location, location. With the IRS, its document, document, document. (Chapter 4 can help you set up a recordkeeping system.)

- **Donations are so unpredictable — why do I still need an operating budget?** Whether your organization is flat broke and you don't know where the next dime is coming from or it has millions in the bank, you always need to have an operating budget. You need to know how much is needed to operate your organization on a weekly, monthly, quarterly, and annual basis. Your operating budget is your financial plan. (Check out Chapter 10 for more advice.)

- **What do I need to know about complying with IRS guidelines to keep my non-profit status?** One thing that applies to all nonprofits, no matter how big or small, is timely filing information with the IRS annually through Form 990. Which version of Form 990 you file depends on your annual gross receipts. (Turn to Chapters 13 and 16 to find out more.)

Chapter **2**

Starting with Basic Bookkeeping and Accounting

Have you ever talked to computer support people about problems you're having with your computer, and they started using terms like *API, ISP, BYOD,* and other acronyms about which you don't have a clue? If you're like me, when people talk over your head, your brain shuts down. Every profession has its jargon, and accounting is no different. But the good news is that the jargon doesn't have to be an impenetrable wall separating you from the bookkeeping and accounting tasks you need to master.

This chapter introduces you to accounting (including basic terms) and explains why you need to understand it and how it works. You also get started with managing your nonprofit's books, selecting the most appropriate accounting methods for your organization, safeguarding against negative compliance results, and protecting your nonprofit's physical and financial assets from theft.

Understanding Accounting and Bookkeeping

Whether you're chief executive officer (CEO) of a multibillion-dollar corporation or the manager of your household, you use accounting every day. *To account* is to record and report a quantity of money or objects. *Accounting* is counting, recording, classifying, and summarizing transactions and events — and then interpreting the results. If you look inside your wallet and count your money, you've accounted for your cash on hand.

Bookkeeping, on the other hand, is the process of accumulating, organizing, and storing information about transactions on a day-to-day basis. When you write a check and record it in your checkbook register, you engage in bookkeeping.

Accounting and bookkeeping have many things in common, but the most basic is evaluating and entering transactions into the records. A *transaction* can be an exchange of value between two or more parties. For example, you walk into a local store and purchase a pack of gum, handing the cashier a $5 bill. That purchase is a transaction.

Accounting transactions also include non-cash events such as booking depreciation or amortization, which move the cost of assets from the statement of financial position (see Chapter 18) to the statement of activities (see Chapter 17). You may also have the need to reclassify donations from those with donor restrictions to those without donor restrictions. (You can find out more about booking transactions in Chapter 8.)

Outlining the differences between accounting and bookkeeping

Bookkeeping is generally the starting point of the accounting process. A bookkeeper is a paraprofessional who records the daily transactions in the accounting cycle such as bill paying, reconciling purchase orders to deliveries, and balancing the checkbook. As part of this process, bookkeepers maintain the following documents:

>> Originals or copies of invoices and receipts

>> Copies of cleared checks and bank statements

>> All other paperwork required for accounting purposes

Bookkeepers perform daily tasks of recording, including

>> Dates of transactions

>> Amounts of transactions

>> Sources of donations

>> Expenses and loss transactions

Bookkeepers accomplish this by memorializing transactions affecting cash in the check register (see Chapter 7) and maybe even preparing journal entries (see Chapter 6). Based on their level of expertise, a bookkeeper may also be in charge of posting journal entries to the appropriate journal and *general ledger* (the recording of all financial transactions within the nonprofit for a particular accounting cycle).

Accounting summarizes the day-to-day activities recorded by a bookkeeper. After reviewing the day-to-day bookkeeping, your accountant will prepare any needed adjusting journal entries and the financial statements. Your nonprofit might distribute the financial statements to an interested donor, use them as a starting point for budgets, or use them for decision making.

Bookkeeping focuses on recording and organizing financial data, while accounting is more about the interpretation/analysis and presentation of the bookkeeping data. That means the accountant evaluates the overall results of economic activity by identifying, measuring, recording, interpreting, and communicating every transaction according to set rules and guidelines.

REMEMBER

An accountant uses *double-entry accounting* to record every transaction because every transaction affects a minimum of two accounts. For example, if you write a check to purchase a printer for $600, your bookkeeper will record it in the check register as cash disbursed to purchase office equipment. Your accountant realizes that writing a check increases your assets (office equipment) for $600 and reduces your cash for the same amount. That's two accounting entries happening with one transaction.

Defining common financial terms

Accounting is the language of business. As with all professions, learning the jargon is key to understanding the process. In the following sections, I define the most common accounting and bookkeeping terms. As you read through the remaining chapters of this book, you'll encounter many more accounting terms, which are defined as you need to know them.

Grasping assets, liabilities, and net assets

You've probably heard the terms *assets*, *liabilities*, and *net assets* before. Here's what they mean:

>> **Assets:** What you own. Assets include things like cars, buildings, savings, and other items of value. A house is generally considered an asset, even when you don't yet own it outright. Common nonprofit assets include cash in the bank, contributions receivable, government contracts and grants, prepaid expenses, and investments. Most nonprofits also have assets in the form of property and equipment like computers, copiers, printers, desks, chairs, and perhaps a vehicle.

>> **Liabilities:** What you owe. Most people who say they're homeowners really aren't; as long as they're still paying on a mortgage, the payment is a liability due every month. Common nonprofit liabilities include accounts payable, accrued payroll expense, and amounts committed to program services.

>> **Net assets:** For a nonprofit, this is the difference between assets and liabilities.

Assets, liabilities, and net assets show up on the statement of financial position (see Chapter 18).

TIP

Put another way, net assets are the difference between what you own and what you owe.

Eyeing nonprofit revenue and expenses

Nonprofit revenue is the inflow of assets received in exchange for goods and services, or from donations, investments, and other miscellaneous sources such as foundation and government grants. Donations will probably be your primary source of revenue. *Donations* come from individuals, corporations, foundations, and government entities to help you fulfill your mission. Cash, grants, time, and services are examples of donations.

Expenses are the cost for current period goods or services. Your nonprofit encounters the same expenses as most for-profit corporations, except for income taxes. You have to account for overhead expenses (rent and utilities), program management expenses (salaries, fringe benefits, and office supplies), and other incidentals.

Some people have a misconception that nonprofits shouldn't make a profit or generate revenue, but no organization can operate without revenue. In the non-profit arena, *operating income* (revenue greater than expenses) increases net assets.

Many profits have nonoperating income and expenses that, combined with operating income, affect net assets. (See Chapter 17 for more information about nonoperating income and expenses.)

Identifying cash flows and operating budgets

To stay afloat, you must identify new streams of cash flow to sustain your organization. *Cash flow* is the amount of money received in and paid out during the same period. In the private sector, corporations are always looking for new ways to increase their cash flow, usually through new or improved products or services.

As a nonprofit manager, you must continuously look for new ways to appeal to your constituents and tap into new streams of cash inflow. What you did last year may not appeal to your donors this year.

An *operating budget* is a financial plan for current operations that includes estimating cash inflows from all sources and the related cash outflows you need to operate. When preparing an operating budget, most nonprofits estimate cash inflows first and budget expenses accordingly. Some nonprofits may opt to estimate expenses first and come up with a plan for revenue based on the amount needed to cover those expenses.

Getting a hold on debits and credits

Debits and *credits* are what's done to accounts to record transactions. To get a grasp on debits and credits, you must first know the normal balances of a few accounts. The *normal balance* is what it takes to increase an account.

Think of this as an equation that has two sides — a right side and a left side. What is done on the right must be balanced by recording the same amount on the left. For example, to debit an account is to charge the left side or left column of your journal or ledger. (A *journal* is a book of original entry where transactions are recorded in the order they occur; a *ledger* contains the transactions according to the account they belong to. Check out Chapter 6 for more info.)

Asset and expense accounts are increased by debits. On the other hand, to credit an account is always done to the right side or right column of your journal or ledger. Revenue, liability, and net assets accounts are increased by credits.

Asset accounts normally have a debit balance, so if you debit an asset account, you increase it. This transaction is placed on the left side of the journal or ledger. If you credit an asset account, you decrease it. Credits are shown on the right side of a journal or ledger.

Assets	
Debit side	Credit side
shows increases	shows decreases

REMEMBER

Asset accounts can be current or long term and include the following accounts: cash, grants, accounts receivable, inventory, supplies, prepaid rent, prepaid insurance, land, buildings, equipment, and accumulated depreciation.

Liability accounts normally have a credit balance, so if you credit a liability account, you increase it. On the flip side, if you debit a liability account, you decrease it. As with assets, debits are recorded on the left side or column of the journal or ledger, and credits are recorded on the right side or column. In fact, this holds true for all accounting processes.

Liabilities	
Debit side	Credit side
shows decreases	shows increases

REMEMBER

To decrease an account, you need to do the opposite of what is done to increase it.

Net assets are handled the same as liability accounts. If you credit net assets, you increase it. If you debit net assets, you decrease it.

Net Assets	
Debit side	Credit side
shows decreases	shows increases

Adhering to generally accepted accounting principles

Before you can play a new game, you read the instructions, right? Well, before you can fully understand bookkeeping and accounting for your nonprofit, you have to familiarize yourself with the ground rules. The ground rules of the accounting profession can be attributed to *generally accepted accounting principles* (GAAP).

GAAP is the standards that accountants follow when making decisions about how to handle accounting issues. You can consider them the rules of the profession. (See Chapter 6 for more on GAAP.)

Choosing Your Accounting Method

The two main accounting methods are cash and accrual. Before starting to keep track of things, you need to decide which of the two methods you'll use to account for your activities. You'll also decide if you need to use *fund accounting*, which means you further organize your accounting transactions by purpose.

When you choose the *cash basis,* transactions are recorded only when cash changes hands. That is, if you pay for something or receive an unrestricted donation via cash, check, or credit card, the transaction shows up in your books immediately. A slight twist on this is that if your nonprofit receives an unconditional promise to contribute, you must record that income in the same period as the promise regardless of whether cash was received. It's never easy, but you find out more about booking income in Chapters 8 and 17.

REMEMBER

When you present a check for payment, you're affirming that enough cash is in your checking account for the check to clear. The same rational holds true for credit card payments — you're responsible for paying your credit card company when the charge goes through. Thus, both modes of payment are treated like cash.

For example, you run to your nearest office supply store to stock up on pencils, paper, staples, sticky notes, and whatever other fun items you run across. You pay for these items by cash, check, or credit card. Under the cash basis, you record the transaction immediately. Alternatively, you may have a store account and decide to have the goods charged to that account, which you'll pay later. If you decide to charge the same supplies to your account, under the cash basis, you don't record the transaction until the bill is paid.

If you're using the *accrual basis* of accounting, purchases are recorded when they occur, regardless of when they're paid. So, if you buy those office supplies on store credit on June 1 and pay the bill four weeks later on July 1, the transaction records on June 1 when you bought the supplies, not on July 1 when you issue a check for the payable.

In most instances you can choose to keep your accounting records on the cash or accrual basis. Many small nonprofits use the cash basis. Medium and larger non-profits usually use the accrual basis. The major difference between cash basis and accrual basis has to do with when you record the transactions.

TIP

The cash basis is often used when there is little difference in the bottom line under cash or accrual basis, or if the nonprofit spends all revenue it received in the same year and doesn't have any large unpaid bills or uncollected income left over at year-end.

Keeping track of the cash

Cash is a medium of exchange. Cash is currency, and in accounting, cash is a current asset. Cash equivalents are instruments that can be immediately converted into cash and include

>> Petty cash, usually kept to make small office purchases

>> Checking account balances

>> Certificates of deposits (CDs)

>> Savings account balances

Recording transactions using the cash method means that you record revenues only when cash is received and record expenses only when they're paid. This is the easiest method to use because if you make a purchase on account, and the bill doesn't come out until next month, you don't record the transaction until you pay the bill.

When preparing your organization's financial statements, a certified public accountant (CPA) can easily convert your cash-basis accounting information into GAAP-required accrual-basis information.

TIP

Maintaining accrual-based books

To accrue means to accumulate or increase. Under the accrual basis, you recognize revenues and expenses when a transaction takes place, whether cash exchanges hands or not.

For example, if you buy office supplies on account, you record the transaction in your accounting books when you make the purchase and again when the bill is paid. To record such a transaction, you initially debit office supplies (a current asset account) and credit accounts payable (a current liability account) for the cost of the office supplies. Then, when you pay the bill, you debit accounts payable and credit cash.

The accrual basis gives you a more accurate account of your nonprofit's bottom line because expenses are reported in the same accounting period as the associated revenue. It also requires end-of-the-period adjustments for salaries and other expenses. Your accounting period may close but you may have some expenses such as prepaid subscriptions, prepaid insurance, or salaries, which cross more

REMEMBER

than one period. The accrual basis of accounting charges expenses to the period in which they're used and is required by GAAP if the nonprofit is required to have audited financial statements.

Introducing fund accounting

Depending on the mission and size of your nonprofit, you may want to incorporate fund accounting into your recordkeeping. *Fund accounting* means that you track assets, liabilities, revenue, and expenses by their type, or *fund*.

Two biggies in the world of fund accounting are general and restricted funds. A *general fund* refers to any money you receive or use that has no conditions to its use that you must abide by. On the flip side, a *restricted fund* is just that — money you receive that has been earmarked by the donor to be used only for a specific purpose. For example, if you run a nonprofit child-wellness center, the donor may specify their contribution be used only for child education.

TIP

If you decide to use fund accounting, the accrual method of accounting primarily applies (although, in some instances, you can use the cash method) using the guidance about the cash versus accrual method detailed earlier in this chapter. You record using cash or accrual and then divvy up those transactions into your different funds.

Running Numbers on Your Assets

When you buy items such as printers, computers, cars, or other things that last more than a year, you need to place these items on your books as assets. To record an asset, you record it in your books at the price you paid for it.

Because some assets, such as computers, may last for several years, you need to write off the cost (*depreciate*) over the item's life span. For example, if a computer is expected to last three years, you'll need to depreciate it over three years. *Depreciable assets* are commonly referred to as *plant, property, or equipment* (PPE). The following sections explain how to put a number to your assets and how to depreciate them.

REMEMBER

When writing off the cost of assets, you never depreciate the cost of land. You need to depreciate the costs of all other assets classified as PPE that last longer than a year.

Booking assets

Prices can fluctuate. You may pay $1,000 for something on Tuesday and then discover that it went on sale the next day for $500. When this happens, how much is the item worth? What amount should you record in your books?

The answers to these questions are simple. The *historic cost* principle states that all assets should record at their original cost. *Original cost* is generally what you paid to acquire the asset. It's an approach that keeps assets on the books at their purchase price with no regard for inflation or the economy.

REMEMBER

Original cost includes sales tax, shipping, and any costs associated with placing the asset in service, such as installation.

Presently, GAAP requires depreciable assets to be recorded at historic value, which incorporates depreciation. Depreciation is used to reduce an asset's value due to the asset's use over time. You can't take any additional adjustments for estimated changes in the asset's market value because market values for depreciable assets are only estimates. Estimating a higher or lower market value of an asset isn't done to avoid the possibility of someone using the information to manipulate reported financial results.

In contrast to historical value, *fair market value* is the price that an interested buyer would be willing to pay and an interested seller would be willing to accept for a particular asset. If you had to liquidate all your assets tomorrow, fair market value would be very important to you.

Recording most equity investments at fair market value and adjusting for changes in their value is allowed under GAAP. An example of an equity investment is *trading securities*, which are purchased to sell in the short term for profit. Qualifying equity securities are recorded initially at cost. Then, as their value goes up and down, you make an adjustment to record them at fair market value, recording the unrealized gain or loss on your statement of activities. In this instance, market values aren't estimates — they're readily determined, so there is no room to manipulate financial results.

Learning about depreciation methods

To depreciate means to write off the expense of an item over its expected useful life, less any *salvage value* (the amount that can be recovered after an asset's service life). When you purchase equipment or a building, you pay a set amount. As time passes, these assets are assumed to lose some of their value through use.

Therefore, you systematically write off a portion of an asset's cost by depreciating it as an expense. For example, suppose you buy a computer for $1,450, and the computer is expected to be useful to you for three years, at which time its salvage value will be $50. You have $1,400 ($1,450 − $50) of depreciation expense to write off for the computer over those three years.

You get to choose which depreciation method you use, although after you choose a method, you generally have to stick with the same method until the asset is fully depreciated. Therefore, the amount of depreciation expense you write off in any year depends on which depreciation method you choose. Because depreciation is an expense, it directly reduces your operating income carrying over to an associated reduction to your net assets.

The executive director and board, with the advice of an accountant, decide which depreciation method to use. You can use a different method for different assets. The most important thing to remember here is that you want to reflect the most accurate value of all your assets. It's important for you to know the value of the assets you own.

In all that you do, you want to fairly present your financial information in the most accurate way. Some financial types have started discussing how assets are valued on the books compared to their market value. Some organizations have assets that are overvalued on their books, and then when those assets are evaluated, the previous value that has been indicated on the organization's statement of financial position isn't correct.

Choosing declining balance depreciation

Declining balance depreciation is an accelerated method of depreciation. That means there is a larger depreciation expense in the early years of an asset's life and smaller amounts in the later years. Declining balance depreciation can be used on any item classified as PPE.

When to use this type of depreciation method depends on many different factors, two of which are the use and life of the asset. Assets with shorter lives (less than ten years) usually lose most of their value in their earlier years, so declining depreciation methods are warranted. Longer-lived assets tend to lose their value evenly over time, and straight-line depreciation is adequate for these assets (see the next section). Although the Internal Revenue Service (IRS) and GAAP offer some guidance, use your professional judgment or solicit the advice of an accountant or CPA.

For tax purposes, the IRS provides useful lives for classes of assets and tables of depreciation percentages for various depreciation methods and asset lives. Office equipment has a useful life of five years; so do most automobiles. Office furniture and fixtures have useful lives of seven years. The IRS system doesn't take salvage value into account, but the tables are useful and can be applied to amounts adjusted for salvage value. IRS Publication 946, "How to Depreciate Property," is a good source of information about depreciation methods. You can find the publication online at www.irs.gov/publications/p946.

Going with straight-line depreciation

The easiest method of depreciation is the straight-line method. The *straight-line depreciation method* allocates the same amount of depreciation for each year over the expected life of an asset.

REMEMBER

Residual value is the same as salvage value. It's the value placed on an asset after it's fully depreciated. For example, suppose you expect to use your computer system for three years, and you pay $30,000 with an expected salvage value of $3,000. Plug these numbers into the equation, and your depreciation expense using the straight-line method is $9,000 per year:

($30,000 – $3,000) ÷ 3 years = $9,000 depreciation per year for 3 years

Selecting double-declining balance depreciation

The *double-declining balance depreciation method* is twice the rate of straight-line. The major difference between the double-declining balance and the straight-line method of depreciation is the amount of depreciation in each year of an asset's useful life. With double-declining balance, as opposed to straight-line, more depreciation is expensed in an asset's early years, and less is expensed in its later years.

To calculate the double-declining balance method, you must first compute the rate of depreciation for the straight-line method; then double this rate. You don't deduct the salvage value from the original cost of the asset when computing the asset's depreciable base. However, you stop taking depreciation expense when the asset's *net book value* (the original cost minus the accumulated depreciation) reaches the asset's salvage value. GAAP doesn't allow a depreciable asset's net book value to be less than its salvage value.

Returning to the example from the previous section, suppose your computer system has a total cost of $30,000 and a salvage value of $3,000, and it's expected to last three years. Figure 2-1 shows a comparison of the straight-line and double-declining balance depreciation methods.

Straight-Line Depreciation Method		Double-Declining Balance Method	
(Cost - Salvage Value) divided by useful life		Straight-line rate is 1/3 or 33.33% per year	
$27,000 ($30,000 - $3,000)/3 years = $9,000		Double-Declining Balance Method = 66.66% (33.33% x 2)	
2023 Depreciation	$9,000	2023 Deprecation $30,000 x 66.66%	$19,998
2024 Depreciation	$9,000	2024 Depreciation $30,000 - $19,998 = $10,002 $10,002 x 66.66%	$6,666
2025 Depreciation	$9,000	2025 Depreciation Limited to $27,000	$336
Total Depreciation	$27,000	Total Depreciation	$27,000

FIGURE 2-1:
A comparison of the straight-line and double-declining balance depreciation methods.

TIP

When in doubt about which method to use to calculate depreciation, choose an accelerated depreciation method such as double-declining balance. Under GAAP, it's the most conservative approach.

Keeping an Eye on Your Assets

It's virtually impossible to know if an employee will steal. To limit the possibility, you can do a background check on potential employees and give them assessment exams to find out what type of people they really are. Some major retailers ask a series of questions that give them a good indication of a person's moral character. You can order or design a similar test for your staff. Also, you can install security cameras in your building that record everything that takes place.

In addition to implementing protective procedures regarding who your nonprofit organization hires, you can institute internal controls that directly monitor your organization's financial holdings. A good system of internal controls puts some checks and balances in place to protect against employee theft. The following sections give you some ideas about how to keep your assets safe.

TIP

Before you hire an employee, perform a background check on them. Often this can be done through your state's attorney general's office or other law enforcement agencies.

Protecting your nonprofit's physical assets

Tracking and keeping up with inventory is a must to protect your nonprofit's assets. Portable equipment like a laptop computer is so easy to walk away with. To safeguard your valuables, require all equipment to be checked out before leaving the building. Some organizations have their employees sign statements agreeing to have their final paychecks withheld until all equipment is returned in good condition.

Limiting access to certain areas of interest can protect your assets. Consider installing security cameras and key access cards, as well as keeping your petty cash drawer locked and a book handy to record all transactions with receipts to support them.

Setting internal controls

Internal controls are procedures and policies that you establish to limit the possibility of accounting errors, fraud, theft, or *embezzlement* (taking something of value from someone who trusts you).

Keeping some office doors locked and some areas off-limits is just one kind of internal control to protect important records and data from manipulation. Other internal controls are less obvious than locked doors.

Establishing checks and balances

The founding fathers of the United States knew that human nature is subject to error, so they established the system of checks and balances to provide constant oversight and accountability within the federal government. You can apply a similar system of internal control by which you have checkpoints to balance your books. One example may be doing a physical count of all inventories to see if anything is missing or unaccounted for.

Checks and balances in your organization not only protect your assets but also can help you avoid an unfavorable audit finding. Start with the following checks and balances and then expand on them for protections that are tailored to your organization and its operations:

» Require two signatures on all checks over a set amount (usually more than a typical payroll tax deposit amount).

» Separate duties between your recordkeeper and the person handling cash.

» Record employees' hours on time sheets on a daily basis.

» Require all invoices for payment to be reviewed and authorized.

Your nonprofit's policies and procedures manual should present and explain your organization's checks and balances in such a way that all the steps are clearly defined. Most nonprofits have written policies about personnel, travel, and purchasing procedures. Put steps in writing about how to deal with personnel matters. Include the limits on travel pay for mileage, lodging, and meals. Also, create rules to deal with large purchases of, say, more than $500. You need to have a plan for how these types of situations should be handled to bring structure to your organization.

Separating employees' duties

You can place some roadblocks in your accounting system that prevent employees from stealing from your nonprofit (or at the very least, make it really hard) by establishing segregation of duties, which is a type of internal control. *Segregation of duties* assigns different steps of a process to different people. So, for example, you don't allow the same person who opens the mail to be responsible for making deposits. Think about how easy it would be for the person opening the mail to divert cash receipts.

Here are some examples of segregation of duties that you can apply to your nonprofit:

>> **Accounts payable and purchasing:** The person approving vendor payments shouldn't be authorized to make purchases without some oversight by a second party.

>> **Business mail and check deposits:** One person can open business mail and log in each check that's received, but someone else should be responsible for making deposits into your bank account.

Insuring or bonding nonprofit employees

Checks and balances and segregation of duties establish some internal controls, but you can take your internal protections a step further with risk-management strategies. Insuring or bonding your employees ensures that your organization faces minimal risk of loss in case of mistakes or malfeasance by the people who manage and work for your organization.

A *bond* is a debt security that guarantees to pay you for acts committed by board members or employees, and it protects you from employee or board theft. A bond is actually paid to you by the bonding company, but the person bonded reimburses the bonding company. Any reputable bonding entity will share some helpful tips about bonding your employees.

You determine the type and degree of insurance and bonded protections your nonprofit needs based on an assessment of your organization. First, you need to evaluate the potential risk and think about how much money is being handled. What is the value of your nonprofit's assets? How much equity has your nonprofit accrued? How much money does your nonprofit have in its savings and checking accounts? These are some of the questions you'll need to answer to determine how much insurance your organization needs.

Do some research by consulting with a few insurance companies and comparing rates. Your board of directors is responsible for finding an insurance company and approving the purchase of bonding insurance. As with most things concerning the management of your nonprofit, your board is responsible for making key decisions.

Chapter **3**

Introducing Financial Statements

I f you've ever made a major purchase or tried to secure a large sum of money to purchase a home, the lending institution, mortgage company, or bank probably asked for personal financial information about what you earn (your income), what you own (your assets), and what you owe (your liabilities). This is because the lender wants to know if you have the ability to timely make the loan payments on the debt. Although this example is on a personal level, for-profit businesses, and nonprofit organizations need to provide similar information via financial statements.

Financial statements describe and summarize operating activities, obligations, and economic resources for a given period. This can be monthly, quarterly, or yearly. A wide assortment of individuals and entities evaluate these statements to get a clear picture of your nonprofit's true financial position. Donors, investors, creditors, and even some governmental agencies evaluate these reports when they're deciding whether to donate or lend money to your organization.

This chapter gives you a quick overview on why these financial statements are important and which statements your nonprofit will generally need to prepare. The chapters in Part 4 then delve deeper into these statements and show you how your nonprofit can use them.

Explaining the Importance of Financial Statements

Nonprofits are granted tax-exempt status by the federal government to enable organizations to provide services in the public's interest. In exchange for tax-exempt status (generally owing no federal or state income taxes), these organizations are expected and required to perform and record financial functions in an effective, efficient manner. (See more about tax-exempt status in Chapter 16.)

Even though your nonprofit generally doesn't pay income taxes, you're required to submit information to the IRS about your activities — annually. Your nonprofit will file a Form 990, Return of Organization Exempt from Income Tax, that tells where your money came from, who you paid, and how much you paid. Don't worry — no money is due, just information. You need to file this information every year by the 15th day of the fifth month after the end of a tax-exempt organization's fiscal year. For a calendar year, the deadline is May 15. (Refer to Chapter 16 for more on Form 990.)

Not only are state and federal regulatory agencies interested in how you're managing your nonprofit, but the public also has your organization under close watch. The very reason for a nonprofit's existence — to serve the public's interest — opens up your financial information for public review. Therefore, your financial records are considered public domain. Because every move you make and every transaction you record is subject to public scrutiny, it's very important to properly track every transaction and keep materially correct books.

If you want continued support from the public, disclosing and reporting your organization's operating activities, economic resources, and obligations are in your best interest. (They're also required by law via a tax return.)

A complete set of financial statements for nonprofit organizations can include the following:

>> Independent auditor's report (see Chapter 14)

>> Statement of activities, reporting revenues and expenses, both operating and nonoperating (see Chapter 17)

>> Statement of financial position, reporting assets, liabilities, and net assets (see Chapter 18)

>> Cash flow statement, reporting cash receipts and payments (see Chapter 19)

>> Statement of functional expenses, which classifies expense by program or function (see Chapter 20)

>> Notes to financial statements, which provide the users expanded information about line items showing up on the financial statements (see Chapter 21)

I explain each of these reports in the "Identifying the Financial Statements" section later in this chapter.

When you have a small block of time, log on to www.guidestar.org and look up your favorite (or your own) nonprofit organization. You can find out where its money came from, who it paid, and how much. All Form 990s are open for public review.

In the following sections, I provide a brief overview of how you can use these statements to benefit and sustain your nonprofit. Tracking your income and spending helps you stay financially on track. Proper management of assets and liabilities is a hallmark of good stewardship. Keeping an eye on cash flow ensures that you'll have the cash to pay your employees, vendors, and long-term obligations. Eyeing all the financial reports is essential for you to know where your nonprofit's money comes from and where it goes.

Seeing the benefits of tracking the money

Financial statements summarize and describe nonprofit activity over a period of time. They should show that you've fulfilled your end of the bargain in being held accountable. They also indicate whether you've been a responsible steward or a sloppy manager of your nonprofit's resources.

WARNING

Sloppy management or inadequate accounting records can prove detrimental to your organization's reputation. The bulk of your support comes from contributions made by private donors, government entities, foundations, and corporate givers. If they see that you haven't been responsible with their money, they're likely to stop supporting you.

These statements also serve folks within the organization. People within your nonprofit use these financial statements to forecast the organization's needs and create plans to address those needs.

Using the financial statements

Without financial statements, planning and forecasting your organization's future needs is nearly impossible. Internal and external users rely on a nonprofit organization's financial statements to make important decisions. Managers of nonprofit organizations use financial statements to make decisions concerning the organization; people outside the nonprofit use the documents to decide whether to donate.

Internal users

The following individuals are examples of internal users of nonprofit financial statements:

- » **Executive director:** This person is hired by the board of directors to preside over the day-to-day management of a nonprofit. They use financial statements to see the big picture of the organization's finances.

- » **Nonprofit executive manager:** This person oversees accounting, information systems, marketing, personnel, and fundraising. They're likely to follow the organization's finances more closely.

- » **Nonprofit accountant:** They track and account for your financial activities. Their work forms the basis of your financial statements.

- » **Board members:** These folks are responsible for oversight of the entire operation. They use your financial statements to make sure the nonprofit is headed in the right direction.

External users

External users also rely on your nonprofit's financial statements. Those external users are

- » **Bankers/creditors:** Your banker will be primarily interested in your statement of financial position and statement of activities. Just like all creditors, your banker wants to know if you have something of value to secure a loan and the ability to make payments on the debt.

- » **Public donors:** They're public charities and government entities.

- » **Private donors:** They're individuals, corporations, and private foundations that donate to your organization. They invest in your cause.

- » **Independent auditors:** Your independent auditor needs copies of your financial statements to verify the fairness of representation of your finances. External auditors have an audit process under generally accepted auditing standards (GAAS). During this process, the auditor will ask your nonprofit to provide varying amounts of substantiation to verify assertions you make via the financial statements. (See Chapter 14 for more about audits.)

>> **Public watchdog groups:** These groups keep an eye on nonprofits. Their underlying motive is to expose your nonprofit to the general public as being a fraud or counterfeit if you're not being a good steward and doing what you're supposed to be doing. Public watchdogs go to extreme measures to expose you if you're not doing the right thing. After the media gets wind that you may not be doing what you should be doing with the money, you may be tried in the court of public opinion.

REMEMBER

Internal users have a greater day-to-day need than external users do to review financial statements. For example, internal users compare actual versus budget data on a month-by-month basis. Actual refers to results that have happened, and budget refers to anticipated results. A budget is a projection — it predicts future anticipated revenues and expenses that may change. Past financial information can be a good gauge of future revenues. (Check out Chapter 10 for more on projecting a budget.)

Board members and executive directors rely on financial statements to guide their decision making. Comparative financial statements tell how much money the organization received in the past year and how much it spent as compared to the current year. They also reveal whether an organization can pay its debt. For example, the last figure on the statement of activities is either a positive or a negative number. This number reveals how well the organization is performing financially. Information like this helps executive directors and board members do financial forecasting.

TIP

Information from current statements should be compared to prior years. Many nonprofits prepare a comparative analysis of at least three years if such records exist. That's why consistency in your treatment of accounting events and adding proper notes to the financial statements is key. Without these things, comparing year-over-year results may be like comparing apples to oranges.

Using Financial Statements to Your Advantage

Have you heard the phrase, "Everyone has to answer to someone"? Well, it's true for nonprofits, too. Life would be easier if nonprofits could just focus on the people and causes they serve and not have to worry about finances, but that isn't the case. Your financial statements are your financial scorecards — if you don't keep score, someone else will tally it for you and you may not be happy with the results.

The quickest way to identify problems in an organization is through frequent review of the financial statements, budget variances, and notes to the financial statements. For internal users (such as managers), that analysis allows them to identify and take corrective actions in a timely fashion. For external users (such as grantors or donors), that review is tailored to evaluating whether your nonprofit uses its funds responsibly. The statements should be accurate, easily readable, understandable, and done in a timely fashion.

REMEMBER

The headings on all financial statements answer the who, what, and when. The who is the name of your organization; the what is the name of the statement; and the when is the time period covered.

The following sections cover important things that financial statements can be used for.

Assisting with grant proposals

Whenever you submit a grant proposal, you're usually required to attach copies of your organization's audited financial statements. Audited financial statements must be compiled by an independent accounting firm or certified public accountant (CPA). The CPA provides an opinion on whether the information in the financial statements can be relied upon. (See Chapter 14 for more on audits.)

Government entities (federal agencies), corporate, and foundation grant makers require an overview of your nonprofit's financial activities and its ability to properly manage its finances. Many of these groups want to see if your organization has the capacity to manage a grant. Being a good steward of your organization's finances has its rewards. Grant makers know just what to look for to determine if your organization is a wise investment.

Review of your financial statements clues the grant makers into the reasonableness of your grant application. For example, if your organization has an operating budget of $25,000 and you're applying for a $150,000 grant, it most likely will matter to the funder that you've never managed such a large sum of money.

Tracing donations

Accurate financial statements allow internal users to project and anticipate potential changes in donor and contribution trends. You need to keep a close eye on changes in donation volume and amounts to properly address future financial problems. Analyzing giving trends allows internal users to make timely decisions about increasing fundraising goals.

The negative difference between projected or pledged donations versus actual donations affects a nonprofit's ability to pay bills and meet payroll. Balancing the inflow with the outflow can feel like a juggling act. Your ultimate objective is to ensure you have enough cash to pay the bills.

All nonprofit organizations are required to keep a donors list on file. Your auditor will test your list by randomly contacting some of the donors to make sure what your nonprofit reports reconciles with donor records. In the audit cycle, independent verification such as this isn't an option for the auditor; it's a requirement. (For more information about tracking donations, see Chapter 12.)

Following nonprofit activities

Many nonprofit organizations receive income from government grants, foundations, corporate grants, fundraising activities, and donations. The financial statements let you keep track of important nonprofit activities, such as how much income will be allocated to pay for specific needs. For example, the cash flow statement (see "Developing the cash flow statement," later in this chapter), reports cash inflows and outflows, reconciling to cash in bank.

Nonprofit organizations must track income and expenses carefully to know and understand their financial situation. If you're keeping manual records (see Chapter 8), a good place to start is by balancing the nonprofit checkbook, which tracks cash receipts made into and cash payments made out of your checking account.

Record transactions in the checkbook register when transactions take place. Your checkbook register will contain records of every donation, all expenses paid, and a running balance of cash on hand. Chapter 7 covers how to balance your nonprofit's checkbook.

Identifying contingent liabilities

Accurate financial statements also provide important information about potential liabilities. One type of potential liability is contingent liabilities, which is a possible obligation/loss pending the outcome of an uncertain future event, such as a court matter to be decided by a settlement, a judge, and/or a jury.

Generally accepted accounting principles (GAAP) lay out the criteria for when and how to report contingent liabilities. In a nutshell, losses should be accrued if the pending event is known prior to the preparation of the financial statements, the likelihood of an unfavorable outcome is probable, and the amount of loss can be reasonably estimated. Clear as mud? Don't worry — see Chapters 17, 18, and 21 for more information about booking contingencies.

PROTECTING YOUR NONPROFIT WITH LIABILITY INSURANCE

At the very least, if your nonprofit has direct contact with vulnerable people (such as children, the elderly, or individuals with developmental disabilities), you should protect yourself from potential lawsuits. To protect your nonprofit from potential disaster, consider speaking with your board about liability insurance. Liability insurance is important because it protects your assets.

Insurance can protect against lawsuits for any of the following:

- Alleged violations
- Breach of contract
- Discrimination
- Fraudulent conduct, reports, or financial statements
- Improper self-dealing
- Misuse of restricted funds
- Personal injury
- Sexual harassment
- Violation of state and federal laws
- Wrongful termination

If your organization has any of the preceding charges pending litigation, you should consult with an attorney.

Without this information, users of your financial statements won't have an accurate picture of your true financial status and any potential liabilities. Check out the nearby sidebar on how insurance can safeguard your nonprofit from lawsuits.

Identifying the Financial Statements

In order to show an accurate picture of your nonprofit's bottom line, you prepare financial statements. These statements show how much revenue has come in, what your expenses are, and whether you're in the red or black. The following sections give a quick outline of the different financial statements your nonprofit needs to compile and prepare at the end of your accounting period. To make the information more understandable, I also provide detailed examples of each.

Reading the statement of activities

The statement of activities (in the for-profit world known as the *income statement,* the *statement of revenues and expenses,* or the *profit-and-loss statement*) reveals where the nonprofit's money came from, where it went, and whether your organization had an increase or decrease to net assets for the year.

It must show the nonprofit entity as a whole and report the change in net assets with and without donor restrictions. All grants, contributions, interest income, and gains on the sale of marketable securities or sale of stock — basically, any money you bring in — are revenues, gains, and other support line items on the statement of activities. This is followed by all expenses *and losses* — for example, any money you spend, whether it's for salaries, new programs, events to raise more money, or losses on disposal of fixed assets.

The first item to pay attention to when reading a statement of activities appears at the end of the statement. Adding all the revenues and gains and subtracting all the expenses and losses results in the change in net assets. A possible change is when revenues and gains are more than expenses and losses, while a negative change is when expenses and losses are more than revenues and gains.

To start your orientation to this report, Figure 3-1 shows an abbreviated statement of activities with columns for net assets with and without donor restrictions and totals. The multicolumn format is becoming more popular than the single-column format. Turn to Chapter 17 to walk through a fully developed statements of activities with figures, so you can see the relationship between the categories.

There is no particular format for the statement of activities required by GAAP as long as all categories are correctly classified by net asset and the change in net assets is also correctly presented. You can use a single-column format, which is helpful if you're reporting prior year results. It's also okay to break out your statement of activities between operating income and expenses and nonoperating gains and losses.

Figure 3-2 presents the same financial information as Figure 3-1 in the single-column format. The big difference between the multicolumn format and the single-column format is the presentation of donor-restricted items. Because the single-column format doesn't have a dedicated donor restricted column, these items are listed as unique single-column line items. Regardless of the format you're using, end-of-period net assets are the same.

TIP

If you're using a spreadsheet or accounting program, it's very easy to add a column to the right to drop in prior-year results and another column to show the difference between current- and prior-year results.

	Jay & Top Community Cat Project Statement of Activities For Year Ended December 31, 20XX		
	Without Donor Restrictions	**With Donor Restrictions**	**Total**
Revenue, gains and other support:			
Contributions	XX,XXX	XX,XXX	XX,XXX
Event Income	XX,XXX		XX,XXX
Net assets released from restrictions:	XXX		XXX
Total revenue, gains, and other support	XXX,XXX	XX,XXX	XXX,XXX
Expenses and losses:			-
Program	XX,XXX		-
Management and general	XX,XXX		-
Fundraising	XX,XXX		-
Total expenses	XXX,XXX		-
Fire loss on furniture and fixtures	XX		XX
Total expenses and losses *	XXX,XXX		XXX,XXX
Change in net assets	XX,XXX	XX,XXX	XX,XXX
Net assets January 1, 20XX	XX,XXX	XX,XXX	XX,XXX
Net assets December 31, 20XX	XXX,XXX	XX,XXX	XXX,XXX

FIGURE 3-1:
A statement of activities, multicolumn format.

Finally, at the very bottom of the statement of activities, you find the change in net assets added to the beginning net assets to come up with ending net assets. The ending net assets figure is transferred to the statement of financial position (see the "Working with the statement of financial position" section for more on these statements).

REMEMBER

Anytime you see the word net in relation to financial statements, it means whatever remains after subtracting other items affecting the main account. For example, net interest income would indicate expenses relating to earning the interest income are deducted from the gross interest income figure on the statement. A good way to think of net is to think of a paystub. You have gross pay less deductions, with the difference between the two being your net pay.

WARNING

Although the statement of activities may be the first statement that comes to mind when you think of financial statements, the information is useful but limited. The statement of activities doesn't give the full financial position. You also need to rely on the other financial statements I explain in this chapter.

```
┌──────────────────────────────────────────────────────────────┐
│                  Jay & Top Community Cat Project               │
│                      Statement of Activities                   │
│                  For Year Ended December 31, 20XX              │
│                                                                │
│  Change in without donor restriction net assets:             │
│     Revenue, gains and other support:                          │
│        Contributions                                 XX,XXX    │
│        Event Income                                  XX,XXX    │
│        Net assets released from restrictions:           XXX    │
│           Total revenue, gains, and other support   XXX,XXX    │
│                                                                │
│  Expenses and losses:                                          │
│        Program                                       XX,XXX    │
│        Management and general                        XX,XXX    │
│        Fundraising                                   XX,XXX    │
│           Total expenses                            XXX,XXX    │
│  Fire loss on furniture and fixtures                     XX    │
│           Total expenses and losses                 XXX,XXX    │
│              Increase in without donor restrictions net assets  XX,XXX │
│  Change with donor restrictions net assets:                    │
│        Contributions                                 XX,XXX    │
│  Net assets released from restrictions             (XX,XXX)    │
│  Increase in net assets                              XX,XXX    │
│  Net assets January 1, 20XX                          XX,XXX    │
│  Net assets December 31, 20XX                       XXX,XXX    │
└──────────────────────────────────────────────────────────────┘
```

FIGURE 3-2:
A statement of
activities,
single-column
format.

FIGURING OUT FASB AND GAAP

Resulting from some criticism of the standard-setting work being done by the American Institute of Certified Public Accountants (AICPA), the Financial Accounting Foundation (FAF) was established in 1972, which in turn established the Financial Accounting Standards Board in 1973.

FASB is current the U.S. private-sector body setting GAAP for all nongovernmental agencies. There are seven FASB members, selected by FAF and elected to five-year terms. The members collectively are knowledgeable in the fields of accounting, finance, accounting education, business, and research.

Governmental entities follow procedures set up by the Governmental Accounting Standards Board (GASB). And at present, the Securities and Exchange Commission (SEC) authorizes FASB to establish financial accounting and reporting standards for publicly held companies.

Working with the statement of financial position

The statement of financial position (which is the for profit business equivalent of the balance sheet) reports the amounts of a nonprofit's assets, liabilities, and net assets as of a specified date (see Chapter 2 for explanations of these terms). The statement of financial position shows the nonprofit's ability to continue to provide services, gives the necessary information for ratio analysis (see Chapter 18), and provides a clue as to whether the nonprofit has the need to seek outside financing to meet its obligations.

Therefore, a quick glance at the statement of financial position reveals the organization's solvency. Solvency indicates whether an organization can meet its obligations on time. If current assets are less than current liabilities, then you need to sell some investments, borrow some money, or hold a fundraiser to meet contemporaneous obligations such as paying employees or vendors.

The statement of financial position should present assets, liabilities, and net assets either by sequencing assets and liabilities or by breaking them out between current and noncurrent. To refresh your memory, current assets are ones you anticipate converting to cash or using within 12 months of the statement date. Current liabilities are those you expect to settle within 12 months of the statement date.

And noncurrent? You guessed it — these are accounts you don't anticipate liquidating within 12 months of the statement date. Examples of noncurrent liabilities are any liabilities whose payments extend out further than 12 months, such as car notes and mortgages.

Figure 3-3 shows an abbreviated statement of financial position broken out between current and noncurrent assets and liabilities. Head to Chapter 18 to review fully developed statements of financial position prepared using the sequencing and classified methods, including figures so you can see the relationship between the categories.

Developing the cash flow statement

The *cash flow statement* records cash receipts and cash payments. You prepare the cash flow statement using certain components of both the statement of activities and statement of financial position. It serves as a bridge between the accrual method and cash method of accounting, giving the user a basis for understanding how noncash transactions showing up on the statements affect the amount of cash the nonprofit has at its disposal.

```
                    Jay & Top Community Cat Project
                     Statement of Financial Position
                          December 31, 20XX


                 Assets
              Current Assets
                 Cash                               XX,XXX

              Long-term assets
                 Fixed assets (net)                 XX,XXX
              Total fixed assets                     XX,XXX

              Total Assets                          XXX,XXX

         Liabilities and Net Assets
              Current Liabilities:
                 Accounts payable                   XX,XXX

              Net Assets                            XX,XXX
               Without donor restrictions           XX,XXX
               With donor restrictions              XX,XXX
              Total Net Assets                      XXX,XXX

              Total Liabilities and Net Assets      XXX,XXX
```

FIGURE 3-3:
A classified statement of financial position.

The cash flow statement has three sections:

>> **Operating:** Operating shows items pulled from the statement of activities.

>> **Investing:** Investing lists items such as the sale and purchase of long-term assets and other nonprofit investments like securities. This information is usually drawn from the statement of financial position.

>> **Financing:** Financing reflects the cash effects of long-term liability items, such as paying or securing loans beyond a period of 12 months from the statement date in order to fund the nonprofit.

There are two different methods to prepare the statement of cash flows:

>> **Direct:** Lists cash receipts and cash disbursements.

>> **Indirect:** Starts with change in net assets and accounts for noncash items reflected on the statement of activities, such as depreciation, which is the allocation of the cost of long-lived assets over their useful life.

Figure 3-4 shows a very basic cash flow statement prepared using the direct method. Chapter 19 provides full-blown examples of cash flow statements prepared using the direct and indirect method.

FIGURE 3-4:
A basic cash flow
statement.

Jay & Top Community Cat Project Statement of Cash Flow For the Twelve-Month Period Ending 31, 20XX	
Cash flows from operating activities	X,XXX
Cash flows from investing activities	(XXX)
Cash flows from financing activities	XXX
Increase (decrease) in cash	X,XXX
Cash balance January 1, 20XX	X,XXX
Cash balance December 31, 20XX	XX,XXX

In a nutshell, the cash flow statement reveals how liquid your organization is. Liquidity refers to the ability to easily convert current assets into cash. Liquid assets have the following characteristics:

>> The sale of a liquid asset doesn't result in significant loss.

>> A liquid asset usually can be converted into cash within a very short period of time.

Grasping the statement of functional expense

Most nonprofit organizations report their expenses by functional category, either by segregation via the statement of activities or by the notes to the financial statements. However, voluntary health and welfare organizations must report on a separate financial statement called the statement of functional expense. The statement of functional expense groups expenses by mission program and support services. *Support services* include management, general, and fundraising expenses.

The grouping is generally done using an allocation method adopted by the nonprofit, such as time spent. At the end of the day, everyone wants to know how you spent your time and money. Allocating expenses provides an accurate gauge when analyzing expenses.

Figure 3-5 shows an abbreviated statement of functional expense. Turn to Chapter 20 for a fully developed statement of functional expense.

FIGURE 3-5:
A partial
statement of
functional
expense.

Jay & Top Community Cat Project
Statement of Functional Expenses
Year Ending December 31, 20XX

Program services	Salaries, Employee Benefits and Taxes	Professional Fees and Other Expenses	Travel and Staff Development	Grants and Awards	Rent, Telephone, Postage and Supplies	Depreciation and Amortization	Total Expenses
Mentoring	XXX,XXX	X,XXX	X,XXX	XX,XXX	X,XXX	XXX	XXX,XXX
Tutoring	XX,XXX	X,XXX	X,XXX	X,XXX	X,XXX	XXX	XX,XXX
Total program services	XXX,XXX	X,XXX	XX,XXX	XX,XXX	XX,XXX	XXX	XXX,XXX

Documenting the notes to the financial statements

Your nonprofit has the responsibility to provide additional information users need to explain the numbers on your financial statements. Information that can't easily be gleaned from reviewing the financial statements has to be spelled out in your nonprofit's various notes and disclosures to explain how or why your nonprofit handles a transaction. You do this with notes to the financial statements (see Chapter 21) or other supplementary information.

Supplementary information to include covers just about any management discussion and analysis relating to your nonprofit. Accurately reporting your organization's financial statement is a matter of ethics. As a nonprofit manager, executive director, or board member, you have a responsibility to make sure adequate and correctly prepared notes are a part of your financial statements.

Reading the notes provides internal and external users with additional information that may greatly influence their judgment about the future livelihood of your organization. In the notes, you can find the following:

>> **Summary of accounting policies:** This section discloses choices made from different accounting methods, such as cash or accrual basis of recording transactions and selection of the method of depreciation.

>> **Detailed information about line items appearing on all statements:** This section includes info about all financial statements, such as property, equipment, and debts.

>> **Contingencies:** These are future events that may occur but whose occurrence is not certain.

The first order of business when preparing explanatory notes is explaining in general your nonprofit's organization. For example, include when and where your nonprofit was created, your vision and mission, and how you plan to achieve this mission. This would also be a good place to explain fundraising activities.

Next, you should provide a summary of significant accounting policies, such as depreciation methods, valuation of donated property, sources of cash contributions, and types of program revenue. Also important is to includes an explanation of how you classify net assets, revenues, gains, and losses by those with and without donor restrictions.

REMEMBER

According to the GAAP, all important information should be explained to users to help them better understand your nonprofit's financial status. Anything that abruptly changes your financial position must be shared with internal and external users in the notes.

REMEMBER

Your accounting system fulfills the reporting requirements for all internal and external users. Your internal managerial accounting reports may reflect more detail than your published records. This is not to suggest that something is being withheld, but merely that your reports address the needs of the group using them. For planning and strategizing, you may need more detailed reports about expenses and revenues than are required in the statement of activities.

Chapter **4**

Keeping Accurate Accounting Records

Recordkeeping involves entering accounting transactions into your books, tracking your accounts, keeping the documents that support the transactions, and making sure to leave an adequate paper trail. To keep good records, you need a central location where you keep all your source documents and any other paper records. Preparing materially correct reports about your financial position is your objective. This enables you to know how much money you have, how much you've spent, and what you've spent it on.

Choosing the method by which you'll track your income and expenses is a function of the size of your nonprofit. Smaller nonprofits and those first starting out can use a manual system. Larger nonprofits usually use nonprofit accounting software. It doesn't matter which method you choose as long as your financial reporting is accurate and traceable.

So, where to start? This chapter looks at your two options and helps you choose which one is best for you and your nonprofit. You find out how a manual accounting system works, how to convert a manual system into a computerized system, and the benefits of doing so. I also introduce you to three commonly used nonprofit accounting software programs and share with you how to protect your computer from dangerous viruses.

Going the Manual or Computer Route

Whether to use a manual system or computer software is a topic to discuss with your accountant and board after considering how much activity is going on in your nonprofit. Even with all the modern technology and computers, some nonprofit bookkeepers and accountants start with a pencil, pad, and adding machine. A good reason for this is that it allows them to understand how the numbers come together.

"Garbage in, garbage out" is a cautionary tale from all college programming courses. If you enter figures into accounting software incorrectly, all reporting flowing from those entries is incorrect. Keeping records manually at first can help to understand the accounting process and cycle, making it easier to recognize errors in automated reports.

Entering a high volume of transactions using a manual system can leave you feeling overwhelmed and lead to errors. Therefore, most bookkeepers and accountants rely heavily on accounting software programs because the software automatically updates all files when changes are made. For example, accounting software carries journal entries to ledgers and ultimately to the financial statements. This automatically recalculates totals when you make one change to a number or add another one. Using accounting software to keep track of your books saves time and energy.

REMEMBER

Journals are the books of original entry. Any event affecting your nonprofit is first recorded in a journal. Then your journal entries are entered in a ledger. Information in the ledgers is consolidated into financial reports, such as the statement of financial position.

TIP

Some accounting software even "talks to" tax return preparation software, transferring year-end figures from the accounting software to the tax return software. Although you always have to double-check the transfer process and update tax return figures as needed to conform with tax code, this saves you the time of having to completely reenter numbers from reporting software to return software.

TIP

If you're currently keeping your books manually and planning a move to accounting software, it's a good idea to use both systems concurrently for a few weeks to make sure both are providing the same results. The best way to do so is to create a paper file with hard copies of your *working papers* (the numbers added on paper). Then transfer the numbers from your working papers into your accounting software. Use your accounting software to print reports comparing the printout with your manual set of accounting reports making sure both systems give you the same results.

WARNING

Computer systems aren't foolproof. As wonderful as computers and accounting software are at making life easier, they're not immune to problems. Occasionally, things get lost, or users make mistakes. Plus, there's nothing like the sinking feeling of coming back to your laptop after the weekend to find it won't boot up or data that you know you entered isn't showing up on reports. To avoid extra work in reentering figures, you should back up every time you enter a significant amount of data during the day or at least at the close of business each day. That way you can seamlessly transition to a new laptop or restore a prior backup to find the missing data (see the "Making Sure Your System Is Secure" section at the end of this chapter for more information).

Creating a Manual System

A manual bookkeeping system is great if you have a limited number of transactions to record. It's the nature of the beast that you can easily monitor all transactions because you have hard copies of all journals, ledgers, and statements. Furthermore, writing down numbers and transactions helps the brain to remember them. A manual system entails much more than just keeping a check register or organizing all your receipts and canceled checks in an orderly fashion. The following sections take a closer look at the pros and cons of using a manual system and the characteristics of this type of system.

Discussing the pros and cons

Before you can maintain a manual bookkeeping system, you need to have a firm grasp of the advantages and disadvantages of using such a system. Being aware of these important considerations helps you understand what your manual bookkeeping system can and can't do for you and your nonprofit.

Here are some advantages of using a manual system:

>> You have hard copies of your records available at your fingertips.

>> You gain a greater understanding of your accounting system because every step is processed by hand.

Meanwhile here are some important drawbacks to consider as you maintain your manual system:

>> Using a manual system can be time consuming because you have to move numbers from journals to ledgers to reports manually. If you make an error, you can't correct it without redoing everything.

>> Paper files take up space, and if you need something, it can take some time to go through your files to find it.

>> Paper discolors and deteriorates, and paper mites find their way to old files. Older paper tends to smell funny and turns a brownish color. To handle these potential problems, you can scan your documents into your computer if you ever need to restore them to print.

Scanning your paper documents to your laptop and backing up the electronic copies to a flash drive is an excellent way to preserve them for long-term storage. Internal Revenue Service (IRS) examinations follow the statute of limitations, which is generally three years after filing, but I generally keep paper records for five years.

Walking through the parts of a manual system

To use a manual bookkeeping system, you need certain tools:

>> **A checkbook register:** Inside every new box of checks is a checkbook register to document each transaction affecting your account. You use this register to record your written checks, deposits, checking fees, and debit card transactions. Logging every transaction as soon as you know a deposit has been made or a check has been written is good financial management. Maintaining the register takes a little time and effort, but it's important to balancing your finances. (Check out Chapter 7 for more information about keeping a checkbook register.)

Some nonprofits opt to use a multiple-check-per-page register. These registers are usually bound with three stubs and checks per page. You record the check details (payee, amount, and purpose of the payment) on the stub, and then detach and issue the completed check. The stubs stay in the register for future reference.

>> **A ten-key adding machine with tape:** A ten-key adding machine that runs tape is another important component of your manual bookkeeping system. When working with numbers, it's easy to make transposition errors and write numerals down differently than how they appear. The tape that the ten-key adding machine spits out is an excellent tool to verify your numbers after you've calculated them. (You can use a calculator that doesn't print out a tape, but then it's harder to check for mistakes when the numbers don't add up correctly.)

Attach your adding machine tape to the documents you took the numbers from and file everything together.

>> **A journal, ledger paper, and statements:** Record all transactions first in a journal, which you then post to a ledger. The ending ledger figures come together in one of three nonprofit financial reports: statement of activities (Chapter 17), statement of financial position (Chapter 18), or statement of cash flow (Chapter 19). (Chapter 8 walks you through preparing manual journals, ledgers, and statements.)

>> **A filing system:** A key component of a manual bookkeeping system is good organization. You have to keep track of all source documents, such as merchant receipts, written checks, and paid invoices. This creates an audit trail proving substantiation that a transaction took place on a certain date for a certain amount. You correct errors faster and easier by having the necessary papers organized and accessible.

To keep your paperwork organized, I suggest the following:

>> Maintain hard copies of all records.

>> Place all important documents in clearly labeled and easily accessible file folders. Some nonprofits label files by the month and create a cross-reference system if they do a lot of transactions with a large vendor. This system makes it easier to do monthly and quarterly financial reports.

>> Store all records for at least three years for auditing purposes.

Make sure to keep your donors list on file. It's important to keep records of all the income your nonprofit receives and the sources of that income. This information is needed when your books are audited. (For more about donor information, see Chapter 7.)

WARNING

If you decide to track day-to-day operations manually and then deliver the necessary documents to your accountant to prepare your financial statements, they may ask for the underlying documents for purchases, receipts, and other transactions, especially if they're large, unusual, or questionable. If you're not organized and you don't have everything in order, you're in for a frustrating experience.

Using Spreadsheet Programs

If you want to use a computer bookkeeping system for your nonprofit, you don't necessarily have to use an accounting software program like the ones I discuss in the "Exploring Nonprofit Software Programs" section later in this chapter. Even if you're not computer savvy, it's easy to incorporate an electronic spreadsheet program such as Microsoft Excel into your bookkeeping system.

You can use Excel to sort, store, organize, and calculate data. Using the program, you create spreadsheets, which consist of rows and columns. After you enter information into the spreadsheet, you can calculate totals, create tables and graphs, and analyze financial data. The program is also useful for making lists of donors and charts of accounts.

Here are some of the advantages to using Excel:

>> You can use it to compare information from one period to information from another period.

>> You can store your accounting information on your desktop or external storage device.

>> With a little practice, you can put together some professional-looking reports using Excel, including some pretty impressive pie charts and graphs in your financial reports.

Working with Excel isn't all efficiency and automatic calculations, though. Here are some important drawbacks to consider:

>> Excel offers so many options in the toolbar that you may feel you have too many choices until you get familiar with the program.

>> Like any software program, if Excel isn't formatted correctly, you'll have erroneous results.

In the following sections, I show you how you can take baby steps to start using Excel in your bookkeeping. This information shows you how a simple spreadsheet can make your life easier. For more detailed information about how to use Excel and all its bells and whistles, check out *Excel For Dummies*, by Greg Harvey (Wiley), or *Excel All-in-One For Dummies*, by Paul McFedries (Wiley).

Breaking down the spreadsheet

Spreadsheets are the centerpiece of Excel. They're where you enter your data; after you've completed that task, you can crunch the numbers, sort data, track spending and income, and perform countless other functions. This section gives you a quick overview of the all-important spreadsheet.

A spreadsheet is commonly referred to as a worksheet. Every Excel spreadsheet has the following components:

>> **Columns:** Columns run up and down (vertically), and they're identified alphabetically at the top of the spreadsheet.

- » **Rows:** Rows run from side to side (horizontally). Each row is numbered on the left side.

- » **Cells:** The place where a column and row intersect is called a cell, and it looks like a rectangle. A cell is labeled by a letter and a number (so a cell two columns in and three rows down would be labeled B3). You enter the data into the cells.

You can use spreadsheets to make your job easier, no matter your position with your nonprofit. Spreadsheets store the following three basic types of data:

- » **Labels** are written text with no numerical value and are used to identify information. Labels consist of data that begins with a letter, like a list of names. Labels are typically found in the first cell of a column or row. For example, you can create a list of the donors who gave to a fundraiser by entering names of individuals.

- » **Numbers** are digits or entries that have a fixed value. For example, you can enter the amount given by each donor in the cell next to the person's name.

- » **Formulas** are mathematical equations used to make calculations. On the toolbar at the top of the spreadsheet is a button used to do mathematical computations. For example, if you want to know how much a donor has contributed over the year, you can use the AutoSum button to get the total.

Converting your manual system to a spreadsheet

If you've been using a manual bookkeeping system and you want to move to a more automated process, an Excel spreadsheet is a good place to start. You can use Excel to verify your totals in your manual bookkeeping system until you become more comfortable with Excel. Microsoft has issued many versions of Excel since the initial release in 1985, but the following steps will generally be applicable to whatever version you have on your computer:

1. **To open a new spreadsheet, open the Excel app and choose File ⇨ New.**

2. **To set up the spreadsheet, enter labels in the first cell of each column and row.**

   Creating these labels allows you to identify the data. For example, you can enter donor names in the columns (one name per cell) and various fundraising events in the rows (one event per cell).

3. **Enter your data into the appropriate cells.**

   The cell where a column and row intersect is where you enter the data specific to those two situations. So, if John Smith donated money at Fundraisers A, C, and D, you'd enter a number in the appropriate cells, skipping the one for Fundraiser B (or entering a zero in that cell).

   To quickly move from one cell to another, use the arrow keys on your computer keyboard. Another way to navigate through an Excel spreadsheet is by using the Tab key.

4. **After you enter your information, click the AutoSum button (it looks like the Greek letter sigma, or a very angular capital E) to tabulate your totals.**

   When you're ready to calculate totals on your spreadsheet, you'll use formulas. You can use the AutoSum button to have the computer do the math and make your job easier. The AutoSum button is located on the toolbar. Clicking it immediately calculates values in a range of cells. It can add, subtract, divide, multiply, and compute averages and means in a range of cells. All you have to do is enter data into the cells and use the AutoSum button to do the math.

   All math equations or formulas must begin with an equal sign (=). The computer automatically inserts an equal sign when you use the AutoSum button, but if you decide to write your own equations, make sure you start with an equal sign. Otherwise, the computer won't compute anything for that cell. (I don't cover equation writing in this chapter. If you're ambitious enough to tackle that, check out the For Dummies books I mention earlier in this chapter.)

Here's how to use the AutoSum function:

1. **Click the cell where you want your total to appear on your spreadsheet.**

2. **Click the AutoSum button on your toolbar.**

3. **Drag your mouse over the cells that you want to add and press the Enter button on your keyboard.**

   The total should appear in the cell you clicked in Step 1.

Figure 4-1 shows donor information by name, fundraiser, and amounts for John Smith and three other donors. Donor names show up as column labels, with fundraising events showing up as row labels. To make the spreadsheet easier to read, I inserted a column between each donor with a reduced column width of 2.

	A	B	C	D	E	F	G	H	I
1									
2	Donor		Smith, John		Jones, Mary		Topal, Liz		Salz, Joey
3	Fundraiser A		50				25		
4	Fundraiser B				60				
5	Fundraiser C		25						100
6	Fundraiser D		100		75		25		
7	Total		175		135		50		100
8									

FIGURE 4-1: Donor information captured in Excel.

TIP

You can use the AutoSum button to do more than add numbers. You can click inside a formula and change the colon to

>> A minus sign (–) to subtract numbers

>> An asterisk (*) to multiply numbers

>> A backslash (/) to divide numbers

For example, if you want to know how much money you've got left at the end of the month, you need to subtract your expenses from your income. First, add all your income in one column, and then add all expenses in another column. After you have those totals, you can select those two cells and tell Excel to subtract the expenses from the income just by changing the colon to a minus sign. (If you get a negative answer, you probably need to reverse the order of the cells in the formula.)

Cell formulas show up in the Excel formula bar, but sometimes it's helpful to be able to view the formulas directly in the cells and have the formula show up if you print the spreadsheet (see Figure 4-2 for an example).

You can accomplish this by first selecting the relevant cells. Then, on your keyboard, press CTRL + ` (` is the grave accent mark key, which is normally located at the left of your keyboard by the number 1). Press the same combination of keys when you're ready to switch back to the calculated figure.

	Smith, John
Fundraiser A	50
Fundraiser B	
Fundraiser C	25
Fundraiser D	100
Total	=SUM(C3:C6)

FIGURE 4-2: AutoSum cell formula.

TIP

If you need more help getting started with Excel, just click the Help button on the toolbar to access tutorials. The easy-to-follow information will help you navigate your way around a spreadsheet. The best way to get comfortable with using Excel is to play with a spreadsheet by entering information and clicking different icons on the toolbar. Do this on simple numbers when you've got some time before trying to use the software to meet a deadline.

If you aren't a fan of Excel, there are many other spreadsheet programs from which to choose. Some are *open source* (also called *freeware* or *shareware*), which means they're free to use. For contemporaneous alternatives to Excel, use your favorite search engine to search for "spreadsheets options other than Excel" or "open-source spreadsheet options." You can also try Google Sheets; go to www.google.com/sheets to check it out.

TECHNICAL STUFF

A lot of open-source software is the free version of a commercial product and lacks the advanced features of the paid version. The hope is that you'll like it so much that you'll decide to upgrade to a fully functional paid version.

Exploring Nonprofit Software Programs

If your nonprofit is larger or has more than a few accounting transactions each period, you'll want to seriously consider using accounting software. Many accounting programs are available to make bookkeeping and accounting much easier for your organization. Though these programs can greatly help, they do require you to invest some time in reading up on the software and spend some money to purchase the software. However, any time you spend in the learning curve will be more than offset by the amount of time saved keeping your books.

The following are accounting programs commonly used by nonprofits.

TIP

Although this section mentions QuickBooks, Aplos, and ACCOUNTS, there are many other nonprofit software packages, such as Sage Intacct, NonProfit Plus, and Zoho Books, that you may be interested in exploring.

QuickBooks

QuickBooks is widely used by smaller organizations because of its price and ease of use. Although QuickBooks Online Plus and Advanced are not specifically designed for nonprofit organizations, you can tailor both for nonprofits. By making small changes such as changing the company type to nonprofit and labeling customers as donors, the software will use terms, reports, and forms applicable to nonprofit organizations.

QuickBooks can help you

>> Manage donations

>> Categorize expenses and budget items by program or funds

>> Track bank account balances

>> Calculate payroll and sales taxes

>> Prepare payroll

>> Create and print financial reports

>> Track credit cards

>> Write and print checks

Chapter 9 walks you through tailoring QuickBooks for a nonprofit, entering transactions and running reports. For more information about QuickBooks Online, go to https://quickbooks.intuit.com/online. If you're interested in checking out how it can help your organization, check out the latest version of *QuickBooks For Dummies,* by Stephen L. Nelson, CPA, MBA, MS (Wiley).

Aplos

Aplos is cloud-based software specifically tailored to churches and nonprofits. Features include fund accounting, donation, membership, and event management. The software allows for automated donation reminders and receipts, as well as thank-you emails. It's helpful in preparing federal tax returns 990-N and 990-EZ (see Chapter 16).

Plus, all Aplos packages include donor portals, event registration, credit card processing, and customizable reporting. Turn to Chapter 9 to learn more about the different Aplos nonprofit software packages. That chapter also takes you on a guided tour of Aplos's nonprofit features. For more information, go to www.aplos.com.

ACCOUNTS

Less robust than QuickBooks or Aplos, Software4Nonprofits ACCOUNTS does basic bookkeeping and fund accounting. Tailored to churches and charities, it tracks income, expenses, and fund balances, and creates reports.

ACCOUNTS is much less expensive than QuickBooks or Aplos, but in order to track donors and donations, issue receipts, prepare reports, and perform mail-merges you have to also have the ACCOUNTS sister program, DONATION. The good news is you can use DONATION for free if you have 50 or less donors during the calendar year. Head to Chapter 9 to learn more about using ACCOUNTS and DONATION. For more information, go to www.software4nonprofits.com/accounts-features.

Making Sure Your System Is Secure

Your nonprofit's financial records contain important and confidential information that you can't risk losing, damaging, or having fall into the wrong hands. Security is especially important when bookkeeping and accounting records are on a computer system. If your system becomes contaminated with a virus, you may lose your files and never be able to recover them. In the worst-case scenario, if you store bank account information on your computer, someone may hack into your computer and steal the information they need to liquidate your nonprofit's (or even your donors') bank accounts.

That's why ensuring that your computer system is secure is essential. Although nothing is 100 percent secure, you can take the measures I outline in the following sections to give yourself some peace of mind.

TIP

You can choose from all sorts of programs to protect your computer system. When selecting virus protection software, look for recommendations from your nonprofit board, independent accountant, or information technology (IT) contractor.

Maintaining data integrity

In securing your computer system, two of the first lines of defense are a firewall and antivirus software.

Firewall

A *firewall* is a barrier preventing outside users from accessing protected areas of your computer system and tampering with or peering into sensitive materials. A firewall allows you to control who has access to materials you deem for public or private use. Firewalls come in two types:

>> **Software firewalls:** Programs installed on a single computer protecting against outside unauthorized users attempting to access or control the computer.

>> **Hardware firewalls:** Network-wide, dedicated equipment that acts as a barrier between your computer network and the internet. (A *network* is a group of computers that can transmit information between themselves.) Hardware firewalls keep certain types of traffic from entering your network. They also stop certain types of traffic from leaving your network.

To figure out which type of firewall you need, talk to the person in charge of maintaining your computer system.

Antivirus software

An antivirus software program protects your data by preventing, detecting, and removing malware from your computer. It runs in the background, monitoring and scanning information that comes into your computer from outside your firewall, as well as stored information within your network.

When the antivirus software finds malware, its job is to stop it before the malware spreads to your computer and network. *Malware* is any type of computer virus or other unwanted software that installs itself on your computer without your knowledge or consent.

You can set up a regular schedule telling your antivirus software to automatically perform a scan of all files and directories on your computer. Just about all antivirus software allows you to manually run off-schedule scans, allowing you to scan specific files and folders.

Some places where malware may lurk is in email links or attachments, downloads from the internet, and shared files. Malware can affect your computer by:

>> Slowing down your computer

>> Stealing personal data

>> Making your computer unable to perform its normal tasks

>> Crippling your system enough that soon it stops working altogether

>> Allowing hackers to take over your computer

As a protective measure, be cautious when opening emails from people you don't know. Unless you're 100 percent confident in the identity of the sender, it's not a good idea to click links within emails or open attachments. For example, if you receive an unexpected email from your bank, instead of clicking the link within the email, use your browser to go directly to the bank's website to view any important information.

Limiting user privileges

In ensuring your computer system's safety, another line of security is user privileges and file sharing. *User privileges* and *file sharing* mean allowing users in your nonprofit to access only the files they need. User privileges determine who can view, read, write, copy, modify, and print files, and which files may be shared by and with whom.

Sometimes only one person has control and access to everything, but your nonprofit may require that more than one person has access to all files. This person, called the *administrator,* sets up the user privileges and file-sharing protocols. The IT manager is usually the administrator. Other users are given certain rights and privileges for accessing and sharing files. These users can be in your network, as well as people outside your firewall who are granted limited access to information.

Most computer systems use password protection and identification to allow users the right to access certain files. It's a good idea to have your administrator set up your computer system so users have to change their passwords every 90 days. This security measure can keep intruders from accessing your computer files.

Backing up your system

Backing up your computer system is an essential and vital part of securing it. When you *back up* files, you save and archive important documents for potential future use. You should back up essential files that are used to run and maintain your nonprofit. This way, you have duplicate copies of files in the event of a system failure due to a power outage, equipment failure, inadvertently deleting files and folders, user errors, natural disaster, and malicious activities from within and outside your firewall. System backup is usually done by one of the following two methods:

>> **Automatic backup:** The automatic backup can be set to perform backups at a specific time every day. The automatic backup uses a software program to search for and find system files and folders to save for you. Most computer operating systems come with automatic backup programs to restore your computer to a state before it became corrupt or inoperable.

You can back up your info to different media as long as your system can access these modes. Some options for automatic backup include

- **CDs:** Files are copied onto media and stored in a safe place. You need to have the correct equipment and software to read and write to CDs.

- **Your computer's hard drive:** The hard drive comes as an external and internal piece of equipment. The hard drive is the ideal storage place for multiple files because it has a large storage capacity and provides easy access to files.

- **Third-party software:** This type of backup duplicates your computer storage system as a mirror image of computer files and folders. This option is a good choice if you live in an area prone to natural disasters because you can access the storage from another computer if yours is destroyed or inaccessible.

- **USB drive:** Also referred to as a *flash drive, jump drive,* or *thumb drive,* these storage tools are about the size of a lipstick tube. They don't hold as much data as a hard drive, but they hold a lot and can be transported conveniently.

>> **Manual backup:** In this process, you choose to save only certain files and folders or certain aspects or elements of your files and folders. For example, you're midstream working on a grant proposal. At the end of the day, after saving the in-process grant proposal on your laptop, you also copy the file to a USB drive as a second layer of protection against having to start all over again if your laptop fails to boot up the next workday.

TIP

Other security measures are available for your nonprofit's use, depending on how sophisticated of a system you want. To determine whether you need advanced security measures, you must first look at the data you have. Consider whether your information, if hacked, could be damaging to your nonprofit or others such as donors if it were to be viewed by the public. Third-party companies offer the necessary software online or at most retail stores that sell office software. Your IT administrator can check into some of the other available programs.

2

Balancing Your Nonprofit's Books

Set up a chart or list of accounts that you'll use during the accounting cycle.

Record transactions in your journals and ledgers.

Maintain and balance your nonprofit's checkbook.

Walk through keeping your books using both manual and automated systems.

Manage cash flow using a financial plan, the budget that supports your programs.

Chapter **5**

Setting Up the Chart of Accounts for Nonprofits

To keep track of both where money is coming from and where it's going to in your nonprofit and other nonmonetary transactions, you use a chart of accounts. The *chart of accounts* is a list of each account that the accounting system tracks; it captures the information you need to keep track of and use to make good financial decisions.

The chart of accounts is like a big reference card that contains numbers, or codes, and names of accounts; no transactions or specific financial information is recorded on the chart of accounts. An account code from the chart of accounts is recorded into the financial records, and from there into financial reports. For example, when you receive a donation, you code it with one account number. When you owe a vendor, you code it with another account number.

This chapter runs down the different accounts in a typical chart, how you can personalize your nonprofit's chart of accounts, and what you need to do to code funds coming in and going out of your nonprofit.

Identifying and Naming Your Nonprofit's Main Types of Accounts

When I talk about naming accounts, I don't mean choosing monikers like Sally, Sam, or Susie, so you can put away the book of baby names. Choosing names for your nonprofit accounts depends on the type of products or services you provide. Your chart of accounts consists of accounts found on your financial statements. Knowing which accounts go with which statements helps you to identify the main types of accounts. For example, the statement of financial position has assets, liabilities, and net assets (see Chapter 18). The statement of activities has revenues, expenses, and increases or decreases in net assets (see Chapter 17).

A typical chart of accounts is divided into five categories: assets, liabilities, net assets (fund balances), revenues, and expenses. Each account is assigned a unique identifying number for use within your accounting system. I explain these five categories in the following sections.

Figure 5-1 shows a sample chart of accounts for nonprofit organizations. Your nonprofit organizations might have most of the following accounts plus others as well.

```
Assets                                          Long-Term Liabilities
Current assets:                                     2210  Mortgage payable
    1110  Cash                                      2220  Bonds payable

            1111  Cash in checking account      Nonprofit Equity
            1112  Cash in savings account           3110  Net assets
            1113  Cash on hand (petty cash)
    1120  Notes receivable
    1130  Grants receivable                     Revenue
    1140  Accounts receivable                       4110  Federal grants
    1150  Inventory                                 4200  Corporate grants
    1160  Prepaid rent                              4300  State grants
    1170  Prepaid insurance                         4400  Program fees
                                                    4500  Interest income
                                                    4600  Fundraising
Long-Term Assets                                    4700  Individual donors
    1210  Land
    1220  Building
    1221  Accumulated depreciation: building    Expenses
    1230  Equipment                                 5110  Fundraising
    1231  Accumulated depreciation: equipment       5200  Salaries expense
                                                    5300  Depreciation expense
Liabilities                                         5400  Rent expense
Current liabilities                                 5500  Interest expense
    2110  Notes payable                             5600  Office supplies
    2120  Accounts payable
    2130  Salaries payable
```

FIGURE 5-1:
A typical chart of accounts.

Keep in mind that you name and chart your accounts based on their function. For example, Federal Grants is definitely revenue to your nonprofit. Assign revenue an identifying number starting with 4. The "Assigning Numbers to the Accounts" section at the end of this chapter gives a full-blown numbering guide.

REMEMBER

Your chart of accounts belongs to you — it's an internal system you use to keep track of where transactions post. Aside from certain conventions regarding numbering and the order in which information is presented, you can tailor your chart of accounts to your organization's specific needs. The chart classifies accounts by giving them a name and a number, and it's the first thing any bookkeeper needs to keep your books in order. All similar accounts list together. As you add new accounts, you can assign new numbers. The example chart of accounts in Figure 5-1 is merely a suggestion of how you can set up your chart. You must decide what's best for you.

Accounting for assets

The first grouping of accounts in a chart of accounts is assets. *Assets* are the items an organization has as resources, including cash, accounts receivable, equipment, and property. Basically, assets provide economic benefit to your organization. The following are the main types of assets:

>> **Current assets:** An asset that will be sold or depleted in the near future (within one year) or a business cycle. An example of a current asset is cash.

>> **Fixed assets:** A fixed asset is a long-term tangible asset your nonprofit uses that will mature or be used up more than 12 months after the date of the statement of financial position. Examples of fixed assets are computer equipment or office furniture and fixtures.

>> **Other assets:** This is a statement of financial position classification that covers miscellaneous assets. Prepaid expenses is a good example of other assets and one that you'll probably have for your nonprofit.

All assets start with the number 1 in the chart of accounts (refer to Figure 5-1). Assets are usually listed in descending order of liquidity. This means that cash and other assets that are easily converted to cash are listed first. Receivables and inventory are typically not as liquid as cash, so they're normally listed after cash accounts, followed by long-term assets.

The following are asset accounts:

>> **Checking account:** This is where you record cash on deposit in a checking account with a bank.

- **Petty cash, change funds, undeposited receipts, cash on hand:** This account includes cash used by the nonprofit organization for revolving funds, *change funds* (cash used to supply change to customers and others; can also be used to cash payroll checks), petty cash funds, and undeposited receipts at year-end.

- **Savings accounts, money-market accounts, certificates of deposit (CDs):** This category records funds on deposit with banks and other financial institutions that usually are interest bearing.

- **Contributions receivable:** When people give you pledges, you record them here, even if the donor restricts the pledged contribution to use in a future period. *Note:* If the pledge won't be paid until a future period, it should be classified as a noncurrent asset.

- **Land:** This account records the amount paid for the land itself, costs incidental to the acquisition of land, and expenditures incurred in preparing the land for use.

- **Buildings and improvements:** This account records the cost of relatively permanent structures used to house people or property. It also includes fixtures that are permanently attached to buildings you own that can't be removed without cutting into walls, ceilings, or floors, or without in some way damaging the building.

- **Furniture and equipment:** This account records the cost of furniture and equipment, such as office desks, chairs, computer tables, copy machines, large printers, and the like.

- **Data processing equipment:** Here's where you record the cost of data processing equipment used by your nonprofit, such as flat-screen monitors, desktop computers, hard drives, and such.

- **Leasehold improvements:** These costs usually include improvements made to facilities or property leased by your organization.

- **Accumulated depreciation:** This account records depreciation that has accumulated over time by periodic adjustments for annual depreciation. When an asset is sold, depreciation recorded for the item is removed from the records.

Labeling liabilities

Liabilities are obligations due to creditors; in other words, they are bills your nonprofit owes and, thus, indicate how much debt the nonprofit is obligated to pay. Liabilities are either current or long term:

>> **Current liabilities:** These are obligations that are due within one year or within the business cycle. An example is accounts payable.

>> **Long-term liabilities:** These are liabilities that aren't due within one year or within the current business cycle. A long-term notes payable is an example of a long-term liability.

Like assets, current liabilities are listed first, followed by long-term liabilities. All liabilities start with the number 2 in the chart of accounts (refer to Figure 5-1). In this example, the current liabilities' second digit is a 1. The long-term liabilities' second digit is a 2. (Check out the section "Assigning Numbers to the Accounts" at the end of this chapter for more about numbering.)

The following are common liabilities:

>> **Accounts payable:** This account records current liabilities, which represent debts that must be paid within a relatively short period, usually within 30 to 90 days of the statement date.

>> **Salary and wages payable:** Here's where you record the liabilities for salaries, wages, and employee benefits the employee has earned but not yet paid to the employee because payday may not be for another week or two.

>> **Accrued payroll:** This account records the liability for payrolls accrued at year-end. The accrual should include all salaries and wages earned by employees; thus, this entry would include all time worked by employees up to the end of the year.

>> **Payroll taxes payable:** These accounts record liabilities for various payroll taxes payable to governments arising from salaries and wages and payroll withholdings.

>> **Unearned revenue:** This account records amounts that have been received by your nonprofit, but the earning process hasn't been completed. For example, if your nonprofit offers subscriptions for one year to your inside newsletter and people pay for them annually, you may have revenue that has been received but not yet earned. That is, if you have only issued four in a series of ten newsletters, you still owe the subscribers six issues.

>> **Notes payable:** You use this account to record the outstanding principle due within the next year on notes owed by your organization. As the amount of the payable is due with one year, classify it as short term.

>> **Mortgage payable:** This is just what it sounds like. You record the outstanding principle due within the next year on mortgages. As the amount of the payable is due with one year, classify it as short term.

- » **Accrued interest payable:** This account records interest due on notes, capital leases, and mortgages at the end of the accounting period.

- » **Grants payable:** If you owe outstanding grant awards to outside organizations, you record it here. The figure represents amounts owed but not paid at year-end.

- » **Long-term debt:** This account records noncurrent liabilities, which represent debts that must be paid in a future period that is at least one year or more after the current fiscal period. This includes the balance on any note or mortgage payable that is due beyond 12 months of the statement date.

Explaining net assets

Net assets (your nonprofit's equity) show the financial worth of the organization. It represents the balance remaining after liabilities are subtracted from an organization's assets. (Accounting software designed with for-profits in mind may report net assets under the heading *equity*.) Net asset accounts begin with the number 3. (Check out the section "Assigning Numbers to the Accounts" at the end of this chapter for more info about numbering.) They are classified as:

- » **Net assets without donor restrictions:** This account records net assets with uses not restricted by the donor and can be used at the discretion of the nonprofit board. It includes revenues derived from providing services, producing and delivering goods, receiving unrestricted contributions, and receiving dividends or interest from investing in income-producing assets, less expenses incurred in fulfilling any of those tasks.

- » **Net assets with donor restrictions:** This account combines temporarily restricted and permanently restricted net assets.

   Donors' temporary restrictions may require that resources be used in a later period or after a specified date (time restrictions), or that resources be used for a specified purpose (use of purpose restrictions), or both.

   Permanently restricted assets have donor-imposed restrictions that don't expire with time or with the completion of activities that fulfill a purpose.

REMEMBER

Only people and organizations outside your nonprofit can place restrictions on grants and gifts. Your board of directors may designate a gift for a specific use, but it can turn around and undesignate it. Your nonprofit can't place restrictions on gifts. Restrictions are only enforceable when imposed by outside entities.

Calculating the change in net assets

The statement of activities reports the change in net assets as either a positive (increase) or negative (decrease) figure and is comparable to net income. Generally, you record revenue as increases in net assets and expenses as decreases in net assets. For example, if January 2023 revenue is $100,000 and expenses are $75,000, the change in net assets is $25,000 ($100,000 – $75,000).

Next, calculate ending net assets by taking the January 2023 change in net assets and add it to or subtract it from to your beginning net assets. For example, if the beginning net assets on January 1, 2023, is $45,000 and the current period change in net assets is $25,000, the ending balance in net assets on January 31, 2023, is $70,000 ($45,000 + $25,000).

TIP

The statement of activities reports revenues, expenses, and a change in net assets. The statement of financial position reports assets, liabilities, and net assets. (Chapters 17 and 18 provide more information about both statements.)

Recording revenue

Revenue accounts measure gross increases in assets, gross decreases in liabilities, or a combination of both when your nonprofit delivers or produces goods, renders services, or earns income in other ways during an accounting period. Keeping different sources of revenue (donations and other income) separate is important because you may have to account for what you did with the income.

For example, you'll account separately for government grant revenue, which can be set apart using your chart of accounts. You may have to account for gifts received with restrictions on them. So, assign account numbers that clearly identify all revenue sources because this will serve as documentation for you during an audit.

Your chart of accounts helps you keep track of revenue sources through the assignment of unique account numbers. Revenue accounts start with the number 4 and are further classified by subaccounts such as federal grants, private gifts, and investment income. (See the section "Assigning Numbers to the Accounts" at the end of this chapter for more info about numbering.)

Here are common nonprofit revenue accounts:

>> **Federal grants:** This account records revenues earned for grants from federal agencies. Generally, revenues are earned for operating grant programs and by incurring qualifying expenses. Establish a subaccount for each federal grant.

- **State grants:** This account shows revenue earned from grants from one or more states. The revenue/expense relationship is similar to that of federal grants. Establish a subaccount for grants from different states.

- **Private gifts and grants (contributions):** Here's where you record revenues from private gifts and grants, including corporate gifts, grants from private foundations, and contributions from individuals. This account can also be used for pledges that aren't contingent on future events. Set up a subaccount for each corporation (unless anonymity is requested).

- **Fees from special events:** When you collect membership fees and funds raised through special events, you record them in this account. Subaccounts should be established for each type of fee collected.

- **Special events (net revenue):** This account records the net proceeds (gross collections less expenses) from special events. Establish subaccounts to record receipts and expenses.

- **Investment income:** This account records income from investments. The balance of these accounts should include investment income received during the year, as well as accrued investment income earned but not received by year-end.

Your nonprofit may also receive donations and contributions of nonfinancial assets, also known as *in-kind contributions.* These include donated goods, buildings, below-market rent, and pro bono legal and professional services.

TIP

Wondering how your nonprofit accounts for in-kind contributions? Well, there is an FASB for that! Financial Accounting Standards Board (FASB) Accounting Standards Update (ASU) No. 2020-07 is effective for all financial statements with a June 30, 2022, year-end and after. (Turn to Chapter 13 for more about FASB ASU No 2020-07.)

Booking costs

You can't make money without spending money. *Expenses* are expired costs, the using up of assets, or incurrence of liabilities from operations. Examples include personnel costs, costs of supplies, and the costs associated with accounts payable. If you're using the accrual method (see Chapter 1 for an explanation of the accrual method and its counterpart, the cash method), expenses are recognized when incurred, and revenues are recognized in your accounting books when they're earned. Expense accounts start with the number 5. (See the section "Assigning Numbers to the Accounts" at the end of this chapter for more info about numbering.)

Here are some common expense accounts:

>> **Salary and wages:** Here's where you record the cost of salary and wages paid to employees of your nonprofit. This account includes both full- and part-time personnel costs.

>> **Payroll tax expense:** This account records the employer's share of Social Security and Medicare taxes based on the amount of salary and wages paid to employees.

>> **Unemployment insurance contribution:** This account records the employer's contribution for employees' costs of the state unemployment insurance program.

>> **Workers compensation:** Here you record the cost of workers compensation insurance premiums for your nonprofit.

>> **Board member compensation/stipends:** When you pay stipends to board members, you record them here.

>> **Accounting and tax services:** This account records accounting and tax services for bookkeeping services, payroll, and preparation of tax returns.

>> **Legal services:** This account is used to record legal services either for specific services or the used-up portion of retainers.

>> **Temporary services:** If you use temporary services (like temporary clerical or secretarial personnel) from workforce agencies, you record the expense in this account.

>> **Management services:** This account records the costs of management services acquired by the organization (for example, consulting services).

>> **Honorariums:** When you pay an *honorarium* (a sum paid to a professional for speaking engagements or other services for which no fee is set), you record the amount in this category.

>> **Supplies and materials:** This account records the cost of supplies and materials used in the daily operations of your organization.

>> **Travel:** Here you record the costs of employee travel, including food, lodging, and transportation.

>> **Communication:** This account records the costs of landlines, cellphones, high-speed Internet, and postage.

>> **Utilities:** This account records costs for things such as electricity, water and sewer, and gas.

>> **Printing and binding:** This account records the cost of printing, binding, and copying documents used or distributed by the nonprofit.

>> **Repair and maintenance:** This account covers the costs of routine repairs and maintenance, including service contracts.

>> **Employee training:** Here you record the cost of employee training, including tuition, conference registration, and training materials.

>> **Advertising and promotion:** This account records the cost of advertising program services, solicitation of bids, obtaining qualified applicants, or advertising fundraising events.

>> **Board member expense:** Here's where you record the cost of board member travel and per diem expenses.

>> **Office rent:** This account records the cost of office rent.

>> **Furniture and equipment rental:** This account records the cost of furniture or equipment rental. Lease-purchase agreements that meet the criteria of a *financing lease* (a lease recorded as an asset accompanied by borrowing of funds) should be recorded as *capital outlays* (a liability intended to benefit future periods).

>> **Vehicle rental:** You record the cost of vehicle rental in this account. Lease-purchase agreements that meet the criteria of a capital lease should be recorded as capital outlays.

>> **Dues and subscriptions:** Record the costs of professional fees for organizations your nonprofit is a member of in this account.

>> **Insurance and bonding:** This account records the costs of insurance on facilities and liability insurance.

>> **Depreciation:** This account records the estimated periodic charge against asset values for use, deterioration, or obsolescence.

>> **Contracts, grants, and stipends:** This account records contracts, grants, or stipends with outside organizations or individuals.

>> **Other expenses:** This account records any other expenses not classified in the other categories.

Assigning Numbers to the Accounts

To recap, your chart of accounts is a list of all accounts used in the five categories I discuss in the "Identifying and Naming Your Nonprofit's Main Types of Accounts" section. The chart of accounts assigns specific account names and numbers to each account found on your statement of activities and statement of financial position.

You recognize account types by looking at the first digit or leading number. To number your accounts, remember this basic numbering system:

>> Asset accounts begin with the number 1, so 1000 to 1999 are assigned to asset accounts.

>> Liability accounts begin with the number 2, so 2000 to 2999 are assigned to liability accounts.

>> Net assets (nonprofit equity) begin with the number 3, so 3000 to 3999 are assigned to equity accounts.

>> Revenue accounts begin with the number 4, so 4000 to 4999 are assigned to revenue accounts.

>> Expense accounts begin with the number 5, so 5000 to 5999 are assigned to expense accounts.

TECHNICAL STUFF

Referring to Figure 5-1 you may be thinking, "Why does that typical chart of accounts start numbering at 1110, 2110, 3110, 4110, and 5110, rather than the numbering sequence listed here?" Well, it's because accountants and bookkeepers look to the future and the possibility of having to add accounts as the nonprofit evolves. It's easier to add accounts if you leave the space to add accounts.

For year-over-year comparative analysis and audit procedures, you can't just willy-nilly delete accounts or change the names of accounts. That will totally destroy an audit trail. The example chart of accounts in Figure 5-1 is merely a suggestion of how you can set up your chart.

As a suggestion to maintain a great audit trail and controls, within each category of accounts, the second digit identifies the subclassification. For example:

>> Within 1110 to 1231 of asset accounts, you could have the following:

• 1111 to 1170 as current assets

• 1210 to 1231 as long-term assets

>> Within 2110 to 2220 of liability accounts, you could have the following:

• 2110 to 2130 as current liabilities

• 2210 to 2220 as long-term liabilities

You use your chart of accounts to code accounting transactions. This chart also helps you locate accounts in your ledger. It's important that you follow a systematic approach of assigning numbers to your accounts. Having a systematic method to identify your accounts helps when errors are made while preparing your trial balance. (For more about your ledger and trial balance, see Chapter 6.)

IN THIS CHAPTER

» **Getting an overview of the accounting process**

» **Making entries in the journal**

» **Transferring information to the general ledger**

» **Making sure everything balances**

» **Finding and fixing errors**

Chapter **6**

Recording Accounting Transactions

J
ust like a coin has two sides (a head and a tail), an account has two sides (a debit and a credit). When your nonprofit makes a transaction, you have to record it in two or more accounts: the *debit* (the left side of an account) and the *credit* (the right side of an account). When you record the transaction in your accounting books, you're making a *journal entry*.

This chapter touches on the basics, including the different types of accounting and an overview of the accounting process. With this information you can make journal entries, prepare a worksheet, make adjusting entries, and find errors in your books.

Explaining the Recording Process

You can't enter transactions in your book work until you select a basis of accounting. Some industries use hybrid methods, but for your nonprofit, you need to decide between using the cash method and using the accrual method. Bookkeepers generally find the cash method easier to maintain. However, if you anticipate applying for any grants, I suggest you strongly consider using the accrual method.

In this section, I also highlight the nuts and bolts of the accounting process and what the general recording process looks like. Although accounting can be quite maddening at times, it follows a clear logic. As you work to get a firm grasp of the accounting process, start with the end in mind first. In the end, you prepare and issue financial statements to customers such as donors. Your donors care that your financial statements fairly represent your true financial position for a given time period as of a certain date.

Choosing your basis of accounting

Your nonprofit's *basis of accounting* is the method by which you account for things. Most organizations can choose between two bases of accounting to track their transactions: cash or accrual. Depending on the basis you choose, you account for things when they happen or you wait until later. The method you choose affects when you make journal entries about transactions and is centered on how and when you recognize revenues and expenses.

Choose between the two following methods:

>> **Cash-basis accounting:** The cash-basis method is simple to use because you usually only recognize transactions when you receive or distribute cash.

>> **Accrual-basis accounting:** The accrual-based system recognizes revenues when a promise or pledge is given and recognizes expenses when they're incurred.

Check out Chapter 1 for more on the ins and outs of these two types of accounting methods.

TIP

Using the accrual method of accounting may be your best choice. All grant applications ask for a set of audited financial statements, which are prepared according to generally accepted accounting principles (GAAP). GAAP usually uses the accrual method.

If you're running a small nonprofit and you're keeping your own books or you have a part-time bookkeeper doing the work, you may want to account for your transactions on the cash basis and pass the books on to your accountant or certified public accountant (CPA) at the end of the year to compile your financial statements. Your CPA can convert your cash-basis books to accrual basis for the necessary audit report.

Eyeing the specifics of the process

To fully understand how to record and track your nonprofit's financial transactions, you need to understand the ins and outs of the process. You also need to know what the different accounts are and how putting them together creates your nonprofit's bottom line.

So, how does the process work? It usually starts when your organization receives a donation. You enter the donation into a journal and post it to the general ledger (check out the later sections in this chapter for more how-to info).

Once a month or when the accounting period is over, you (or your bookkeeping and accounting staff) prepare a trial balance. A *trial balance* is a listing of all accounts and their balances. If the total of the accounts' debit balances equals the total of the accounts' credit balances, then your accounts are in balance (refer to the section "Reaching the trial balance," later in this chapter, for specifics).

At the end of the accounting period, you take your *unadjusted trial balance* (a trial balance prepared before you put together any necessary adjustments) and make adjusting entries. *Adjusting entries* are made to your accounts to bring them to their actual balance. For example, adjustments are made for prepaid accounts and for expenses incurred but not yet paid.

Common adjusting entries include the following:

» Accrued revenue (earned revenue that hasn't been recorded because payment hasn't been received)

» Accrued salaries that are unpaid and unrecorded

» Depreciation (allocating the cost and usage of assets as expense)

» Prepaid expenses, such as insurance

» Office supplies used

» Unearned revenue (payments received in advance)

After you finish adjusting the entries and everything balances, you're ready to prepare an *adjusted trial balance.* Your adjusted trial balance verifies that the accounts are still in balance. If your entries are out of balance, then you must find and correct your errors. For help with this, see the section "Correcting errors" later in this chapter. Figure 6-1 provides a snapshot of the accounting process.

WARNING

If you keep your books on the cash basis, you'll have a limited number of adjusting entries because you only recognize revenue when it's received and expenses when they're paid. One example of an adjusting journal entry made while using the cash basis is depreciation expense. (See Chapter 8 for more information.)

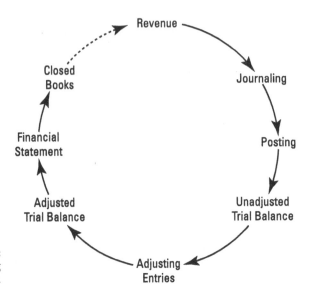

FIGURE 6-1:
The accounting process.

Looking at the two sides of a transaction

Before you begin preparing journal entries to record transactions, you need to understand debits and credits, which is how accounting transactions are originally entered into your nonprofit's books. When you fully understand debits and credits, you'll be able to do journal entries like a pro.

To prepare journal entries, you need to know the law of debits and credits:

» Asset and expense accounts increase by debiting and decrease by crediting.

» Revenue, liability, and equity accounts increase by crediting and decrease by debiting.

For example, you pay cash to purchase $100 of office supplies. To enter this transaction into your books, you debit (add to) office supplies for $100 and credit (subtract from) cash for the same amount — $100.

Consider the debit and credit outline in Table 6-1. This table shows you how normal balances affect accounts on the statement of financial position and statement of activities. *Normal balances* indicate what you do to increase the accounts. To decrease the accounts, you do the opposite. For example, because a debit increases an expense account, to decrease an expense, you credit the account.

TABLE 6-1   **Understanding Normal Balances of Accounts**

Balance Sheet Accounts	Normal Balance
Assets	Debit
Liabilities	Credit
Net Assets (Equity)	Credit
Income Statement Accounts	Normal Balance
Revenue	Credit
Expense	Debit

Stepping Through the Accounting Cycle

Now that you understand the law of debits and credits, the rest of this chapter provides a quick walk through to writing journal entries, posting to the ledger, and preparing and adjusting the trial balance. Chapter 8 has detailed information on the process and many journal entries nonprofits commonly prepare.

Recording journal entries

Many people write in a personal journal to reflect on the events of their daily life. In accounting, you use a *journal* to record transactions in the order that they occur. A journal is often referred to as the *book of original entry* because it's the first place where you record transactions in the accounts.

Figure 6-2 shows how to prepare the journal entry for the $100 office supply purchase from earlier.

General Journal

	Date	Account Titles & Explanation	Debit	Credit
FIGURE 6-2: Journal entry recording $100 cash purchase.	April 20, 20XX	Office Supplies	100	
		Cash		100
		To record purchase of copier paper		

The first step you take when preparing journal entries is to record the transaction date. You need to know when transactions take place to help keep your books up to date and maintain an audit trail. Record journal entries in the order of their occurrence.

The second step of recording your journal entries includes writing the names of the accounts to be debited and credited. You write the name of the account to be debited first, and write the name of the account to be credited indented about 1 inch. Doing so helps readers identify quickly which accounts have been debited and which have been credited.

In the third step, you write the debit amount in the debit column opposite the name of the account to be debited, and write the credit amount in the credit column opposite the account to be credited. So, if doing one thing to one side of an account increases the account, then the opposite happens when you record the entry on the opposite side.

TIP

When recording journal entries and ledger postings, don't use dollar signs because the only thing you can debit and credit to accounts is money. Everyone knows you're talking about money.

Each transaction has an explanation. The last step to recording a journal entry is to state the reason for the transaction. Write the explanation on the next line, indented about ½ inch. Keep this explanation short and to the point, but be sure to include enough information to explain the transaction.

Posting to the general ledger

The *general ledger* shows all the accounts in your chart of accounts ordered by account number and reflects all transactions affecting each account. You keep track of any changes to the different accounts by posting journal entries to your general ledger.

Assets, liabilities, and net assets, which are statement of financial position accounts, are placed first. Next are revenues and expenses, which are statement of activities accounts.

Here's an example of how usual accounts in the general ledger are arranged:

>> **Cash:** This includes coins, currency, checks, money orders, checking and savings accounts, and short-term certificates of deposit (CDs).

>> **Donation receivables:** These are promises and pledges to give.

>> **Prepaid insurance:** Here is what you've paid in advance for insurance coverage that expires as the days go by.

>> **Inventory:** This account records the price paid for any product sitting on your shelves that you plan to sell.

>> **Land:** This account includes land purchased or owned by your organization. Although a valuable asset, land should not be depreciated (see Chapter 2 for more on depreciation).

>> **Buildings:** This includes your office building if you're buying or you already own it. Buildings usually have a depreciable span of 39 to 40 years.

>> **Equipment:** This account records the purchase of copy machines, computers, vehicles, office furniture, file cabinets, and similar items. Equipment usually has a useful life span of three to seven years.

>> **Accumulated depreciation:** This account shows how much depreciation has occurred on assets so far. The flip side of accumulated depreciation is depreciation expense. (You learn more about expenses in Chapter 17.)

>> **Accounts payable:** These are short-term liabilities usually paid within a month or two. They're considered a current liability.

>> **Salaries payable:** These are usually recorded on the statements of financial position and activities because employees have earned salaries but have not yet been paid.

>> **Notes payable:** These are liabilities or promises to pay a certain amount on a certain date.

>> **Mortgage payable:** This is a long-term liability to a creditor for a large purchase of land or buildings.

>> **Bonds payable:** This is a long-term liability between the issuer and the lender. Some organizations borrow large sums of money to finance large purchases, equipment, and other assets. The money is obtained by issuing bonds. Bonds are paid back, and usually you have a bond payable and interest payable account to account for bonds payable.

>> **Revenue:** These accounts are established for all sources of income: donations, grants, fees from services rendered, and interest income. For most nonprofits, donations from individuals, corporations, foundations, and state and federal grants are each recorded in a separate account.

>> **Expenses:** These are usually the last group of general ledger accounts. You name your expense accounts according to their purpose. Typical expenses are rent expense, supplies expense, insurance expense, salaries expense, and so on.

Keep in mind the accounts in the general ledger vary from one organization to another. Which accounts you set up depend on many variables including the nature of your organization, the way you operate, the size of your nonprofit and regulatory requirements.

When transferring entries from your journals to your general ledger, you post information following these steps:

1. **Find the account name and number in your ledger.**

2. **Copy the date of the transaction as written in the journal to your ledger.**

3. **Enter a description of the transaction.**

4. **Enter the posting reference, letter G (general journal).**

5. **Write the amount as shown in the journal in your ledger as either a debit or a credit following the guidance given earlier in this chapter in the "Looking at the two sides of a transaction" section.**

6. **Enter the new balance after making the entry in your ledger.**

Referencing Figure 6-2, check out Figure 6-3 for an example of what the cash in checking account general ledger page looks like after you've posted the transaction from that general journal to the general ledger.

General Ledger

Account Name: Cash in checking account				Account #: 1111	
Date	Description	Post Ref.	Debit	Credit	Balance
April 1, 20XX					645.00
April 20, 20XX	Office Supplies	G		100.00	545.00

FIGURE 6-3:
A sample general ledger page.

Reaching the trial balance

At the end of your accounting cycle, after you post the last entry to your general ledger, it's time to prepare a trial balance. Your *trial balance* lists the balances of all the general ledger accounts. The sum of the debits in the trial balance must equal the sum of the credits.

To prepare a trial balance, you write down all your account titles from your general ledger and the ending debit or credit balances in each. You have two columns for the figures. Debit ending balances are in the left-hand column and credit ending balances are in the right-hand column. (See Chapter 8 for more information about preparing a trial balance and an example of a trial balance.)

Adjusting entries

Most likely after you prepare your trial balance, you'll need to prepare adjusting entries. *Adjustments* are journal entries of changes in accounts. You may have to make adjustments to correct errors, book depreciation, or to make any changes required by your independent CPA or auditor.

For example, if operating on the accrual basis, generally accepted accounting principles (GAAP) require you to assign revenues to the period in which they're earned, regardless of whether they've been paid to your nonprofit. Expenses incurred are reported in the same period as the revenues earned (the matching principle), regardless of whether you've paid the expense. If it's time to close your accounting period and you have salaries that have been earned but not paid, you need to make adjusting entries to record that salary expense.

You may need to prepare adjustments for the following accounts:

>> **Prepaid expenses** include payments in advance of use. A prepaid expense is considered an asset until it's consumed in the operation of your business. An example of a prepaid expense is paying an insurance premium for 12 months and you're only 5 months into the policy period. The remaining 7 months is considered prepaid insurance.

>> **Accrued expenses** are expenses incurred but not yet paid. For example, at the close of your accounting period, some expenses may be unrecorded because the payment is not yet due. Examples of accrued expenses are utilities, telephone bills, and unpaid wages.

>> **Unearned revenues** include payments prior to delivery of the product or service; for example, the sale of tickets for a benefit dinner or golf tournament. You may collect money weeks in advance of the event.

>> **Depreciation** is an allocation of the purchase price of an asset based on its useful life. Assets are expensed over their useful life through depreciation. As they lose their value, a portion is written off as an expense.

Correcting errors

No matter how meticulous you are with your accounting, you're going to make mistakes. There's no way to avoid it. If you find an error in your trial balance, don't despair. It happens to everyone. You know you have an error when your figures don't balance when you total all debits and all credits.

Your general ledger is only as accurate as your journal. If you entered incorrect data while journaling, you probably transferred the same incorrect information to the general ledger. Go back to the beginning and compare journal entries to general ledger entries. If you still can't find the error, go back over each transaction, and look at receipts, invoices, checks, and bills. Carefully review each item to ensure you recorded the correct information in your journal and in your ledger.

TIP

If you find that your trial balance is still out of balance and the difference is evenly divisible by 9, you've made a transposition error. A *transposition error* occurs when you switch the order of the digits; for example, you write 428 instead of 482, resulting in an error of 54 (482 − 428).

Even if your accounting system is computerized, you or one of your staff members has to enter the numbers. Occasionally, the person entering the information makes a mistake that throws things off. One of the objectives of an audit is to find errors that have a material effect on an organization's financial statements.

Do the following to locate errors:

>> Refer to your journal and check the posting and totals.

>> Check the posting and balances in your general ledger accounts.

>> Check all balances in the trial balance.

Keep in mind that some errors are hard to find. For example, if you forget to record a transaction, or if you copy the incorrect debit amount and credit amount in accounts, it's highly unlikely these errors would be immediately apparent.

Some errors cancel each other out. If you make a $1,000 error twice, the two may cancel each other out. Or you may make an error by debiting the wrong account within the same account group. For example, if you charge something to Vehicle Expense that should have been charged to Office Supplies, you might not detect this error. However, your auditor will detect material amounts. They'll also define for you what's considered material for your nonprofit.

TIP

One way to reduce the chance of errors like these is to create a monthly trial balance. Tracking your accounts by creating a monthly trial balance can save you lots of time and energy. If you keep everything in balance month by month, you'll breeze through the final process at the end of the year. (See Chapter 21 for more on closing the year-end books.)

So, after hunting through your transactions, you find your error. Although some errors are easier to find than others, most are easily correctible. Errors made in calculations and balancing, posting to the wrong side of an account, entering the wrong amounts, or simply forgetting to enter a transaction can be easily corrected. The trial balance can show these errors quickly. How you correct the error depends on whether it's in the journal and the general ledger or in your journal only.

Making a journal correction

Where and when you find an error in the journal affects how you correct it. Usually you can correct it by drawing a line through the error and writing the correct amount or title above the error. If the data has been journalized and not posted to the general ledger, that's all you have to do.

For example, say you see the following entry in your journal:

Date		Debit	Credit
20XX			
Oct. 8	Office Furniture and Fixtures	75	
	Cash		75

To record the purchase of office supplies.

If you made that entry when you purchased office supplies on October 8, then the following entry is needed to correct the error.

Date		Debit	Credit
20XX			
Oct. 8	Office Supplies	75	
	Office Furniture and Fixtures		75

To correct entry of Oct 8 when the Office Furniture and Fixtures account was debited in error instead of Office Supplies.

The debit to Office Supplies records the purchase in the right account and the credit to Office Furniture and Fixtures cancels out the error of the first entry. There's no need to bother with cash because it was handled properly.

If the incorrect information from the journal has already been recorded in the ledger, you have to take a few more steps to make everything right. The next section shows you how.

Making a ledger correction

If you find a mistake after it's been posted to the general ledger, you need to correct both the journal entry and the general ledger to fix the problem. Using the

Office Furniture and Fixtures/Office Supplies example from the preceding section, "Making a journal correction," there are two steps to carry that correction to the general ledger:

1. Post the $75 adjustment to the Office Supplies general ledger account following the same steps as in the earlier section "Posting to the general ledger."

2. Draw a line through the erroneous posting to the Office Furniture and Fixtures, hand-write in a brief explanation, and adjust the balance.

   In this case you decrease the Office Furniture and Fixtures ending balance by $75.

See Chapters 8 and 9 for an adjusted trial balance and partial general ledger.

IN THIS CHAPTER

» **Understanding the checkbook register**

» **Taking in and tracking donations**

» **Paying bills and recording expenses**

» **Reconciling your checkbook register**

» **Ferreting out and fixing errors**

Chapter **7**

Keeping Tabs on Your Checking Account

The center of many transactions in nonprofit organizations starts and ends in the checkbook register. In fact, you can find keys that unlock your non-profit's financial position in the checkbook register and bank statements. Having more money than you thought you had in your checking account is okay, but having less money can cost you if a check bounces.

The bank records every donation deposited and expense paid out of your checking account and sends you a monthly statement showing this activity. All deposits are considered *credits* (additions) to your account, and all withdrawals are considered *debits* (subtractions). The difference between credits and debits equals your checking account *balance*.

Having a checking account saves you time and energy. For example, driving to each utility to pay your bill in cash would take a lot of time away from bigger duties — serving your community. It makes it easier for bookkeeping and record-keeping if you pay bills out of a checking account instead of using cash. That's why organization is necessary. Having a plan to track all donations and expenses is essential; if you don't have a plan, you'll inevitably run into major problems because you won't know whether you have enough money to cover your expenses and pay your bills.

Writing a check creates a paper trail between your checkbook, the bank, and the vendor or bill you're paying. It's easier to trace your steps when you have a bank that provides a bank statement. This paper trail comes in handy during your nonprofit's audit.

This chapter focuses on how to use the checkbook register to balance your nonprofit's checking account and shows you how to record and log transactions when they occur.

WARNING

If you just opened a checking account, balancing the account in your head may seem like a practical approach when only a few transactions are taking place. Don't rely on this system as an adequate method. You'll regret it later. Not balancing your checkbook can cost you returned check fees and overdraft fees and cause you to lose your credibility.

Getting the Lowdown on Your Checkbook Register

Before you can balance your nonprofit's checkbook register, you first need to know what the register is. You're probably familiar with your personal checking account register — it's where you record the payment and deposit details to keep track of your money. With your nonprofit's checking account, the checkbook register holds valuable information, too.

You use a checkbook register to record the following:

>> Each check when written

>> Each deposit when made

>> Each withdrawal either from an ATM or from a bank teller

>> All bank service charges

Figure 7-1 shows you an example of a checkbook register for a fictional nonprofit organization. In this figure, you can see entries for the transactions that take place in the checking account. The rest of this chapter discusses how you record information in your register to balance your nonprofit's checkbook.

Date	Check #	Payee/ Description of Transaction	Withdrawal Debit	Deposit Credit	Balance
Beg Bal					$ 1,000.00
01-10-2023		Donations Received		500.00	1,500.00
05-10-2023		ATM Withdrawal	50.00		1,450.00
08-10-2023	255	George Rembert Supplies	100.00		1,350.00
08-10-2023		Bank Charges	8.00		1,342.00
08-10-2023		Fundraiser		750.00	2,092.00
09-10-2023	256	Web Design	25.00		2,067.00
10-10-2023	257	Salaries Paid	925.00		1,142.00
13-10-2023		Donations Received		300.00	1,442.00
Balances			1,108.00	1,550.00	$ 1,442.00

FIGURE 7-1:
A nonprofit's checkbook register.

TIP

Duplicate checks can be a lifesaver when it comes to recording information in your checkbook register. *Duplicate checks* create a copy of a check as you fill it out, so you have all the details of the check after you hand it over to pay for something. These nifty copies help you stay on top of your account balance because you can look at the copies and transfer the transaction information to your register.

TIP

Another lifesaver to keeping your register balanced is online banking. You can see an updated and current balance in your account when you access your account online. But even with online banking, you still need a paper trail because one day you may be audited, and you'll need to have all deposits and withdrawals from your checking account recorded in the check register. Even if you're not a number cruncher, you still need to keep a checkbook register because you need to stay on top of your finances.

Tracking Nonprofit Donations

To have a complete picture of how much money your nonprofit has on hand, you need to keep an accurate picture of the money coming in. Most of what comes in is in the form of *private donations* (charitable contributions that individuals, as well as organizations, give to your nonprofit) or *grants* (funds received from foundations and government agencies that are generally secured via an application process).

Discussing donation methods

People can write checks, hand you cash, or pay by credit card when they donate money to your organization. Larger groups, such as the United Way, may give you a grant to finance your mission. This section takes a closer look at the diverse types of donations you record as deposits.

Cash donations

The best way to handle the rare event of receiving a cash donation is to give the donor a receipt if the donation is made in your office. In the unlikely event of receiving cash in the mail, you should send the donor a receipt. Your nonprofit should have some checks and balances in place to properly account for cash donations. (See Chapter 2 for more on setting up checks and balances.)

Donations made by check

Most of your donations will come in the form of a check. Although these are more secure than cash donations, your nonprofit must establish and follow a procedure for recording and depositing donations made by check. (See the section "Entering donations in your register" later in this chapter for more about depositing donations.)

WARNING

Watch out for bad checks! Occasionally, donors will write you checks that they don't have enough funds in their checking accounts to cover. It may appear that you have a good working balance in your checkbook register because you've received and recorded donations made by check as deposits. But don't count your chickens before they hatch. Until those checks clear your bank, don't count them as available cash.

TIP

If you can afford it, purchase a *check-swiping system,* such as TeleCheck, to speed up the check-clearing process. These systems connect directly to banks and reject a check if the money isn't in the account. This is the best way to avoid delays in waiting for checks to clear your bank account. The cost of the terminal and printer varies based on the vendor and factors unique to your nonprofit. You'll also have transaction fees and monthly customer service fees. For more about TeleCheck quick check-clearing processing, visit `https://getassistance.telecheck.com`.

Credit card donations

Credit card donations are another popular way you receive donations. When reporting these donations, remember that when someone donates $1,000 on their credit card, you don't receive $1,000. So, you can't record credit card donations for the total amount donated. The major credit card companies — American Express, Discover Card, Mastercard, and Visa — all charge a merchant fee or percentage (anywhere from 1 percent to 5 percent) for processing the payment. When a donor contributes to your organization by using their credit card, you won't get the total amount. For example, if a donor uses their credit card to give you a $100 donation and the bank charges a 2 percent fee, you only receive $98 in your bank account. The donor has given a $100 donation, but you have to pay a $2 bank fee.

WARNING

Don't count credit card donations until they're deposited into your account. The amount of time it takes for credit card transactions to hit your bank account depends on the bank, the credit card company, and the day of the week. Usually it takes up to three business days.

Direct bank draft donations

Direct bank draft donations allow people to donate a lump sum broken into smaller amounts over a longer period of time. For example, under a payroll program, each pay period the employer takes the designated, approved amount out of an employee's paycheck as a payroll deduction and sends the money to the nonprofit. These types of donations are a win-win; the donor can make small donations that add up over time without feeling a big difference in take-home pay, and the nonprofit receives a donation that's often larger than a one-time donation would be. Many nonprofits arrange with employers to do direct bank drafts from employees' paychecks.

Grants

A grant affords your organization sums of money you don't have to pay back. Some foundations and corporations donate grant money in the form of a check, while some government grants reimburse you by direct deposit after you submit substantiation that you disbursed some or all of the award. No matter how you receive the grant money, remember that a good steward manages grant money by tracking and monitoring how the money is used.

All contributions received from the grant should be deposited into your bank account and recorded in your checkbook register. I recommend you make a copy of the check before you deposit it for audit trail purposes. Some nonprofits open a new account just to manage the grant, but this is up to you. Whether to open a separate account depends on how much money the grant is for and how likely it is that you'll have problems keeping transactions separate.

Your nonprofit may have other sources of income (check out the nearby sidebar, "Identifying other potential income sources," for more info). However, you should deposit all donations and other sources of income into your nonprofit checking account.

The following sections focus on how to log monetary donations into your checking account, the diverse types of donations you may encounter, and why you need to differentiate between them.

Entering donations in your register

As your nonprofit receives donations, make sure you write them down (or *log* them) in your checkbook register as soon as you deposit them. Keeping your checkbook register current is necessary to avoid *overdraft fees* (fees the bank charges you when you write a check for more money than you have in your account) and to stay on top of your organization's income and expenses.

WARNING

If you incorrectly record a deposit, such as entering $2,850 when the deposit was actually $285, you may end up being charged an overdraft fee because you may inadvertently write a check for more money than you actually have in your account.

When you receive donations, you need to properly track and record them. You want to ensure that you create a paper trail that leads back to the donors list for auditing purposes. It's important to get those donations in your bank account and write your donor a thank-you letter.

I recommend the following four steps for effective deposit management:

1. **At a preselected cutoff time each day (perhaps after receiving and opening the daily mail), add the donations you received during the day.**

   Record the amounts on a bank deposit slip. If the money came from a new donor, add the person to your donors list. If the donation came from an established donor, open the donor's account, and record the new donation.

2. **Make copies of the checks and deposit slip before you deposit the checks.**

   Banks can make mistakes, so it's important for you to retain proof of every deposit made to your account. Keep copies of the deposited checks and deposit slips in a safe place until you reconcile the monthly bank statement. This is especially important if you make deposits after banking hours through night depositories.

3. **Write down the deposit in your checkbook register.**

   Although forgetting to write down a deposit may not have as dire a consequence as forgetting to write down an issued check, not writing down a deposit will throw your checking account out of whack.

4. **Take the checks and the deposit slip to the bank and make the deposit.**

   If you have a high volume of checks coming in for large amounts, you don't want to keep them at your office any longer than necessary. You open yourself up to possible robbery or some other unforeseen event.

At the end of the month, you'll receive a bank statement that lists all the transactions made on your account. Compare your records against the bank's records using the statement to balance your checking account (see the section "Balancing the Checkbook" later in this chapter for more information).

TIP

To record your deposits in your checkbook register, you enter the date, the source of the deposit, and the amount of the transaction in the corresponding columns. In the sample checkbook register shown in Figure 7-1, there are three deposits. The first deposit of $500 was made on October 1; the second deposit of $750 was made on October 8; and the third deposit of $300 was made on October 13. The total of the deposits is $1,550.

REMEMBER

In addition to tracking donations, you need to keep a list of donors. The donors list should include donors' names and addresses, and the amount donated. You'll need this list for information purposes and to track your donations. Your auditor will use your donors list to randomly verify donations received.

SEARCHING FOR THE RIGHT BANK

Shop for and find a bank that addresses your nonprofit's needs. When selecting a bank, ask yourself what's important for your nonprofit. One factor to consider is how much activity you transact within a given month. Pay attention to banks that offer free services.

Many banks offer overdraft protection — where the bank will pay the check if you overdraw your account. This can save you some embarrassment and bank overdraft fees. Talk with your banker about overdraft protection.

WARNING

To stay in IRS compliance, you must send a written acknowledgment substantiating a charitable contribution that is more than $249. Check out the following to see what information must be contained in the acknowledgment: www.irs.gov/charities-non-profits/charitable-organizations/charitable-contributions-written-acknowledgments.

Subtracting Your Expenses

To balance your checkbook, not only do you record and add all donations (as the previous section explains), but you also record and subtract all disbursements. Every check you write to pay a bill is a deduction from your balance; if you don't carefully record all these payments, your checking account balance won't be accurate, and you may end up overdrawing your account.

The following sections take a closer look at the types of disbursements you may need to subtract from your checkbook register and how to record those transactions in your register. By paying close attention to this information, you have a clearer picture of how much money is in your checking account.

Adjusting the checkbook register

Like death and taxes, bills are inevitable. When you receive them, you can't ignore them. You must pay and record them in your checkbook register right away. If you forget to record just one transaction, you can throw your account out of balance and end up paying unnecessary bank fees.

For example, you have $1,840 in your checking account, and you write checks to cover your utilities for $300, your rent for $1,000, and your insurance for $300. You subtract each check from your total, resulting in $240 left in your account. If you don't write down one of these expenses, such as the insurance bill, you'll think you have $540 in your account, which may think you can write a check for $500 to cover your car payment. Doing so results in an overdraft and potential costly overdraft fees.

TIP

After you pay the expenses, make sure you log them into your checkbook register. Doing so keeps your checkbook register current.

To record your expenses in your checkbook register, you simply log them in as you write the checks. For example, Figure 7-1 shows that check 255 was written for $100 to George Rembert to purchase supplies; check 256 was for $25 to pay the web designer; and check 257 was for $925 for salaries paid. You list each type of information for the transaction in its own column: date, check number, payee/ description of transaction, and withdrawal. For each amount, you subtract it from the running balance in the last column, labeled "Balance."

Now, suppose you pay a $1,500 insurance bill, but you forgot to log in the $100 check written to George Rembert. Your account balance would show $1,542, and you'd think you had just enough money to pay your insurance. As you can see from the account balance, you only have $1,442 in your account. If you forget to log a check for even $100, it can put your account into overdraft.

In addition to keeping track of checks you've written; you need to keep track of expenses associated with the use of a debit card. Most of the time when you open a checking account, the bank sends you a debit card. Because they look like credit cards, debit cards can cause you to forget to track expenses associated with their use.

Identifying common expenses

You can't avoid the dreaded cycle of paying your nonprofit's bills. In fact, it may seem like every time you open your mailbox, you have at least one bill rearing its ugly head.

You need to have a clear grasp of the types of bills your nonprofit may receive so you know what needs to be deducted from your check register. Some common nonprofit expenses paid out of your checkbook include the following:

>> **Rent:** This expense is for your office space or building that you're leasing.

>> **Utilities:** These expenses include telephone, fax, electricity, water, and garbage.

>> **Payroll/wages:** These expenses are incurred when you pay those who provide a service.

>> **Payroll taxes (federal, state, Medicare, Social Security taxes):** These expenses are reported, deducted, and must be paid, if applicable, to federal and state governments.

>> **Contract labor:** This expense is used when additional help is needed, and a contract is issued and signed for a specific time period to complete the task.

>> **Travel expenses:** These expenses occur from going to and from different destinations. They include transportation and lodging, as well as meals.

>> **Licenses and permits:** These expenses are for licenses and permits that allow you to operate and be recognized as a nonprofit organization in your state, county, and city municipalities.

>> **Insurance:** This expense is a necessary component to protect you, your clients, your board, and your organization from potential hazards that could be disastrous to your nonprofit.

>> **Office expenses and supplies:** These expenses include paper, pens, and other small-ticket items, including postage and printing-related supplies.

>> **Office furniture:** These expenses are usually for desks, chairs, tables, and other office furniture.

>> **Computer hardware and software:** These expenses include computers, monitors, printers, and software you use to run your nonprofit.

>> **Website expenses:** These expenses may include web page design, domain name fee, the maintenance and updates of your web page, and the storing and processing of web page data.

>> **Bank service fees:** Banks are competitive, and most allow you to have a free checking account because you're a nonprofit organization. This doesn't mean you get your checks for free, but you won't be charged a fee for the account. Pay attention to the hidden banking fees. Other types of bank fees include the following:

- **Credit card processing:** These fees may be charged by your banking institute for handling monies deposited and withdrawn with credit cards.

- **Transaction fees:** These fees are for using a debit card instead of writing checks to make purchases.

- **Nonsufficient funds (NSF) fees:** Your bank charges these fees for processing a check or credit card transaction when the money wasn't available in your account. This is commonly referred to as a bounced check.

- **Fee per transaction:** These fees may be charged if you go over the number of transactions designated by your bank. For example, If your bank offers free checking with a maximum of 25 transactions, starting with the 26th transaction you may be charged for every transaction thereafter.

- **ATM user fees:** If you use an ATM owned by a different bank, you may be charged.

>> **Building security expenses:** These expenses may include security cameras and security guards, as well as security alarm system installation and monthly access fees.

>> **Miscellaneous expenses:** Any fee not listed in the preceding categories that only occurs occasionally or is incidental may be classified as a miscellaneous expense. For example, this may be the tip you give for prompt delivery of your new computer system or some other small, nonessential expense.

WARNING

Be careful with bills that aren't a fixed amount each month. For example, if the price of natural gas is up, you may want to opt for the budget plan for the gas bill. The *budget plan* (or estimated payment plan) means you pay the same amount for gas year-round, eliminating high or low bills throughout the year, and settle any underage or overage cost at the end of the year.

REMEMBER

Any payment made for an item that could be considered an asset is technically a cost rather than an expense. The payment is still deducted from your checking account balance but does not show up as an expense until it's used or depreciated. See Chapter 2 for more information about assets and depreciation.

Recording direct or automatic bank drafts

You can set up automatic or direct bank drafts with your checking account. These are bills that are paid directly out of your checking account on the same date every month.

Using automatic bank drafts has a few advantages and disadvantages. Some of the advantages are

>> You save time by not having to write a check.

>> You save money by not having to buy stamps.

>> You save time by not having to remember to pay the bill.

Because direct drafts are automatic, they pose the following disadvantages:

>> You may forget to record and deduct the draft in your checkbook register.

>> You may forget to make sure you have enough money in your account to cover the payment.

>> If you don't have enough money to cover the draft, you may be hit with an overdraft fee on your account.

WARNING

Doing a direct draft for bills that vary considerably may not be advisable. A good example of this is your utility bill, which may fluctuate based on the time of year and how much you're running your heating or air-conditioning.

TIP

It's a good idea to subtract direct drafts on your check register at the beginning of the month. If you're really organized, you can make a note to record the draft when the payment is scheduled to be made directly from your account. Forgetting to log these expenses can put your organization's finances in a whirlwind.

Balancing the Checkbook

Balancing your nonprofit's checkbook each month is necessary. Catching an out-of-balance checking account gives you a timely warning that you may have entered a transaction incorrectly in either your manually kept accounting records (see Chapter 8) or your accounting software package such as QuickBooks (see Chapter 9). It also alerts you to the fact that you may have forgotten to enter a transaction.

Most nonprofits hire a bookkeeper or part time accountant to handle the day-to-day accounting tasks such as balancing the checkbook. Whether you're doing the bank reconciliation yourself or you have someone else do it, this section provides information to correctly prepare a bank reconciliation.

Proving your bank balance through the bank reconciliation process verifies you correctly record income and disbursements occurring during the month. Staying on top of this saves you time later when filing returns to the IRS (see Chapters 15 and 16), reporting to your nonprofit's board of directors, and gathering information requested by auditors.

REMEMBER

Don't allow a lot of time to pass without reconciling your checkbook register to your bank statement. Waiting too long can cause you to bounce a check because you were unaware of a deduction on the bank statement that was either not entered or entered incorrectly.

TIP

To help you reconcile your account, order duplicate checks or choose a bank that includes images of your checks either on your paper statement or as a link on your electronic statement. The more records you have as documentation, the easier it is to get everything to balance.

Using the bank statement

At the end of the month, your bank issues a bank statement — either by paper mailing or online, if you've set up online banking with your bank account. Either way, it contains a list of deposits and withdrawals (withdrawals include cash you've taken out, checks you've written, and miscellaneous bank fees) that have cleared your account.

If your bank statement comes in the mail, you can use the handy worksheet on the back of the statement to balance your checkbook. It has a grid and instructions (like those presented in this section) to walk you through the process.

To make sure you know the true balance of your nonprofit's bank account, compare the balance you have in your checkbook register with the balance on the bank statement. Because these two figures probably won't be the same, you reconcile your checking account to the bank statement.

Reconciling your checking account involves accounting for the differences between the bank statement and your checkbook register. Follow these steps to reconcile and see Figure 7-2 for an example:

1. **Compare your bank statement to your checkbook register to figure out which checks have cleared your account, and which haven't; put a check mark next to the checks that have cleared.**

   A check has cleared when the money has been moved from your account to the payee's account.

2. **Repeat Step 1 for your deposits.**

3. **Repeat Step 1 for withdrawals and debit card purchases.**

   If the bank shows something that isn't listed in your checkbook register, check your records to make sure you made the transaction. If you did make the purchase and forgot to record it, write it in now. If you didn't make the transaction, call your bank and ask for more information about it.

4. **Repeat Step 1 for any bank fees or interest the account may have paid or earned.**

5. **List the outstanding checks on a separate piece of paper; also list any outstanding withdrawals and debit card purchases. Then add up the numbers.**

   When a check or other transaction is outstanding, it hasn't cleared the bank yet. The transactions that are outstanding are those you didn't put a check mark next to in steps 1–3.

6. **List any outstanding deposits; add them up.**

7. **Write down the ending balance shown on your bank statement.**

8. **Subtract the amount of outstanding checks and withdrawals that you came up with in Step 5 from the ending balance you wrote down in Step 7.**

9. **Add the total of outstanding deposits you came up with in Step 6.**

   After completing steps 8 and 9, your total should match the balance in your checkbook register.

10. **If the number you came up with in Step 9 doesn't match the number in your checkbook register, you have some sleuthing to do.**

    Double-check your math in your checkbook register; make sure you've accounted for all checks, deposits, withdrawals, and fees in your checkbook register; and then go through steps 1–9 again to make sure you didn't leave anything out or do the math incorrectly.

Bank Statement Reconcilation as of October 31, 2023			
From Bank Records		**From Check Register**	
Indicated balance	$3,700	Indicated balance	$3,964
Add deposits in transit	750	Add interest earned	11
Subtract outstanding checks	−500	Subtract service charge	−25
Reconciled balance	$3,950	Reconciled balance	$3,950

FIGURE 7-2:
Bank statement
reconciliation.

REMEMBER

When reconciling your account, you should rely more heavily on your own records than the bank's. The bank statement only covers a set time period; your records are up to date because you've been tracking every transaction.

The following transactions can make it difficult to balance your checkbook:

>> Checks written but not yet cleared (see the next section, "Considering outstanding checks").

>> Online bill-pay transaction fees. Sometimes utility companies charge a fee to process online payments. It's easy to forget to record these fees in your register.

>> ATM/debit card transactions and fees. You may have recent transactions that occurred between the time the statement was printed and now.

>> Deposits made or recorded after the statement date.

>> Bank fees and earned interest not recorded in the checkbook.

Considering outstanding checks

You also prevent errors in your nonprofit's check register by being aware of outstanding checks — checks you've written that haven't yet cleared the bank. Your bank records only the checks that have been paid out of your account. Your bank doesn't know about the checks you've written but it hasn't yet received. Because these checks haven't made it to your bank, they don't reflect in the bank's balance of your account.

To keep outstanding checks from being a problem, make sure you keep up with your own balance and check your records against the bank's every month. It's your responsibility to manage your money and account for all expenses as accurately as possible. Overlooking outstanding checks can put you in a financial bind. Talk with your banker about overdraft protection to alleviate the fees associated with a bounced check.

HANDLING DEPOSITS IN TRANSIT

Earlier in this chapter, I stress the importance of depositing checks as they're received. However, even if you deposit donations and other checks received on a daily basis, you may still have deposits in transit if you miss the bank cutoff time.

Banks vary, but most have a cutoff time of 2 p.m. That means that even though you make your deposit prior to when the bank closes on the last bank day of the month, if you make the deposit after cutoff, it won't post until the next bank day.

Additionally, your bank may place a hold on out-of-state checks or checks over a certain amount. If the hold spans one month to the next, this creates a deposit in transit as well.

WARNING

Some organizations hold on to checks for long periods of time before depositing them. If you're not keeping track of your own account, when these older checks hit your account, recently written checks could start bouncing.

Some banks have time constraints on how long a check can be held before cashing. Some are only good for 90 days, but you should find out from your bank how long it will honor payments on checks. You may want to consider printing "Void after six months" on your checks to avoid problems with old outstanding checks.

When considering outstanding checks, you also need to account for the timing difference in available funds. For example, when you deposit money, it may not be available for a day or two, but when you write a check, the money could be gone within a day, if not instantly. Make sure that when you pay bills, you have enough money to cover them. Make a note of when you expect the check to clear, and pay close attention to see when it does clear.

Finding and addressing errors

As careful as you are when recording your donations and expenses, and reconciling your checkbook to bank statements, sometimes errors will happen. A few simple tricks can help you lower the chances of encountering errors.

To figure out whether an error is caused by transposing digits and not incorrect math, find the difference of the two sums. If it's evenly divisible by 9, you know you have a transposition error. So, when you subtract $859.98 and $859.89, you get $0.09. Because that amount is evenly divisible by 9, you know you've got a transposition error within the numbers you added to reach the total.

To avoid these kinds of errors, take your time when writing down and adding numbers. A ten-key adding machine can be useful when checking your math; it gives you a tape of what you keyed in. You can also use a computer spreadsheet to check figures. The old pencil-and-paper method is still a good one to use, too.

If you've checked and can't find the difference, consider the following suggestions:

>> **Ask someone else to look at the numbers.** A fresh set of eyes may be able to find the problem.

>> **Call your bank and ask for help.** Because the management values you as a customer, someone will help you.

TIP

Using accounting software programs (see Chapter 9) lets you skip all the manual bank reconciliation steps by using the bank reconciliation command built into the software.

Chapter **8**

Starting with Manual Bookkeeping

I f you're new to the nonprofit arena, you may initially decide to keep your accounting books yourself. There are many reasons this may make sense. For example, doing it yourself allows you to cut your outside accounting fees, freeing up money to fulfill program services. It's also a great way to get a fundamental understanding of the accounting process for your nonprofit. This is especially helpful if you don't have a background in accounting or you've recently taken an accounting class.

Not quite sure how to start? Well, your worries are over! In this chapter, I walk you through basic manual nonprofit bookkeeping and accounting from journals to financial statements. You also get a sprinkling of how to use a spreadsheet program to make your accounting life easier by setting up templates or transferring figures from one worksheet to another.

REMEMBER

I assume that you're using a manual checkbook to record deposits and disbursements. Check out Chapter 7 for more information about maintaining and balancing a checkbook.

After reading through this chapter, if you feel that manual bookkeeping is too much of a hassle, Chapter 9 has suggestions for picking out accounting software for your nonprofit and very brief tutorials on three different accounting software packages: ACCOUNTS, Aplos, and QuickBooks.

Suggesting a Manual Bookkeeping Shopping List

These suggestions are not comprehensive; taking a tour of your local office supplies store will probably add to your list. Before you go shopping, do a tour of your house or home office if you have one. You may already own basics such as a stapler, calculator, or tape dispenser.

>> **Basics:** Pencils and erasers, erasable pens, calculator (I prefer one with a tape so I can check the tape against the source documents), stapler, paper punch, folders, dividers, correction fluid or tape, scissors, notebook paper, ruler, and tape dispenser.

>> **Accounting logbooks:** Accounting journal for recording journal entries (if purchasing online, look for an item that has *book of original* or *primary entry* in its description), six-column ledger book and eight-column ledger book.

>> **Computer equipment:** You don't need a laptop and peripherals to keep your books manually, but you do need this equipment if you want to use spreadsheet programs, which I discuss later in this chapter, in the "Incorporating Spreadsheet Programs" section.

TIP

Compile a list of what you have and compare it to my suggested list to come up with a list of supplies you may need to purchase. Don't start shopping until you completely review this chapter — you may decide to modify what you feel you need to purchase.

Walking Through Journals

Small nonprofits most likely will encounter four different types of journals: cash journals (cash receipts and cash disbursements), accrual journals (such as sales and purchases), and the catchall general journal. Most nonprofits using a manual method to keep their books will use the cash method of accounting and, thus, only need cash and general journals. However, to give you a well-rounded picture, this chapter introduces accrual journals, too, a subject I expand upon in Chapter 9.

Recording in cash journals

In accounting, cash is a generic term for any payment method including paper money, coinage, checks, and credit card transactions. This is because when you issue a check, part of the implicit understanding is that the funds are immediately available to clear the check. Ditto paying with a credit card, which represents an immediate satisfaction of your debt with the vendor.

All transactions affecting cash go into the *cash receipts journal* or *cash disbursements journal.*

TECHNICAL STUFF

Some accountants or software programs may refer to the cash disbursements journal as the *cash payments journal* — no big deal both terms mean the same thing.

Cash receipts journal

The cash receipts journal is the most popular cash journal. After all, your nonprofit loves to receive cash!

Your nonprofit may receive cash in one of the following ways (however, these are just a few of the many instances that can necessitate recording a transaction in the cash receipts journal):

>> **Charitable donations made in cash:** This includes simple unrestricted gifts made by cash, check, or credit cards by the donor. You've probably already either received or made a cash contribution to open your nonprofit checking account. In cash basis accounting this goes in the cash receipts journal as a debit to cash (statement of financial position) and a credit to an income account on the statement of activities. (See Chapters 17 and 18 for more about these two statements.)

>> **Donors making payments on a previous commitment:** Sometimes a donor will make a pledge to donate a certain amount at a later date. If it's an unconditional pledge, this records as income when the pledge is received, which brings in accrual-based accounting — in particular, accounts receivable.

>> **Interest or dividend income:** When a bank or investment account pays your nonprofit for the use of its money in the form of interest or dividends, it's also considered a cash receipt.

TIP

As a technical matter, you could record interest income reflecting on your monthly bank or investment statements in the general journal, which I discuss a little later in this section.

The cash receipts journal will normally have six columns for debits and credits — two columns for debiting and four columns for crediting. Because all transactions in the cash receipts journal involve the receipt of cash, one of your debit columns is always for cash. Most nonprofits won't have a need for the second debit column because it's typically used for *sales discounts*, which reflect a discount for paying early. But it's there for you to use if need be.

To balance these debits, the credit columns in a cash receipts journal are income, accounts receivable, *sales tax payable* (which is the amount of sales tax your non-profit may collects on the transaction — probably not a common event for your nonprofit), and *miscellaneous* (which is a catchall column where you record all other cash receipts like interest and dividends). Your journal log paper also has columns for the number of the transaction, the date the transaction takes place and the name of the account affected by the transaction.

Figure 8-1 shows a cash receipts journal with limited transactions: one donation, one payment on a pledge, and interest income as reflected on the January month-end bank statement. I've left off any columns that weren't applicable.

Cash Receipts Journal

	Date	Account	Donations Credit	Accounts Receivable Credit	Miscellaneous Credit	Cash Debit
1	1-5	Smith Donation	50.00			50.00
2	1-18	Jones Payment on Pledge		200.00		200.00
3	1-31	Interest Income			18.00	18.00
			50.00	200.00	18.00	268.00

FIGURE 8-1: A partial manual cash receipts journal.

Cash disbursements journal

On the flip side are payments your nonprofit makes using a form of cash records in the cash disbursements (or payments) journal. Here are a few examples of transactions you'll see in a cash disbursements journal:

>> **Purchases:** Anything that you buy for use of the nonprofit such as office supplies, furniture, and stamps.

>> **Payments on outstanding accounts:** This includes all cash disbursements your nonprofit makes to pay for goods or services you obtain from another business and didn't pay for when the original transaction took place.

>> **Payments for operating expenses:** This includes the check or bank transfer you may make to pay rent or a utility or phone invoice.

The cash disbursements journal will normally have four columns for debiting and crediting accounts — two each. Because all transactions in the cash disbursements journal involve the payment of cash, one of your credit columns is for cash. The other is for *purchase discounts*, which are reductions in the amount your nonprofit pays to the vendor for any purchases on account (for example, your office supply shop offers customers a certain discount amount if they pay their bill within a certain number of days). You can find more info about purchase discounts in Chapter 9.

To balance these credits, the debit columns in a cash disbursements journal are accounts payable and *miscellaneous* (a catchall column where you record all other cash payments for transactions like payment of operating expenses). You'll also see a column to enter the number of the transaction, the date the transaction occurs, and the entity to whom the payment is made.

Figure 8-2 shows a cash disbursements journal with limited payment transactions: rent, postage, and a payment on account. I have left off any columns that weren't applicable.

FIGURE 8-2:
A partial
manually
prepared cash
disbursements
journal.

Cash Disbursements Journal

	Date	Ck Num	Pay-To	Account	Misc Debit	Accounts Payable Debit	Cash Credit
1	1-10	124	USPS	Postage Expense	32.60		32.60
2	1-15	125	Bob Jenkins	Rent	375.00		375.00
3	1-23	126	Boots Office Supply LLC	Payment to Vendor		89.65	89.65
					407.60	89.65	497.25

Entering to the sales and purchases journals

You commonly enter accrual transactions (see Chapter 2 for more info about the accrual basis of accounting) to sales and purchases journals. These two journals come into play whenever cash doesn't change hands. For example, you purchase something from Boots Office Supply, LLC, with a promise to pay within 30 days.

Using accruals and recording business transactions on the accrual method is the backbone of financial accounting and receiving an audited set of financial statements (see Chapter 13). Don't worry, I walk you through common nonprofit accrual transactions and give you a complete explanation of each later in this chapter, in the "Showing Examples of Common Nonprofit Journal Entries" section.

In the following sections, I cover your two accrual workhorse journals: the sales journal and the purchases journal.

Sales journal

The sales journal records all income your nonprofit brings in via pledges where no money changes hands between the nonprofit and the donor at receipt of the pledge. For example, the donor may commit to a $30 payment each month for six months. Pledges can also be one-time payments, such as an unconditional commitment to remit $400 in 45 days.

A sales journal will affect two different accounts: accounts receivable and, of course, income. Figure 8-3 shows a partial sales journal. In the sales journal, accounts receivable and income will always be affected by the same dollar amount.

Figure 8-3 shows a partial manual sales journal reflecting three pledges.

		Sales Journal		
	Date	Document Number	Name	Accounts Receivable Debit/Income Credit
1	1-13	89	Good Shepherd Animal Center	235.00
2	1-22	90	Jane Birchstone	125.00
3	1-30	91	Penway Park Cooperative	360.00
				720.00

FIGURE 8-3: A partial manual sales journal.

Purchases journal

Any time your nonprofit buys using store credit, it records the transaction in its purchases journal. The purchases journal typically has a column for transaction number, date, invoice number, and amount. It also has the following columns:

>> **Accounts payable:** Because the company is purchasing on account, this current liability account is always affected.

>> **Terms:** This column shows any discount terms the company may have with the vendor. For example, *2/10, n/30* means the company gets a 2 percent discount if it pays within 10 days; otherwise, the full amount is due in 30 days.

>> **Name:** The company records the name of the vendor from whom the purchase is made.

>> **Account:** This column shows to which account (see Chapter 5 for more info about the chart of accounts) the purchase is taken. In the example shown in Figure 8-4, because no other accounts are affected, accounts payable and purchases are for the same dollar amount.

Purchases Journal				
Date	Invoice Number	Name	Terms	Accounts Payable Credit/ Purchases Debit
1 1-5	1993	Vendor 1	2/10, n/30	125.63
2 1-14	2357	Vendor 2		58.27
3 1-26	185	Vendor 3	2/10, n/30	87.42
				271.32

FIGURE 8-4: A partial manual purchases journal.

REMEMBER

In real life, the debit account could possibly be any account on your chart of accounts — not just a generic purchases account.

Using the general journal

The *general journal* is a catchall type of journal where transactions that don't appropriately belong in any other journal, such as adjusting and closing journal entries, show up. Not sure what I mean by adjusting or closing? Here's what each one does:

>> **Adjusting journal entries** convert cash basis accounting books to accrual. They also reclassify transactions — for example, if a transaction was entered correctly initially but facts change necessitating adjusting the original entry (see Chapter 21 for examples of adjusting entries).

>> **Closing journal entries** zero out all the *temporary accounts,* which are all the revenue and expenses, transferring the net to the balance sheet. You do this to set the statement of activities (see Chapter 17) figures to zero, so you know exactly how much revenue and expenses take place during a certain time period. Nonprofits generally have three closing entries:

- Debit all income accounts and credit income summary for the same amount. *Income summary* is a temporary holding account you only use when closing out a period.

- Credit all expenses and debit income summary for the same amount.

- Either debit or credit income summary to reduce it to zero and take the same figure to net assets.

However, smaller nonprofits operating on the cash basis of accounting may find using just the general journal is sufficient for their accounting recording needs, not just adjusting and closing entries.

TECHNICAL STUFF

If you've worked in the nonprofit sector, you're probably familiar with a fourth closing entry to close dividends paid to retained earnings. This should not apply to a nonprofit.

TIP

If you have employees, even if it's just yourself, a payroll journal will come in handy. I discuss this topic in Chapters 9 and 15.

Showing Examples of Common Nonprofit Journal Entries

In this section, I give you a handy reference for preparing journal entries to record income, expenses, and adjustments and to close your books at the end of a financial period, so the concepts I discuss earlier in this chapter really come to life. Before you get into the nitty-gritty, keep in mind that proper journal entries are prepared by offsetting the date of the entry to the left, the account debited in the middle, and the amounts credited on the right.

Proper journal entries always list debits first and credits afterward. Also, journal entries can have more than one debit and credit. You just have to make sure that, in each entry, debits equal credits.

Booking donor transactions

Commonly, you'll have donor transactions to record unrestricted receipt of cash or a pledge to make the donation at a future date. You could also receive restricted donations, which means the donation may be earmarked for a specific program or a condition such as a matching pledge (donor acts on the pledge if the nonprofit raises a matching amount). Figure 8-5 shows how to enter unrestricted and restricted contributions into the general journal.

Recording expenditures

The novice bookkeeper will probably find booking costs and expenses in the general journal easier than revenue for which a restricted or unrestricted determination must be made. Two expenditure examples are that you pay an expense like a phone bill by writing a check from your nonprofit bank account or buy a piece of equipment with a promise to pay at a later date. Figure 8-6 shows how both these transactions record in the general journal, which you can use as a guide to record other cost and expense transactions.

1/15/20XX	Cash	2,000.00	
	Contributions		2,000.00
	To record contribution from Mr. Philips		
1/20/20XX	Cash	50.00	
	Accounts Receivable	50.00	
	Contributions		100.00
	To record contribution and pledge from Ms. Smokey		
1/31/20XX	Cash	1,500.00	
	Contribution - Restricted		1,500.00
	To record matching restricted contribution from Feral Cat League		

FIGURE 8-5: Recording donor transactions in the manual general journal.

1/7/20XX	Cash	69.87	
	Telephone Expense		69.87
	Check #123		
1/28/20XX	Office Equipment	465.00	
	Accounts Payable		465.00
	To record purchase of printer payable in 30 days		

FIGURE 8-6: Recording cost/ expense transactions in the manual general journal.

Posting to the general ledger

At this point, you may be thinking, "Okay, the journals are the books of original entry, but what happens then? How do these journal entries turn into financial statements?" Well, that's the topic of this section of the chapter. The journal accounts and amounts, either debited or credited, affect how the transactions show up in the *general ledger*, which is a listing of each account. To understand the general ledger, picture a big book. Every page of this book has a title that corresponds with an account from your chart of accounts (see Chapter 1 for more information about the general ledger and Chapter 5 for a discussion about the chart of accounts).

As you record accounting transactions in the journals, you also need to update the general ledger for the same transactions, a process that is called *posting*. If a subsidiary journal like the cash receipts journal is the first point of entry, it eventually flows to the general ledger with all other journal entries. Figure 8-7 is a very simple example of a general ledger using the entries I present earlier in this chapter.

Please note that I've only included the relevant general ledger pages, skipping those that aren't affected by this chapter's entries. Also, keep in mind that net assets of $1,538.33 is assumed to be the unrestricted beginning balance carried over from the prior year and, thus, not a product of a journal entry.

Adjusting prior entries

At the end of the financial period, it's time to initiate the process to close your temporary accounts, which are those on the statement of activities. The first step in this process is transferring ending balances from the general ledger to the working trial balance worksheet (see Figure 8-8). Then you make adjusting entries. I walk you through a few adjusting entries in Chapter 21.

Figure 8-8 reflects the Figure 8-7 general ledger ending balances and the adjusting journal entries from Chapter 21. Please note that I've ignored any account balances relating to these adjusting journal entries for purposes of preparing Figure 8-8. As you review Figure 8-8, keep in mind the figure is a very simple example of the worksheet.

Follow these steps when preparing your manual worksheet. To differentiate between work paper and financial statement columns, the work paper columns are alphabetic (A, B, and C), and the financial statement columns are numeric (4 and 5):

1. **Begin with your unadjusted trial balance (see Figure 8-8, Part A).** The unadjusted trial balance is the listing of your account balances in the general ledger before you post any required adjustments to these accounts.

2. **List all your adjustments to the accounts (see Figure 8-8, Part B).**

3. **Post the adjustments, which gives you the adjusted trial balance (see Figure 8-8, Part C).**

4. **Allocates the adjusted trial balance between income statement and balance sheet accounts (see Figure 8-8, Parts 4 and 5).**

After your adjusted trial balance is in balance, you can complete your financial statements. Just move the information from your worksheet (Figure 8-8, parts 4 and 5) into the correct categories on your financial statements. Check out Chapters 17 and 18 to help you put together the different financial statements you need.

General Ledger Page 1

Type	Date	No.	Name	Memo	Debit	Credit	Balance
1110 - Cash in Bank							745.23
Deposit	1/5/20XX	CR	1	Smith Donation	50.00	0.00	795.23
Check	1/7/20XX	123	ABC Cellular		0.00	69.87	725.36
Check	1/10/20XX	124	USPS		0.00	32.60	692.76
Check	1/15/20XX	125	Bob Jenkins		0.00	375.00	317.76
Deposit	1/15/20XX	GJ	1	Philips donation	2,000.00	0.00	2,317.76
Deposit	1/18/20XX	CR	2	Jones pledge	200.00	0.00	2,517.76
Deposit	1/20/20XX	GJ	2	Smokey donation	50.00	0.00	2,567.76
Check	1/23/20XX	126	Boots Office Supply		0.00	89.65	2,478.11
Deposit	1/31/20XX	GJ	3	Feral Cat donation	1,500.00	0.00	3,978.11
Deposit	1/31/20XX	CR	3	Interest Income	18.00	0.00	3,996.11

General Ledger Page 2

Type	Date	No.	Name	Memo	Debit	Credit	Balance
1111 - Accounts Receivable							350.00
Contribution	1/18/20XX	CR		Jones payment		200.00	150.00
Contribution	1/20/20XX	GJ	2	Smokey pledge	50.00	0.00	200.00
Contribution	1/31/20XX	SJ			720.00	0.00	920.00

General Ledger Page 5

Type	Date	No.	Name	Memo	Debit	Credit	Balance
1223 - Office Equipment							689.00
Purchase	1/28/20XX	GJ	2	printer	465.00		1,154.00

General Ledger Page 9

Type	Date	No.	Name	Memo	Debit	Credit	Balance
2110 - Accounts Payable							245.90
Payment	1/23/20XX	CD	3	Boots Office Supply	89.65		156.25
Purchase	1/28/20XX	GJ	2	printer		465.00	621.25
Purchases	1/31/20XX	PJ				271.32	892.57

General Ledger Page 11

Type	Date	No.	Name	Memo	Debit	Credit	Balance
3110 - Net Assets							1,538.33

General Ledger Page 15

Type	Date	No.	Name	Memo	Debit	Credit	Balance
4110 - Contributions							0.00
Donations	1/15/20XX	GJ	1	Philips		2,000.00	2,000.00
Donations	1/20/20XX	GJ	2	Smokey		100.00	2,100.00
Donations	1/31/20XX	CR				50.00	2,150.00
Donations	1/31/20XX	SJ				720.00	2,870.00

General Ledger Page 16

Type	Date	No.	Name	Memo	Debit	Credit	Balance
4111 - Contributions - Restricted							0.00
Donations	1/31/20XX	GJ	3	Feral Cat		1,500.00	1,500.00

General Ledger Page 20

Type	Date	No.	Name	Memo	Debit	Credit	Balance
4115 - Interest Income							0.00
Misc Income	1/31/20XX	CR	3	Bank statement		18.00	18.00

General Ledger Page 24

Type	Date	No.	Name	Memo	Debit	Credit	Balance
5110 - Purchases							0.00
Purchases	1/31/20XX	PJ		Misc purchases	271.32		271.32

General Ledger Page 27

Type	Date	No.	Name	Memo	Debit	Credit	Balance
5210 - Postage Expense							0.00
Payment	1/10/20XX	124		USPS	32.60		32.60

General Ledger Page 28

Type	Date	No.	Name	Memo	Debit	Credit	Balance
5211 - Rent Expense							0.00
Payment	1/15/20XX	125		Bob Jenkins	375.00		375.00

General Ledger Page 30

Type	Date	No.	Name	Memo	Debit	Credit	Balance
5213 - Telephone Expense							0.00
Payment	1/7/20XX	123		ABC Cellular	69.87		69.87

FIGURE 8-7: Recording cost/expense transactions in the manual general ledger.

Work Sheet for Month Ending December 31, 20XX

Account	A) Unadjusted Trial Balance Dr.	Cr.	B) Adjustments Dr.	Cr.	C) Adjusted Trial Balance Dr.	Cr.	4) Income Statement * Dr.	Cr.	5) Balance Sheet ** Dr.	Cr.
Cash in Bank	3,996.11				3,996.11				3,996.11	
Accounts Receivable	920.00				920.00				920.00	
Office Equipment	1,154.00				1,154.00				1,154.00	
Accounts Payable		892.57		50.00		942.57				942.57
Wages Payable				2,000.00		2,000.00				2,000.00
Mortgage Payable				100.00		100.00				100.00
Net Assets		1,538.33				1,538.33				1,538.33
Contributions		2,870.00				2,870.00		2,870.00		
Contributions - Restricted		1,500.00				1,500.00		1,500.00		
Interest Income		18.00				18.00		18.00		
Purchases	271.32				271.32		271.32			
Interest Expense			100.00		100.00		100.00			
Postage Expense	32.60				32.60		32.60			
Rent Expense	375.00				375.00		375.00			
Telephone Expense	69.87		50.00		119.87		119.87			
Wages Expense			2,000.00		2,000.00		2,000.00			
Net Income							1,489.21			1,489.21
	6,818.90	6,818.90	2,150.00	2,150.00	8,968.90	8,968.90	4,388.00	4,388.00	6,070.11	6,070.11

* Statement of Activities
** Statement of Financial Position

FIGURE 8-8: Working trial balance worksheet.

Now all you have to do to finish closing out your year is to post your closing entries, which you learn how to do in the next section in this chapter.

Dealing with net assets

Finally, it's time to prepare your closing entries, which transfer your temporary account balance to net assets. Record closing entries in the general journal. (I completely walk you through closing entry steps in Chapter 21.)

In a nutshell, you first credit each expense and debit Income Summary; then you debit each revenue account and credit Income Summary. Next, you close out Income Summary to Net Assets. Don't forget that Figure 8-8 has unrestricted and restricted contributions which affect Net Assets, too.

Walk through the following three steps, picking up dollar amounts from Figure 8-8 to prepare your closing journal entries:

1. Credit Purchases for $271.32 through to Wages Expense for $2,000. Debit Income Summary for $271.32 + $100.00 + $32.60 + $375.00 + $119.87 + $2,000 = $2,898.79.

2. Debit Contributions for $2,870, Restricted Contributions for $1,500, and Interest Income for $18. Credit Income Summary for $4,388.

   At this point, Income Summary has a credit balance of $2,898.79 – $4,388.00 = –$1,489.21. This figure must be the same as your net income/loss.

3. **Debit Income Summary for $1,489.21 and Net Assets without Donor Restrictions for $10.79. Credit Net Assets with Donor Restrictions for $1,500.**

This reduces Income Summary to ($1,489.21 + $10.79) – $1,500 = $0.

Total ending net assets is $1,538.33 + $1,489.21 = $3,027.54 and is further broken out as follows:

- **Net Assets without Donor Restrictions:** $1,538.33 – $10.79 = $1,527.54

- **Net Assets with Donor Restrictions:** $1,500.00

WARNING

Please keep in mind the entries I go over in this chapter are for illustration purposes only to introduce you to entering transactions manually to journal and ledger paper. It would take an entire book to completely walk through the accounting cycle.

Incorporating Spreadsheet Programs

Whew! After all that manual bookkeeping in the prior section, you're probably ready to find out how spreadsheet programs can make your accounting life easier. It's very easy to set up journal, general ledger, and financial statement templates in a spreadsheet program such as Microsoft Excel.

For those not familiar with Excel, you can use Excel to sort, store, organize and calculate data. Using the program, you create spreadsheets, which consist of rows and columns. After you enter information into the spreadsheet, you can calculate totals, create tables and graphs, and analyze financial data.

Walking through the spreadsheet

In Excel, a spreadsheet is commonly referred to as a worksheet. Every Excel worksheet has the following components:

>> **Columns:** Columns run up and down (vertically), and they're identified alphabetically on the top of the spreadsheet.

>> **Rows:** Rows run from side to side (horizontally). Each row is numbered on the left side.

>> **Cells:** The place where a column and row intersect is called a cell, and it looks like a rectangle. A cell is labeled by a letter and a number (so a cell two columns in and three rows down would be labeled B3). You enter the data into the cells.

Going back to Figure 8-1, Figure 8-9 shows how you could enter the Cash Receipts Journal into an Excel worksheet.

	A	B	C	D	E	F	G	H	I	J	K	L	M	N
1														
2							Cash Receipts Journal							
3										Accounts				
4							Donations			Receivable		Miscellaneous	Cash	
5				Date		Account	Credit			Credit		Credit	Debit	
6		1		1/5		Smith Donation	50.00						50.00	
7		2		1/18		Jones Payment on Pledge				200.00			200.00	
8		3		1/31		Interest Income						18.00	18.00	
9							50.00			200.00		18.00	268.00	
10														

FIGURE 8-9: A cash receipts journal in Excel.

Converting manual records into a spreadsheet

If you've been using a manual bookkeeping system and you want to move to a more automated process, an Excel spreadsheet is a good place to start. If you're in the planning stages of your nonprofit, it would be good practice to enter all the manual journal entries, general ledger, and trial balance I walk you through in the earlier sections of this chapter directly into an Excel spreadsheet.

I go into the nitty-gritty of how to do this in Chapter 4. You may also find it helpful to reference *Microsoft Excel All-in-One For Dummies* by Paul McFedries and Greg Harvey (Wiley).

Setting up financial reporting templates

After you get your accounting information into Excel, it's a snap to prepare your financial statements using your working trial balance and do financial review such as vertical analysis. Going back to Figure 8-8, I've inserted a new worksheet into that Excel file and asked Excel to copy Part 4 to the new worksheet.

To add a worksheet into an existing Excel file, click the plus sign (+) at the bottom of the file. To copy and paste from one worksheet to another in the same Excel file, select a cell or range of cells by left-clicking your mouse on the applicable range of cells, right-clicking your mouse on the range of cells, selecting Copy, clicking in the new worksheet, and then right-clicking and selecting Paste.

I now have an informal statement of activities on my second worksheet that I use to perform vertical analysis. *Vertical analysis* goes up and down the statement of activities for one year comparing all other accounts to income. This type of analysis gives your nonprofit a heads up if any expense appears to be too high when compared to donor contributions and other nonprofit income.

Figure 8-10 shows vertical analysis for both the restricted and unrestricted contributions. The percentages are calculated by dividing expenses by revenue. For example, purchases is 9 percent of unrestricted contributions ($271.32 ÷ $2,870) and the formula for this is E9/E4.

	A	B	C	D	E	F	G	H	I
1									
2		**Statement of Activities**							
3		Revenue:				Unrestricted Contributions	Restricted Contributions	Total Revenue	
4		Contributions			2,870.00				
5		Contributions - Restricted			1,500.00				
6		Interest Income			18.00				
7					4,388.00				
8		Expenses:							
9		Purchases			271.32	9%	18%	6.18%	
10		Interest Expense			100.00	3%	7%	2.28%	
11		Postage Expense			32.60	1%	2%	0.74%	
12		Rent Expense			375.00	13%	25%	8.55%	
13		Telephone Expense			119.87	4%	8%	2.73%	
14		Wages Expense			2,000.00	70%	133%	45.58%	
15					2,898.79				
16									
17		Net Income			1,489.21				

FIGURE 8-10:
Vertical analysis.

TIP

Horizontal analysis compares account balances over different periods of time. For example, if you put prior or subsequent year amounts into Figure 8-10, you'd be able to see percentage or dollar variances year over year. Visit www.fe.training/free-resources/financial-modeling/horizontal-analysis for an example of horizontal analysis.

Chapter **9**

Advancing into Nonprofit Accounting Software

C hapter 8 lays the foundation for using accounting software by walking you through how to record your accounting transactions manually. Keeping your accounting books manually can be quite time-consuming, so in this chapter you build upon your manual knowledge from Chapter 8 by reviewing three different accounting software packages.

First, I introduce you to QuickBooks, which you may already be familiar with. QuickBooks doesn't have a dedicated nonprofit product, like Aplos or ACCOUNTS, but you can tailor QuickBooks Online or the desktop version, QuickBooks Premier Plus (and some of the other QuickBooks options), for nonprofits. The good thing about QuickBooks is that you may have already used a version of it in the past, and there is a good chance that any accountant or bookkeeper you hire has experience using QuickBooks.

Next, I cover Aplos, which is a dedicated nonprofit software package offering fund accounting, donation tracking, online gift forms, financial and giving reports, and event registration. It has an option to help prepare your nonprofit federal income tax Form 990. If your nonprofit received restricted donations, it has helpful management tools for those, too.

Finally, I walk you through some of the features of ACCOUNTS. It's less robust than QuickBooks or Aplos, but ACCOUNTS does basic bookkeeping and fund accounting. Tailored to churches and charities, it tracks income, expenses, and fund balances, and creates reports. There are many other software packages that you can find by doing online research. For the sake of simplicity, I've presented an impartial evaluation of each of these three, and I wasn't compensated by the software companies for mentioning them (just in case you were wondering!).

Choosing Accounting Software

Before you get into the thick of it, keep in mind that the purpose of nonprofits differs from the purpose of for-profit businesses you may have worked for in the past. The goal of any nonprofit is to benefit its constituents, which could be the general public or a specific group. So, you'll encounter slightly different accounts (see Chapter 5), a unique presentation of the financial statements (see Chapters 17, 18, and 19), and a donor transparency aspect.

REMEMBER

To be transparent, nonprofits need to keep organized, accurate, and understandable books so donors can understand how the nonprofit is using their contributions.

For example, your nonprofit's main source of income is not selling a product. You're soliciting donations from contributors and maybe even securing grants in order to pay your program and administrative costs. Donors may gift your nonprofit restricted donations, which have to be accounted for in a specific manner. Plus, you may have a need to allocate income and the related expenses to different programs or funds.

For me, there are three considerations when picking out an accounting software package for a nonprofit: number of transactions, cost, and ease of use. Throughout this book, I show you how to analyze, treat, and record accounting transactions (see Chapters 2, 6, and 8 in particular). If your nonprofit is small and doesn't have a volume of accounting transactions per month, it may make more sense to keep your books manually (see Chapter 8) at present or hand off everything to a bookkeeper or accountant at the end of the month for recording.

You have to weigh the time involved in doing it yourself against the cost of an accounting software package or paying an outside bookkeeper or accountant to record your transactions. Additionally, it's very important that the accounting software you select isn't a burden to learn and has reasonable customer support.

Therefore, I recommend that you walk through a free trial first before buying any software package.

Finally, before you complete the purchase, make sure you understand the software company's cancellation policy. Even with a run-through during the free trial, after you start using the software on a daily basis, you may find it to be just too confusing or too much work, or maybe a better product for your particular nonprofit will come on the market and you'll want to switch.

REMEMBER

Free trials probably have all menu options enabled. If the software is sold with tiered features, make sure the version you're purchasing has the features you need. Confirm this by discussing with the software provider sales or customer service representatives.

TIP

Although doable, it can be time consuming to switch accounting packages midyear. Making the change from one package to another is something you should discuss with your accountant. Best practices dictate you run both software packages concurrently for at least a couple of months to weed out any bugs or errors.

Using QuickBooks for Nonprofits

In my experience, the main reason why nonprofits gravitate to QuickBooks is because it's a recognized name and at least one person in the nonprofit organization has used it in the past. With a little patience, it's not that big of a deal to customize setup for small nonprofits. Plus, there are a bunch of online videos and tutorials on the Intuit website (https://quickbooks.intuit.com) to lend a helping hand.

TIP

One aspect of QuickBooks that I really like is the ability to quickly convert a report to Microsoft Excel that can be searched using keywords or key phrases.

The cost of QuickBooks varies based on version, number of users, and options. To see the current pricing and any special pricing, go to https://quickbooks.intuit.com/industry/non-profits/#pricing. When checking prices for this chapter, QuickBooks Plus was $42.50 per month and QuickBooks Advanced was $100 per month.

Considering the pros and cons

One advantage of QuickBooks is that it offers several plans from which to choose. Another is that all outside accountants realize their clients like to use QuickBooks, so the accountant will have a version running as well. This makes it easy to transfer data back and forth between your nonprofit and your accountant.

On the downside, you will have to customize QuickBooks for your nonprofit — but after you get your nonprofit set up, implementation of the software is straightforward. Making corrections for errors can be time-consuming if you aren't completely up to speed with using the software. Plus, there are less-expensive nonprofit software options out there that may be sufficiently powerful for your nonprofit (see the "Selecting ACCOUNTS" section, later in this chapter).

Customizing QuickBooks for nonprofits

Depending on the version of QuickBooks you have and whether you opt for Business or Accountant view, the menu will look pretty much the same as Figure 9-1, which is the Business view. Here's what the menu items mean:

>> **Get Things Done:** Containing a list of accounting tasks such as bills to pay or pledged contributions due.

>> **Business Overview:** This is your workspace allowing you to toggle back and forth between information links about your nonprofit such as money in/out and reports.

>> **Bookkeeping:** One stop for your bank, receipts, sales, and expense transactions.

>> **Get Paid & Pay:** Go here to prepare donor invoices and set up online or in-person payments from your donors.

>> **Customers & Leads:** Organize existing and new donor information with this option.

>> **Commerce:** Probably not be applicable to your nonprofit; includes Amazon Prime, eBay, and other sales channels.

>> **Payroll:** One stop to track and pay employees. You also manage independent contractors with this menu option.

>> **Taxes:** Probably not applicable to your nonprofit; this is where you manage sales tax.

>> **Menu Settings:** Allows you to customize your menu or switch to Accountant view.

After viewing the menu, it's time to go over two customization basics:

>> You need to set your company type as Nonprofit.

>> You need to change customers to donors.

I walk you through these customizations in the following sections.

FIGURE 9-1:
The
QuickBooks
menu in
Business view.

Per sales staff at QuickBooks, 90 percent of nonprofits use QuickBooks Online. For this reason, all the customization steps I cover in this chapter are based on Quick-Books Online. But they should be applicable to other versions of QuickBooks as well.

TIP

Company type

The first step is to select Nonprofit as your company type by following these instructions:

1. Select Settings (the gear symbol at the top right of your nonprofit's page), and then select Account and Settings.

2. Select Advanced, and then select the Edit function (which is a symbol that looks like a pencil) in the Company type section.

3. From the Tax Form drop-down list, select Nonprofit (Form 990) (see Figure 9-2).

4. Click Save and click Done.

5. Sign out and sign back in to see the change.

FIGURE 9-2:
Changing your
company type
to nonprofit.

Donor type

Your income comes from donors, not customers. Follow these instructions to change customers to donors:

1. Select Settings (the gear symbol at the top right of your nonprofit's page), and then select Account and Settings.

2. Select Advanced, and then select the Edit function (which is a symbol that looks like a pencil) in the Other Preferences section.

3. From the Customer Label drop-down list, select Donors (see Figure 9-3).

4. Click Save and click Done.

FIGURE 9-3:
Changing customers to donors in QuickBooks.

Other preferences		
Date format		MM/dd/yyyy ▾
Number format		$123,456.00 ▾
Customer label		Donors ▾ ⑦

Configuring classes, and tags

In order to allocate expenses and income to your nonprofit's various programs or funds, you configure QuickBooks for fund accounting. Turning on class tracking is the first step:

1. Select Settings (the gear symbol at the top right of your nonprofit's page), and then select Account and Settings.

2. Select Advanced, and then select the Edit function (which is a symbol that looks like a pencil) in the Categories section.

3. Turn on Track classes.

4. Click Save and click Done.

Next, set up a Class for each fund:

1. Select Settings, select All Lists, and select Classes.

2. In the Name field, select New.

3. Click Save and click Done.

   Repeat these steps for all funds/programs you want to track.

The Tags function tracks income, expenses, and assets for multiple sites or areas. Most small to midsize nonprofits have only one location and don't require the Tags feature. To turn off Tags, follow these steps:

1. Select Settings, and then select Account and Settings.

2. Select the Sales tab.

3. Turn off Tags.

4. Click Save.

5. Select the Expense tab.

6. Turn off the Show Tags field.

7. Click Save and click Done.

Providing examples of QuickBooks journals, ledgers, and reports

In accounting, you use a *journal* to record transactions in the order that they occur. A journal is often referred to as the *book of original entry* because it's the first place where you record transactions in the accounts. The general ledger shows all the accounts in your chart of accounts ordered by account number and reflects all transactions affecting each account. See Chapter 6 for more information about journal entries and the general ledger. Your nonprofit has three major financial reports: the Statement of Activities, the Statement of Financial Position, and the Statement of Cash Flows (see Chapters 17, 18, and 19).

The next sections in this chapter show you how to enter a general journal entry in QuickBooks, introduce the payroll journal, provide a quick peek at the QuickBooks general ledger, and list all the reporting available in QuickBooks.

Walking through a journal and entries

Chapter 8 walks you through the cash disbursement and cash payments journals, which you use to report cash transactions. In that chapter, you also learn about accrual journals such as the sales and purchases journals. Use these journals to record purchases your nonprofit makes using store credit and donations pledged with a promise to pay in the future.

The following sections briefly discuss the payroll journal and show you how to enter a general journal entry in QuickBooks.

PAYROLL JOURNAL

The payroll journal records all payroll transactions such a gross wages, taxes withheld, and other deductions like health insurance paid by the employee leading to net pay, which is the amount shown on the employee's checks. Turn to Chapter 15 to see how to figure payroll and payroll tax deposits.

Referencing Figure 9-1 at the beginning of this chapter, you see the Payroll menu option. Selecting this option allows you to enter and pay employees. When you enter a new employee QuickBooks asks you for their name, Social Security number, tax withholding and other deduction information, pay rate, and payment method.

After you enter payroll, you can prepare a *payroll journal*, a listing of all payroll facts by employee. In QuickBooks, the payroll journal goes by the name of Paycheck Summary. Figure 9-4 shows a payroll listing summary.

FIGURE 9-4:
A QuickBooks
Paycheck
Summary.

Gross pay	Pretax deductions	Other pay	Employee taxes	Aftertax deductions	Net pay	Employer taxes	Company contributions	Total pay
$2,935.76	-$73.74		-$430.39	-$75.00	$2,356.63	$344.95		$3,280.71

TIP

The QuickBooks Payroll menu also lets you enter and pay your self-employed contractors.

GENERAL JOURNAL ENTRY

To access the general journal option, at the top left of your nonprofit's home page, click + New. Then select Other **and Journal Entry.**

Figure 9-5 shows how the ABC Cellular journal entry from Chapter 8 appears in the QuickBooks general journal.

FIGURE 9-5:
A QuickBooks
general
journal
entry.

Showing a partial general ledger

Journal entries you enter into QuickBooks affect how the transactions show up in the *general ledger*, which is a listing of each account. As you record accounting transactions in the journals, they automatically update the general ledger for the same transactions, a process called *posting*. Chapter 8 shows the relationship between the journals and the ledger and gives you a look at a manually prepared general ledger. Turn to Figure 9-6 to see what a brand-new, partial general ledger looks like in QuickBooks.

Jay & Top Community Cat Project

General Ledger

DATE	TRANSACTION TYPE	NUM	NAME	MEMO/DESCRIPTION	SPLIT	AMOUNT	BALANCE
Checking							
Beginning Balance							
Total for Checking							
Savings							
Beginning Balance							
Total for Savings							
Accounts Receivable (A/R)							
Beginning Balance							
Total for Accounts Receivable (A/R)							

FIGURE 9-6: A QuickBooks general ledger.

Laying out financial reporting

In QuickBooks Business View, click Get Things Done. In Workspace, scroll down to Accounting and Reports and click See Reports and Trends. There, you find three tabs — Standard, Custom, and Management — and a search option to find various reports.

The Standard option shows your financial statements: statement of activities, financial position, and cash flow. This option also includes accounts receivable (pledges), sales (income from contributions and grants), accounts payable, and expenses.

The Management option includes your company overview (which can be set up as a one-page overview of your need-to-know numbers), sales, and expense performance (allowing you to build charts to see your business performance in QuickBooks).

Use Custom to tailor reports to your nonprofit — maybe your board wants to see information in a particular format.

TIP

Use QuickBooks reports as a template for your Form 990. One issue with QuickBooks is that your net assets may not allocate correctly between restricted and nonrestricted. I always double-check figures before I transfer them to my tax return software, but it's especially important to do this for net assets.

Selecting Aplos Fund Accounting Software

Cloud-based Aplos is tailored to the needs of small to midsize nonprofit and religious organizations. This software does fund accounting, tracks donations, and issues donor statements; it even has a tool for event registrations.

Setting up your free 15-day Aplos trial is easy. Go to the Aplos home page at www.aplos.com. Select the Free Trial link at the top-right side of the home page. Enter your email address, select a password, and enter the day of the month to receive an email to verify your existence. Select the Get Started link in the Aplos confirmation email.

You're then guided through some pages asking for your name, your organization's name, the organization type, phone number, and revenue (I entered Under $100,000). Next, the program asks you questions about what you're trying to accomplish using their software. I checked Explore All Options. After you answer a final question pertaining to your future purchasing plans, you're ready to click the green Begin Your Journey button!

Weighing the pros and cons

The big advantage with Aplos is that it's specifically tailored to nonprofits. Unlike QuickBooks, you won't have to do any customization in your setup in your quest for true fund accounting. It also does budgeting and accounts receivable and allows you to set up recurring transactions.

The lowest-priced software option is Aplos Lite, which as of this writing was $39.50 per month. Lite doesn't do pledge tracking, budgeting, closing, or accrual options such as entering accounts receivable or accounts payable. However, if your nonprofit operates on the cash-based method and has simple donor and expense transactions, the Lite version may be sufficient. Go to www.aplos.com/nonprofit-software for a free trial (scroll down toward the bottom of the page).

The next step up is Core. As of this writing, Core was $69.50 per month. This price point could be a disadvantage for smaller nonprofits with uncomplicated donor transactions. Core does everything Lite does; plus, you can track pledges, budget, close, and access accrual options. However, Core doesn't budget by fund or do income and expense allocations. Whether this is a deal-breaker for your nonprofit would hinge on how many programs you have going at any one time. Go to www.aplos.com/pricing for current pricing.

TIP

Aplos has an advanced version offering fund budgeting and allocations that, as of this writing, starts at $189 per month.

Walking through reporting layers

In this section, I walk you through recording transactions in Aplos, culminating in the preparation of the financial statements. You start by setting up your chart of accounts. If you're on the cash basis of accounting, the check register and general journal options will update your financial statements. If you're on the accrual basis of accounting, there are accounts receivable and accounts payable menu options updating your financial statements as well.

Chart of accounts

The first reporting layer is setting up your chart of accounts, which you use to keep track of where money is coming from and going to in your nonprofit and other nonmonetary transactions. The *chart of accounts* is a list of each account that the accounting system tracks; it captures the information you need to keep track of and use to make good financial decisions.

The chart of accounts is like a big reference card that contains numbers or codes and names of accounts. An account code from the chart of accounts records into the financial records and from there into financial reports. For example, when you receive a donation, you code it with one account number. When you owe a vendor, you code it with another account number.

Aplos has a selection for a building fund and general fund. Most small or midsize nonprofits won't have a need for a building fund chart of accounts, but it's there if you need it. If you need a chart of accounts for another fund or program, there is an option to add one.

Aplos follows the normal chart of accounts numbering sequence with the ability to tailor the standard chart of accounts to your nonprofit. Equity is appropriately broken out between unrestricted and restricted net assets. Because this software is tailored to nonprofits, revenue accounts are correctly listed as income accounts — for example, contributions.

Finally, when you add an account to the standard chart of accounts after you enter the name and account number, you can earmark it as applying to a specific fund.

Also of note is the ability to designate the account as a subaccount. For example, you can have a main telephone expense account with subaccounts (such as mobile, fax, and so on) broken out but still listed under the main account.

Check register

The check register is very simple to use. The same tab selection allows you to record both deposits and payments. On the deposit/payment tab, you enter the same sort of information you would in a manual checkbook, with the additional feature of entering a chart of accounts and fund number. So, after entering this information, it automatically flows through to the financial statements.

There is a second tab to add contributions, which lets you enter donor information. You can enter contact information for the donor, which you use for all communications with the donor (such as the donor acknowledgement letter and letting the donor know about future events). Figure 9-7 shows the check register fields.

FIGURE 9-7:
A check register payment and deposit form.

Figure 9-8 is a partial check register using some of the manual entries from Chapter 8. Note that the beginning balance records at the bottom and the accounting transactions flow upward by date.

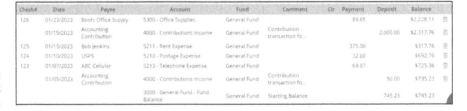

FIGURE 9-8:
A partial check register.

General journal

The general journal is a catchall type of journal for transactions that don't appropriately belong in any other journal, such as adjusting entries. Examples of adjusting entries are to convert cash-basis accounting books to accrual and to reclassify transactions and fix errors.

The Aplos form to enter general journal entries is very similar to recording them manually on journal paper. In addition to having fields to enter the basics (such as the date, accounts affected and by what dollar amounts, and a memo section) there is also a field to apply any of the debits or credits to a fund. The software also keeps track of the journal entry number, automatically entering the next number in a series. See Figure 9-9 for your first general journal entry!

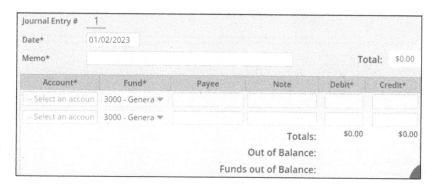

FIGURE 9-9:
A general journal entry form.

REMEMBER

Chapter 8 discusses using the general journal for manually entering closing entries. When using an accounting software program, you don't make closing entries — the software does it automatically when you close the accounting period. In Aplos, this is accomplished with the Period Close option.

Accrual accounting options

If using the accrual method of accounting, Aplos has Accounts Receivable and Accounts Payable menu options to enter and pay your accrual-based transactions. Look to Figure 9-10 to see how I enter one accounts payable transaction from Chapter 8. Enter accounts receivable transactions into Aplos in relatively the same manner.

FIGURE 9-10:
An accounts payable form.

Donor tools

Figure 9-11 shows the Aplos donor menu options. Use these menu options to create donor profiles, communicate with donors, and keep a record of your relationship with the donor. You can also set up events, keep track of pledges, and accept/keep track of online donations. To collect contributions online through Aplos, you have to set up a merchant account through AplosPay and set up online donation forms.

FIGURE 9-11:
Donor menu
options.

Budgeting by fund or tag

For an additional monthly fee, Aplos lets you prepare budgets based on your fund accounting allocation and tags. *Tags* are words or phrases describing a topic. In Aplos, tags only apply to income and expense accounts.

For example, all anticipated expenses and income relating to a certain fund event are given a specific tag such as "Dog Day Fun Run." Run a budget for the "Dog Day Fun Run" event to see how much you anticipate netting with this fundraiser. Then compare actual to budgeted for analysis and potential improvement of results with the next fundraiser.

Budgeting by funds may come in handy if your nonprofit receives grants. You must establish a separate financial account for the receipt, spending, and reporting of the grant funds. You can't combine federal grant funds with funds from other sources. You must also purchase only those items that were approved in your grant application budget. Tagging by fund allows you to substantiate how you anticipate spending grant funds and allows you to compare actual to budgeted.

Allocating costs

Midsize and larger nonprofits may find the allocation feature useful. Allocation involves splitting income or expense items between programs, grants, funds, and locations. For example, a payment including grant allocable costs are chargeable to the grant because the expense is incurred specifically for the grant (see Chapter 11 for more information about determining costs).

There are several steps to this process. Your first step is to create cost drivers which you use to tell the software how to divvy up the income or expense. Next, you create a transaction such as paying a telephone invoice and post the transaction. During the posting process, the telephone expense is allocated in the manner and dollar amount you select using the cost driver. For more information go to www.aplos.com/support/articles/allocations.

Selecting ACCOUNTS

ACCOUNTS, while less robust than QuickBooks or Aplos, does basic bookkeeping and fund accounting. Tailored to churches and charities, it tracks income, expenses, and fund balances and creates reports. As of the research date of this chapter, the Standard version is $129 per year and the OnDemand (cloud-based) version is $199 per year.

Discussing advantages and disadvantages

A huge advantage of ACCOUNTS is the price! ACCOUNTS is much less expensive than QuickBooks or Aplos, but in order to track donors and donations, issue receipts, prepare reports, and perform mail merges, you need the ACCOUNTS sister program, DONATION. Unless you have fewer than 50 donors to track (that version is free), DONATION costs $99 for the Standard version and $149 for OnDemand.

The standard version of ACCOUNTS is commonly selected by smaller nonprofits and comes with a 30-day evaluation period. You can install one version on many different computers with one computer accessing the software at a time. If using the OnDemand version, after one user logs out, your nonprofit database can be accessed virtually by another user on another device.

Ready to get started on your 30-day trial period? Go to www.software4 nonprofits.com. From the top menu bar, select Products and then ACCOUNTS Features. After you decide if you want the 30-day trial for the Standard or OnDemand version, click the appropriate Start Free 30-Day Trial button.

I don't need to share my tutorial with any other user, so I chose Standard. Follow these steps to start using the software:

1. **Download the program.**
2. **Complete the registration.**

3. **Put the software through its paces for 30 days.**

4. **Email support to make your payment if you decide to buy.**

TIP You may have to reboot your system to complete installation, so make sure to save your work prior to starting the download procedure.

Recording income and expense

The first step to record accounting transactions is to set up a chart of accounts. This is done as part of the setup process; my selection during the setup process was Charitable. Figure 9-12 shows a partial chart of accounts, which you can edit as needed.

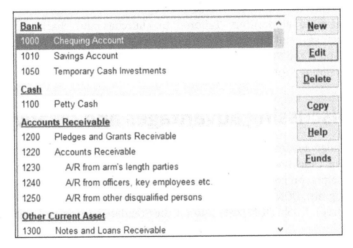

FIGURE 9-12:
A partial chart of
accounts.

Next, you access the main menu for the program, which shows the four Common Actions (see Figure 9-13):

» **Banking:** Record deposits, prepare and print checks, and reconcile your checking account (see Chapter 7 for more information about balancing your checking account).

» **Accounts and Transactions:** Access and modify the chart of accounts, enter journal entries, and drill down into each account to see the transactions affecting the account.

TIP

The Register command pulls up reports similar to the general ledger (see Chapters 6 and 8 for more information about the general ledger).

» **Bills and Vendors:** Geared toward nonprofits operating on the accrual method, maintain a current vendor list, enter vendor invoices, and schedule them for payment.

» **Reports, Backup, and Help:** No surprises here! Run your financial reports, back up your data file, and access ACCOUNTS Help.

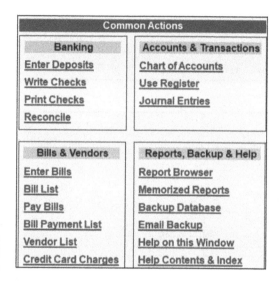

FIGURE 9-13:
The ACCOUNTS
main menu.

Next, let's enter some income deposits and then pay some bills. Select Enter Deposits. This brings you to a pop-up with fields asking for basic checking account information. Going back to Chapter 8, I enter the Smith Donation deposit for $50 (see Figure 9-14). Click Save and Close. When you go back to your main menu, you see that the cash balance automatically increased by $50.

Next, let's enter a check from Chapter 8, payment to ABC Cellular for $69.87. Figure 9-12 shows the check form. Click Save and Close. When you go back to your main menu, you see that the cash balance automatically decreases by $69.87. When reviewing both Figure 9-14 and 9-15 note the ability to allocate both the deposit and the payment between numerous accounts.

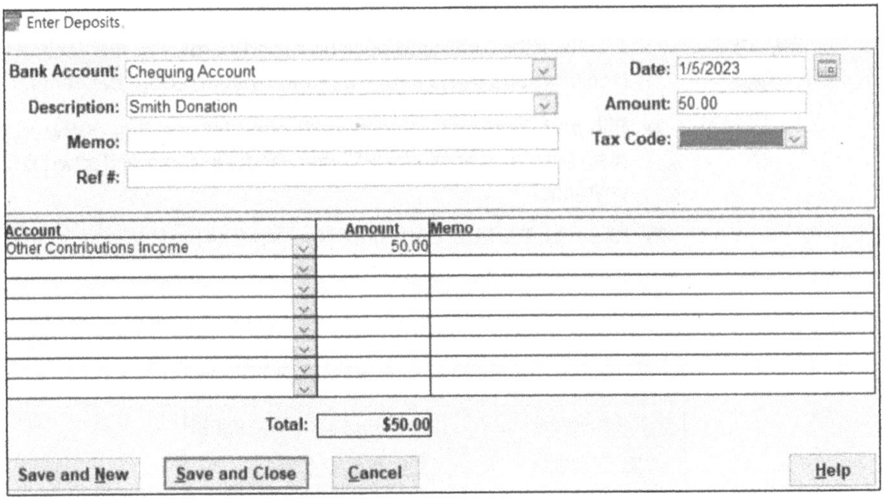

FIGURE 9-14:
The ACCOUNTS
deposit form.

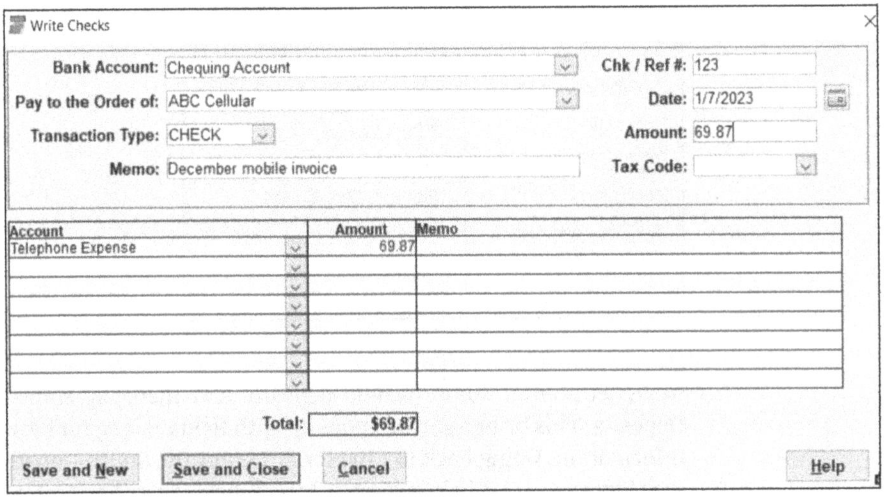

FIGURE 9-15:
The ACCOUNTS
check form.

Tracking fund balances

I briefly discussed fund accounting in Chapter 1. Fund accounting involves tracking income and expenses to your nonprofit's various programs or funds. If your nonprofit has more than one fund and especially if you receive grant money, it's important that your accounting software lets you allocate income and expenses by fund. Allocating in ACCOUNTS couldn't be any easier!

First, make sure the fund to which you want to associate income and expenses appears in section 300 of your chart of accounts. My free trial has three: 3010 General Fund, 3110 Temporary fund #1, and 3210 Permanent Fund #1. Use the New command in the chart of accounts to add a fund specific to your nonprofit, giving it a 3000 series chart of account number.

Associate income and expense accounts with a fund by going to the chart of accounts in the Accounts and Transactions section of Common Actions. Select the income or expense account you want to allocate to a fund and click Edit. Select the Fund field on the Edit pop-up and select the appropriate fund from the drop-down menu.

Creating financial reports

ACCOUNTS has a very well developed financial reports menu from financial statements to log in history and an audit trail. There are nine sections (see Figure 9-16), three of which I've expanded to give you a representative sample. Here's what's in each section:

» **Listing Reports:** Includes the chart of accounts, annual or monthly budget, and income/expenses by fund.

» **Summary Reports:** Lists financial statements such as income statement (statement of activities; see Chapter 17), balance sheet (statement of financial position; Chapter 18), and the ability to pull budget comparisons.

» **Details Reports:** Pull reports by date, amount, account, or payee.

» **Fund Reports:** Allows you to pull financial statements, such as the income statement by fund.

» **Banking Reports:** Lists cleared and uncleared transactions for one selected account and ending statement date for which you performed a reconciliation on that account.

» **Vendors and Bills Report:** Your one-stop shop for all vendor- and bill pay–related items.

» **Accountant Reports:** These reports are the starting point for accountant review. The general ledger shows all accounts and all transactions hitting the accounts for a specific period. The trial balance summarizes that on the general ledger. The audit trial shows who entered what and on what dates.

» **Administrative Reports:** Lists dates and times that any user logged on or off of the program and any transactions that are out of balance (debits don't equal credits).

» **Custom Reports:** Allows you to tailor reports to your nonprofit.

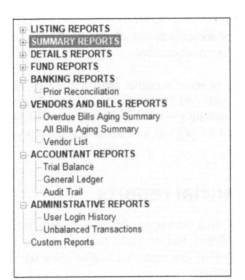

FIGURE 9-16:
The ACCOUNTS
financial reports
menu.

REMEMBER

If you need to track donors and contributions, check out the free 30-day trial for DONATION at www.software4nonprofits.com/donation-features. And best of all, the Standard version of DONATION is free and does not require a license key until your nonprofit has more than 50 donors in the current year.

TIP

For those who only need to automate their donor management and online contributions, check out Little Green Light at www.littlegreenlight.com. Two other fantastic options offered by this software is a one-hour on-demand demo at www.littlegreenlight.com/demo. The company also offers a robust free trial — see www.littlegreenlight.com/signup to find out more about the free 30-day trial.

Chapter **10**

Balancing Cash Flow with an Operating Budget

Your organization needs to know where it's going, whether you put it in writing or not. However, to spend money without thinking or planning indicates a lack of control and responsibility. A budget helps you manage your money and prioritize your spending; it also serves as a check to impulsive buying. It shows projected revenues and the amount set aside for planned expenses. You need a budget to keep cash flow in balance.

Basically, your budget is your organization's financial plan. Without a detailed budget, your nonprofit's risk of failure increases significantly. Not to worry, though. This chapter explains why your nonprofit needs a budget, what you need to do to create a budget, and how to create, track, manage, and evaluate your financial plan.

Understanding the Importance of Having a Budget in the Nonprofit World

A *budget* is an itemized list of what income you expect to receive and what you expect to pay out during a given time period, whether a month, quarter, or year. It expresses in monetary terms what your objectives are. Knowing when you've reached your target goal is nearly impossible if you don't know what you need. For your nonprofit to survive and thrive financially, you must create and follow a budget.

REMEMBER

Without a budget, you're on a cross-country road trip without a map. If you start out on a trip with no planned destination, who knows where you'll end up. Your nonprofit is too important to allow things to just randomly happen. You need to control as much about your finances as you can. A budget can tell you

>> The amount of revenue you're expecting to receive from grants, fundraisers, contributions, and investment income or gains

>> An estimate of program expenses, fundraising expenses, and losses

>> How much you need to cover management and general expenses

Operating on a budget is important at all times, not just when money is tight. Following your budget means you're planning for income and expenses and controlling your money. Your budget is a prediction or forecast based on prior events and expected future events. Not only does a budget include projections, but also, after time expires, you have the reality of what actually happened.

Use your budget to manage costs and run your organization more efficiently. It's smart management to look at your income and expenses to determine how you can reduce your overhead expenses. For example, if a program grant is discontinued, you need to know the impact on your organization. Without a budget, you won't know how much the loss of that revenue is going to affect expected outlays and you won't have a clue about any steps you need to take to smooth out the decrease in revenue by cutting back on costs.

REMEMBER

Many people feel that having a budget limits their spending ability. But contrary to popular belief, a budget means you're aware of and in control of your money.

Large corporations monitor and control their spending. They're always assessing and reassessing how they manufacture products and how they can reduce expenses. Although you don't operate your nonprofit in the same manner as a for-profit business, your organization can't be successful without enough money to cover expenses. Therefore, it's important that you have a financial plan or budget.

Preparing to Create an Operating Budget

If you were planning a monthlong trip to Europe, you wouldn't wake up on the morning of your flight and run to the airport with only a carry-on bag. Weeks in advance, you book your flights and hotels, pack accordingly, and have a general travel plan.

Likewise, before you can put together your nonprofit's operating budget, you have to make the necessary preparations. Do this by determining guidelines, setting your priorities and goals, and keeping everything organized.

Your budget is your resource allocation road map. In a nutshell, the operating budget helps you determine how much you need to secure in contributions to sustain your nonprofit. By creating your operating budget, you'll know how much money you have, how much you plan to receive, how much you need, and what you can plan to achieve. You also use your operating budget to plan for future purchases.

Your financial statements indicate what has already happened (check out chapters 17 through 19 for putting together your nonprofit's financial statements) and are the starting point to help you predict your budget for the upcoming fiscal year. Use your financial statements to figure out why things happened and then analyze the figures to come up with your new operating budget to offset some of the occurrences that occurred (and may occur again). Creating an operating budget gives you another chance to plan and control what happens in the upcoming year.

TIP

Start your budget process by forming a team that includes your executive director, chief financial officer, and finance committee or budget task group. Make sure to have a copy of your mission statement handy. The team assigned to draft your budget uses your mission statement to come up with the guidelines, priorities, and goals needed for the budgeting process.

The following sections walk you through the different steps your organization needs to take before creating your nonprofit budget.

Setting clear guidelines

Start your budgeting process by looking at your organization's vision and purpose, as defined in your mission statement. Your budget guidelines are centered on your mission and what it takes to accomplish your organization's goals. They guide your nonprofit in developing a budget that shows how your funding priorities support your strategic plan. Most strategic plans cover three to five years, defining steps to achieve goals with charts that direct the process. Your strategic plan should be in writing so you can look at it and see whether you're on track.

Budget guidelines allow you to review and evaluate budget requests and submit recommendations to your board of directors. These guidelines help you make measurable progress toward your goals. All budget items should be tied to performance indicators so you can measure their outcomes.

Your guidelines define how you plan to improve the effectiveness of your current system. Some of the items included in budget guidelines are

>> Guidelines for salary increases

>> Budget for operations

>> Line-item transfers

>> Guidelines for adjustments

>> Annual fundraising goals and priorities

Remember that these budget guidelines are just that — guidelines — and they're not written in stone! You may have to make adjustments as your fiscal year progresses.

REMEMBER

Having clear guidelines helps you recognize the importance of budget maintenance for your organization. Your budget allows you to focus on items and issues that are relevant to your board's fiscal priorities.

Identifying your nonprofit's objectives

As you're creating your budget and setting and following your guidelines, it's important for you to establish and know the importance of your objectives. These objectives are what your organization wants to achieve — in other words, your organization's priorities. You need to identify your objectives and put them on paper so you can track your progress and see what objectives require your immediate attention.

With so much to do every day and so many distractions, having clear goals and objectives for your organization and for each program is important. What may be a priority for you may not be for the next person. Knowing your priorities makes day-to-day decisions easier.

REMEMBER

Planning and strategizing aren't just for the for-profit industry. As a nonprofit, you need a plan for your future. A five-year plan with set priorities is an excellent road map.

Commonly stated budget priorities include the following:

>> Maintain financial stability of the organization.

>> Nurture commitment to your target population.

>> Assess and ensure quality of program delivery.

>> Improve and expand your capital campaign.

To identify your priorities, do the following:

1. **Write down the activities that are most important and rank them in order.**

    Ask yourself what your organization's most important activities are.

2. **Make a list of current and future activities that you plan to achieve.**

    Ask yourself what the benefits of the activities are. Determine the purpose and goals, and rank your list according to the greatest benefit to the groups that will be helped.

TIP

Many organizations assign a score for priorities within each program. For example, you can assign a number to each priority on your list indicating its importance.

Making and prioritizing goals

Without a vision, organizations perish. Your nonprofit's goals are visionary statements that motivate you and others to do something. Goals are end results that you want to obtain, and you can't obtain them without the right budget in place. So, before you can put together your operating budget, you need to know what your organization's goals are. Don't forget to factor in evaluating your progress toward goals.

REMEMBER

Defining clear goals and having a plan in place to reach them can save you from going into financial crisis mode, which is when you operate day to day with no definite plan for sustainability. To avoid operating in crisis mode, set clear, concise goals for your organization as a whole, as well as for each of your programs.

To obtain your goals, you must have objectives that are tied to those goals. Activity makes goals happen. But if you do nothing but think about your goals and take no action, nothing will happen.

Ideally, your goal statement starts broadly by first identifying the overall goals for the organization and then indicating on a program-by-program basis what the major actions should be for the upcoming budget year. Start with goals for the entire organization and then look at goals for each program.

Organizational goals

Your nonprofit's goals are the big picture of success for your organization. They may include growth in personnel, effectiveness in the sphere of influence or the ability to partner with other organizations.

You, as the director of your nonprofit, and your board need to set your organization's goals. To do so, take the following steps:

1. **Decide what you want the end results to be.**

2. **Set a measurable way to indicate performance.**

3. **Assign a number by which you can gauge whether you've met your goals.**

   This number serves as a checkpoint of sorts. You need to decide and set realistic measurable performance numbers, such as 10 percent more people will be served in the upcoming year.

After you set your organization's goals, you have to prioritize them. Some people assign numbers to their goals based on priority. To prioritize, you need to rank in order the steps needed to accomplish your goals. Whatever the first step is to reach your goal can be assigned number one. Your top priority is the first step toward reaching your goals. Just work on your list by moving on to Step 2 and so on.

Setting goals alone doesn't yield results. You have to do something to bring your goals to reality.

You can't accomplish your organization's goals without a clear funding plan. Your funding plan defines how much money you need to raise from all sources to operate. You need the following to organize a funding plan:

>> Mission statement defining your purpose or vision

>> Funding goals

>> Funding objectives

>> List of potential funders

>> Action plan

To create a funding plan, simply write down the five preceding items manually on a sheet of paper or electronically on your computer using your document program. Your funding plan contains information about where you plan to get the money (a list of potential funders) to fund your programs. I suggest you do your budget first, so you can identify what your goals, objectives, and needs are, and then do your funding plan.

Individual program goals

You also need individual program goals to keep you and your staff motivated. These program goals are performance levels of what you see as the end result of a particular program. The only difference between organizational goals and program goals is that organizational goals include program goals, whereas program goals are only for one particular program. For example, if your program is a mentoring project, your goal may be that 5 percent more children will be mentored this year than last year.

Program goals require much of the same thought process as setting organizational goals. You need to have clearly defined goals, a well-written plan in place to keep programs up and running, and innovative ideas to attract funders. You can then use these goals to help you establish a program budget.

Creating a separate budget for each program shows good fiscal management. Separate program budgets allow you to see which programs are sustaining themselves and which ones are experiencing cash shortages. Tailored budgets also help when a program needs to be cut or budget items have to be reduced. You create a budget for a program the same way you create a budget for your organization, except you may have different categories. (Check out the section "Coming Up with an Operating Budget," later in this chapter, for how to develop your program budgets.)

After you set a goal, begin working toward achieving it right away. Every activity you do should lead to accomplishing your goal. A good way to reach your goals is to break them down into smaller steps. So, if you have a fundraising goal of $15,000 for the year, you may want to see how much you've raised after each quarter. When you get to each quarter, you can check to see whether you've achieved one-quarter, one-half, and three-quarters of what you plan to achieve. If you haven't, you can make adjustments to the budget or look for ways to increase funding.

As you reach your goals, cross them off the list. If you reach your goal of raising $15,000 at the midway point, you can cross that goal off the list, because you've achieved it.

TIP

Your program goals don't have to stay the same year after year. As your organization changes, you have to reevaluate your goals and priorities.

Staying organized

In order to achieve your goals for your organization and programs, you can't let important details slip through the cracks. Staying organized is key to meeting your goals and staying on budget. Planning and getting organized helps not only with your goals and budget, but also with your stress levels. Being organized allows you to find things, so it saves you money. Remember the old saying, "Time equals money, and money equals time." If you spend less time looking for things, you'll be more productive and focused on operating your organization.

Staying organized requires paying attention to details, time frames, and deadlines. It's a process that takes time, energy, and motivation. The following tips can help you stay organized.

Use a detailed calendar with time frames and deadlines

To stay organized, calendars on which you note time frames and deadlines are essential. You handle many tasks within your organization that have beginnings and endings. Knowing these dates allows you to schedule time to work on them so you don't miss important deadlines.

Your budget and work plan should be scheduled so everyone involved is on the same page. Developing a budget calendar with a timeline can help your board, finance committee, budget task group, and treasurer stay on track. You can use helpful tools such as planners and address books, smartphones, and client databases to keep calendars updated.

You want to schedule the timeline for creating next year's budget based on your fiscal year. Most people allow at least three months from preliminary to approval. So, if your fiscal year starts in May, you'd start working on the new budget no later than February 1. Some larger tasks can be broken down into smaller tasks, and the due dates for those incremental steps should be noted and shared with everyone.

File all paperwork in a timely manner

You evaluate your budget and monitor your progress throughout the year. Therefore, you need to create a set of files to keep up with the changes so you can easily access the information. Organizing your papers helps organize your thoughts. You can purchase a filing cabinet, a file box, and some hanging file folders, and manila folders to sort the papers. You can label files by month. Filing the paperwork month by month saves time and reduces stress. Make sure you keep up with receipts for major purchases and supplies, as well as documents related to payroll taxes.

Throw away what you don't need

As your board meets to discuss changes needed to the budget and new programs that need to be implemented, you may find yourself swimming in paperwork. It may not be a good idea to hold on to the paperwork from the first budget meeting 15 years ago. At some point, you need to clear out the old and make room for the new. Throw away anything more than five years old. Declutter your storage files and cabinets. Consider throwing away or donating items you don't need. Manage your mail. Pick up a magazine rack and throw away magazines more than a month old.

Outline your tasks

When you outline tasks, you create a systematic way to know when to start and complete something. You can make a to-do list and prioritize which tasks need to be done and when. For example, creating a daily to-do list can help you organize your work and time. Even if you don't finish everything on the list, at least your priorities are already organized for the next day. When you complete a task, you can cross it off your list and then manage the remaining tasks to know which ones you can realistically expect to complete.

As you set your goals, you establish an outline of tasks to ensure that you reach the goal. As you accomplish a goal, cross it off the list and start on another one.

To complete your tasks, you use both time and money. If you know how much of each is needed, assign that portion so you can get an overall idea about what is needed financially to accomplish each task and ultimately reach your goals.

Your spending plan is your budget. To outline your spending plans for the coming year, you want to review the following tasks:

>> Starting new programs

>> Expanding existing programs

>> Creating fundraising recommendations

>> Securing funding for new projects through grants

>> Designing a dedicated website for donations

>> Developing an application to accept donations

>> Enabling online donations through services such as PayPal, Venmo, or Zelle

>> Locating in-kind funding to match grants

TIP

Some people like to group tasks into phases. Phase one is usually the planning phase. Phase two may be securing funding for a project. Phase three may be implementation of a project.

Coming Up with an Operating Budget

After you make the necessary preparations by establishing guidelines, identifying your priorities, and setting goals, you're ready to put everything down on paper in the form of a budget. You want to look at what your expenses are and how much money it takes to cover them. Also, consider new programs that are needed and think about how you might fund them. With these points in mind, you're ready to create your organization's operating budget (see Figure 10-1).

The following sections explain the simple steps of how to put together an operating budget, including details on what to include.

20XX Operating Budget

	Year to Date		
	Actual	Budget	Variance	
Income:				
Private Donations	50,000	45,000	5,000	F
Public Donations	75,000	71,000	4,000	F
Special Events	6,000	7,000	(1,000)	U
Investment income	5,000	4,500	500	F
Total income	$136,000	$127,500	8,500	F
Expenses:				
Management and General	23,500	22,300	1,200	U
Travel	2,000	3,500	(1,500)	F
Supplies	6,000	5,300	700	U
Rent	12,000	12,000	-	
Fundraising	13,000	9,500	3,500	U
Telephone	600	700	(100)	F
Salaries	67,500	67,500	-	
Payroll Taxes	5,200	5,200	-	
Total Expenses	129,800	126,000	3,800	U
Excess of income over expenses	6,200	1,500	4,700	F

FIGURE 10-1:
A sample operating budget.

U = Unfavorable
F = Favorable

REMEMBER

You may wonder how your operating budget differs from the financial statements you're required to prepare. Your budget shows what you expect to happen financially; it's based on predictions. Your financial statements show how much you collected and how much you spent; they're based on the reality of what happened.

Walking through the steps to the budget

Creating a budget isn't complicated. Start with ledger or journaling paper (see Chapter 8) or open a word doc on your laptop and follow the steps in this section. Use the following steps to set realistic goals.

Step 1: Prioritize and determine the need

Look at last year's budget and compare it to every new item to be added to this year's budget. Ask yourself the following questions:

>> Is there a need for this activity?

>> How important is it that we do it?

>> What is the anticipated cost?

>> Are there ways we can reduce the cost of running a program?

This process is time-consuming and one of the reasons many organizations don't create a budget. However, by not taking this step, you miss things that need attention, like how you fund your activities and whether there's a way to provide more services for the same amount of money or less. You then refer to the results of these questions as you start talking numbers.

Step 2: Make a list of everything coming in and going out

Write down your actual revenue amounts and their sources — the grants and donations you already have — followed by your actual expenses and their amounts. Refer to Figure 10-1 for an example.

You have two types of expenses to consider:

>> **Variable expenses:** These are amounts you pay that change over the period of your budget. An example is the cost of utilities.

>> **Fixed expenses:** The cost of these expenses is the same over the period of your budget. A rent payment is generally considered a fixed expense.

TIP

To make more expenses fixed, such as utilities, see if the provider offers a budget plan (also called an estimated payment plan). The budget plan takes an average of a year's worth of utility costs and charges you the average amount each month. It stops fluctuations in bills. Going on a budget plan can help you stay in balance with your expense projections.

If you're not sure how much to budget for, take a look at your budget and receipts from last month, last quarter, and last year. Use these documents to make realistic predictions about what will happen next month, next quarter, and next year.

Step 3: Separate actual income versus projected income

Your budget is an estimate of your expected cash flow. Based on prior periods, you can gauge what will happen in the future. When creating a budget, you focus on these two items:

>> **Actual amounts:** Your actual amount is what you've already received or a fixed amount. (Fixed amounts are those things that are preset and not subject to change, such as money you already have in reserve, and existing grants and contracts.)

>> **Projected amounts:** Your projected amount is what you expect to receive, such as a large donation. Your projected income includes your actual income plus your expected income.

One of three things is going to happen: You'll get what you expect (project), or you'll get more or less. Yet, forecasting your expectations is crucial to your organization's budgetary process.

So, when separating actual and projected income, do the following:

1. **Take realistic projections.**

   Begin with amounts you feel somewhat sure about, like grants and contracts you've received in the last year. Make sure these amounts are realistic projections, not merely a wish list, because what you plan to purchase and how you plan to pay your employees are contingent on you being realistic.

2. **After the time period expires, list what actually happened.**

   Track your income and spending periodically. You can do so at the end of the month, quarter, or year. Just make sure you compare what you projected with what you received. Keep a close eye on your budget as time passes, so you can be prepared to adjust it as needed. You want to know how well you've planned things to help you plan better the next time.

3. **Evaluate the difference between what you projected and what actually took place (that is, what was budgeted versus actual).**

   Subtract what happened from what you expected to happen and look at the results. Sometimes you may get more than you expect, which is good. Other times you may have less. So, plan an alternative way to raise the money, which may be another fundraiser or loan. It's a decision that you and your board need to discuss.

Step 4: Compare income to expenses and make adjustments as necessary

After you know what your expenses are likely to be and how much money you expect to bring in, you can figure out your projected bottom line for the period. In other words, you can subtract your projected expenses from your projected revenues and see whether you'll have a net increase or decrease in assets (refer to Figure 10-1).

If your budget shows a positive number, you've got a net increase in assets, meaning you have some money left over. You can increase your spending in one of the expense categories, or you can plan to save the additional revenue in case something unexpected happens — the economy takes a nosedive, you have to replace the heating and cooling system, you lose grant funding, or some other unfortunate event takes place.

If your budget shows a negative number, you have a net decrease in assets, meaning your expenses are larger than your revenues. You can handle this a couple of ways:

>> Look at your expenses and see where you can cut some costs.

>> Look at your revenues and determine how to increase the amount of funding you're bringing in.

Getting your budget approved

Your organization's finance committee should have a budget timeline for preparing, reviewing, and getting board approval of your budget. Most nonprofits will plan budget meetings anywhere from two to eight weeks in the future.

If you're the executive director, you and the finance committee discuss and assess the organization's priorities and present the budget to your board of directors. Your board of directors reviews and evaluates your operating budget to assess how it aligns with your budget priorities, mission, and strategic plan. Your board of directors adopts your annual budget through recommendations and an approval process.

REMEMBER

As things happen or change, you can update the existing budget. For example, evaluate your budget as new grant programs are funded, as old grant programs expire, and any other time something happens in your organization that directly affects your revenues and expenses. Just keep in mind that any changes to a board-approved annual budget will probably require updated board approval.

Reviewing Budget Performance

Throughout the year, your board and executive staff compare the expected amounts to the actual results. Your board and management staff carefully evaluate the gap between actual and budget performance and use it as a tool for future endeavors.

REMEMBER

Your board must be prepared to immediately assess and map out corrective action when actual versus budget is materially off and it's clear that the original budget can't be met. Of course, this primarily applies when expenses exceed the budget and income has not increased enough to cover the increase.

Establishing a budget task group

Many nonprofits have a budget task force in place that brainstorms ways to increase income or decrease costs. One task force function is usually to come up with ways to motivate old donor groups or attract new ones. Another is to brainstorm ways to streamline operations to cut costs during the following year.

If you don't already have a budget task group, it's to your advantage to get one in place prior to the next budgeting process. As the task force is involved in the formation of the original operating budget, it's ideally positioned to evaluate the budget versus actual results. This is because they know the background story and rationale of different budget line items. If a new idea didn't pan out as expected, the task force can dig into their notes to identify what may have caused the variance.

Making adjustments

Make sure to review your budget regularly to see how budgeted figures are different from actual results. For example, based on your best estimate at the time, you budgeted a repair expense for $1,000. An unexpected storm did some damage, increasing your repair expense to $3,200, which may be an extreme variance for your nonprofit. If variances are extreme, either good or bad, it's time to make adjustments by revising tasks and schedules.

If you have a *budget deficit* (a shortage of funds or when expenses outweigh income), devise a plan to manage down the deficit. Some programs may have to be canceled or scaled back. Capital improvements or the purchase of fixed assets may have to be delayed.

On the flip side, if you received an unexpected inflow of cash, some new programs on your wish list could be implemented based on your organization's goals and the needs of your target population. Or maybe you can go ahead and buy that new copier! Flexibility is key.

TIP

Keep in mind that a written narrative report should be prepared explaining why certain deviations from the budget occur. For example, "After the budget was approved, we had some unexpected facility repairs resulting in exceeding budget by $2,000. We are confident that our annual budget will not be exceeded."

3

Accounting for Nonprofit Situations

Access grant money and pay special attention to the federal grant system if you receive any federal grant money.

Comply with all the rules after you access grant money.

Prepare for a grant audit, which makes sure you're spending Uncle Sam's money wisely.

Pay employee payroll taxes and file yearly federal Form 990.

Chapter **11**

Introducing Federal Grants

M ost nonprofit executives spend sleepless nights worrying about finances and wondering if donors will continue to support the organization's mission. Have you been one of those directors or managers who tossed and turned, wondering where the money for your next project is coming from?

Applying for and using federal grants are wise moves to secure more dependable sources of revenue. Being awarded a federal grant is just like money in the bank. Although the check doesn't come in the mail, the money is reserved for you at the U.S. Treasury.

Some nonprofit directors openly express a disinterest in federal money. One of the reasons is that they don't understand the process. Another reason is the stiff federal penalties and serious repercussion for abuse and mismanagement of federal grant funds.

Nevertheless, I wouldn't attempt to operate a nonprofit without federal money. The federal government is holding our tax dollars and has set aside funding to fulfill needs addressed by nonprofit charitable organizations like yours. Don't wait any longer to take advantage of this money to help your organization!

Receiving federal money does have strings attached. In this chapter, you discover how to comply with federal grant submission requirements to take advantage of the grant money available.

Grasping Why Federal Grant Money Is Important to Nonprofits

Finding money to fund your nonprofit's projects can be a time-consuming and stressful experience. However, exploring grants is worth the time because a significant amount of federal grant money is available if you know where to turn and how to apply for it.

If a for-profit business needs to generate more cash, all it has to do is sell a product or service or perhaps issue more stock. For nonprofits, current regulations and tax codes are very specific about how nonprofits can obtain money. That makes federal grant money particularly important for nonprofits for the following reasons:

>> **Grant money has been set aside for nonprofit use.** Congress allocates our tax dollars to federal programs. Grant funds are allocated to states based on the following numbers:

- Unemployment rate

- Inmate population

- Low-birth rates

- Number of unwed mothers

- Juvenile delinquency statistics

- High school dropout rates

>> **The government relies on nonprofits to address the needs in their respective communities.** Because of the nature of nonprofit organizations and their underlying purpose, the government looks to you to fill the gaps in society by addressing your community's needs.

>> **Grant funds provide a stable, reliable cash flow for nonprofit organizations.** The funds allow nonprofits to focus on their missions and not worry about finances.

REMEMBER

In 2022, the federal government awarded more than $700 billion in the form of grants that help:

>> Further the common good by supporting nonprofit organizations so they can fulfill their intended purpose

>> Expand social programs for educational and cultural enrichment

>> Support human health and protect the environment

Unfortunately, grant dollars are susceptible to waste and abuse. Therefore, strict guidelines have been established to provide oversight of financial management of agencies' programs that are supported by federal grants. Even with all the strict guidelines and hoops to jump through, if your nonprofit isn't taking advantage of this money, you're losing out on funds that can make a real impact on your organization.

Spelling Out the Basics

Right now people are sitting in federal offices writing and rewriting legislation, rules, and guidelines concerning federal grants for nonprofits. You may be overwhelmed by information overload and hate to read the fine print. It may be possible to initially just scan some data, but much of it is essential to knowing how your nonprofit effectively accounts for federal money.

Federal grants are awarded for a specific project and require strict financial oversight. Because grants are closely monitored, you want to ensure you properly account for them. The good news is there are clearly spelled out rules to assist you along the way. Check out the "Managing Federal Grant Money" section, later in this chapter, for more specific advice about managing grant money. As long as you know and understand the accounting requirements, you can effectively account for grant funds.

This section gives you a clearer picture of federal grants and answers several questions, including what these grants are, who can take advantage of them, how to apply for them, and what you have to do if your nonprofit receives federal grant money.

Defining a federal grant

Before your nonprofit can take advantage of federal grant money, you first need to understand what federal grant money is. A *federal* grant is financial assistance in the form of money issued by the U.S. government to carry out a public purpose of support or stimulation authorized by law. Federal grants are available to nonprofits depending on their ability to implement, manage, and meet the obligation.

REMEMBER

To be eligible for federal grants, your organization must meet the federal government's definition of a nonprofit, which is generally covered under your specific Internal Revenue Code (IRC) 501(c)(3) designation, and your nonprofit is any corporation, trust, association, cooperative, or other organization that

>> Operates primarily for scientific, educational, service, charitable, religious or similar purposes in the public interest

>> Is not organized primarily for profit or operated for the benefit of private interests

>> Uses its net proceeds to maintain, improve, and/or expand its operations

TIP

For more information about IRC 501(c)(3), visit the IRS Exemption Requirements page at `www.irs.gov/charities-non-profits/charitable-organizations/exemption-requirements-501c3-organizations`.

The federal grant process has three phases: pre-award, award, and post-award. Figure 11-1 gives a thumbnail sketch of each phase in the grant life cycle. For more detailed information about each phase, go to `www.grants.gov/learn-grants/grants-101/award-phase.html` and click the links in the Award Phase menu. That menu also has a link to a fantastic Getting Started Checklist.

FIGURE 11-1:
The grant
life cycle.

Grant Lifecyle
Pre-Award Phase: Grant announcement and application review
Award Phase: Review complete, grantees selected and NoA letters issued
Post-Award Phase: Fulfillment, reporting and close out of the grant

UNCOVERING OTHER (NONGOVERNMENTAL) STONES FOR GRANT MONEY

The government is the biggest grant maker in the nation, but there are some other large givers that I want you to consider. Many large corporations and foundations give grants, too. For instance, the Gates Foundation gives money for health services and education. Some large corporations make so much money that they give it away — sometimes altruistically, sometimes to reduce taxable income. I suggest you first look in your own community for grants to help your nonprofit. Identify any large corporations in your area and ask whether they have any sort of grant program for which your nonprofit may qualify. You can find information about all the foundations in the world by visiting the Foundation Center's website at `https://fconline.foundationcenter.org`.

If you're lucky enough to get a grant, you're a grant recipient. At a minimum a grant recipient is expected to:

>> Be a good steward of the grant money.

>> Use the grant money for its intended purposes.

>> Keep copies of all bills and expenses paid for with the money.

Finding and applying for federal grants for your nonprofit

If you're like me, you receive tons of spam emails about grants to pay your bills, buy a house, start a business, and so on. Federal grants aren't a joke or scam though. They're given to organizations that fulfill a need in society. The federal government knows it can't address people's needs by itself; therefore, it awards grants to nonprofit organizations that benefit society.

So, where can your nonprofit locate these federal grant monies? Here are three primary places to find grant opportunities for your nonprofit:

>> **Grants.gov:** Grants.gov is the one-stop shop designed to provide a level playing field for all organizations. Every funding opportunity offered by the 26 federal agencies can be found at www.grants.gov.

>> **SAM.gov:** The Assistance Listings section of SAM.gov provides a complete tally of federal assistance programs. Check it out at https://sam.gov/content/assistance-listings.

>> **The specific federal agency's website:** All 26 federal agencies have information on their respective websites about grant opportunities. A simple way to find any federal agency is to use an online search engine.

WARNING

Challenges flowing from the COVID-19 pandemic have caused nonprofits to be stretched rather thin. Due to the decline in the stock market since 2022, industry experts reckon less money will be available for grants. Nonprofits have to take measures to counteract any anticipated reduction in grant awards such as networking, seeking out new grant opportunities, or increasing fundraising events.

TIP

There is a handy page at FederalGrants.com listing the 25 categories of grant funding. Select the one that most closely matches your nonprofit to see what grants are currently available. Find this page information at www.federalgrants.com/Category.

Accessing federal grant money isn't as easy as shopping at your local discount store. Although it is somewhat of a process, the good news is, all organizations follow the same six steps. Go to www.grants.gov/web/grants/applicants/apply-for-grants.html for more information about each of the six steps:

1. **Review the grants learning center.**

   Your first stop is to find basic information about the grant process, grant-writing tips, and other topics from determining grant terminology to grant fraud.

2. **Verify your eligibility.**

   You don't want to waste the time applying for grants for which your nonprofit doesn't meet the grant criteria. Follow the links in Steps 4 and 6 of this list to get the details on how eligibility is determined and generally what types of grants your nonprofit can apply for.

3. **Search for grants that align with your mission statement.**

   This page lists available grants by opportunity number and title, what federal agency is sponsoring the grant, what the status of the grant is, and the application opening and closing dates.

4. **Register.**

   Organization must register with both SAM.gov and Grants.gov. SAM.gov captures your nonprofit information and is where you obtain the unique entity identifier (UEI) that you need to proceed to Grants.gov. Grants.gov manages the grant application process. For more information about both, go directly to www.grants.gov/web/grants/applicants/registration.html.

5. **Apply for grants using Workspace.**

   Workspace is the standard tool you use for all grant applications; it can be found at www.grants.gov/applicants/workspace-overview.html. Be sure to view the "How to Create a Workspace" video on the Workspace home page; it explains how to set up Workspace and submit your grant application.

6. **Track your application.**

   You've successfully navigated SAM.gov and Grants.gov and successfully uploaded your grant application using Workspace. Now the waiting starts. The waiting period for finding out whether you've been awarded a grant is usually three to six months. You can track your application at www.grants.gov/web/grants/applicants/track-my-application.html.

Documenting where the money goes

If your nonprofit receives federal grant money, federal regulations require strict documentation of grant expenses. Uncle Sam wants to know how and where you're spending his money. You have to document costs for verification purposes, both for requesting payment for expenses and for audit purposes. As your nonprofit incurs program expenses related to the grant, you need to account for every transaction with supporting documentation to justify and verify expenditures.

In the wake of government accountability, federal grants are under serious scrutiny. Although opening a separate bank account for grant funds isn't required, federal auditors and monitors require that nonprofits account for and keep track of every purchase, sale, and payment separately.

REMEMBER

Tracking expenses separately can help you gather financial information for reports required by the federal government. These reports monitor your progress (see Chapter 12 for more about required reports), and all discrepancies will be documented in audit findings (see Chapter 14 for more about grant audits).

Nonprofits must do the following to account for federal grants:

>> Report as required on the use of grant funds.

>> Use grant funds only for the purpose intended.

>> Keep records showing use of grant funds.

>> Have supporting documentation showing use of grant funds (bank statements, checks, invoices, paid bills, and receipts).

>> Establish and maintain internal controls, which protect you from employee theft by segregating employees' duties. (For more about internal controls, see Chapter 2.)

In federal terminology, these accountability practices are called administrative requirements. Administrative requirements refer to matters common to grants in general, such as financial management, type and frequency of reports, and retention of reports.

REMEMBER

It's very important to dot your *i*'s and cross your *t*'s by leaving a paper trail for every transaction that uses grant money. The federal government wants to help you meet your organization's mission but also needs to be sure you're a good steward of federal monies. For every grant awarded, a budget is attached showing how the money is to be spent — receiving a federal grant award is a contractual agreement between your organization and the federal government. (Check out Chapter 10 for more on creating a budget.)

When you applied for the grant, you stated that you had a need. Thus, the government has signed a binding agreement with you to provide the necessary funds to address the need. Your responsibility as the grant recipient is to properly account for every dollar by keeping backup documents that prove good stewardship.

Auditors and program managers will at least want to see the following documents:

- Grant receipts

- Grant-paid invoices

- Bid quotes and records of procurements

- Time and attendance reports for employees

- Payroll (salary and fringe benefits) expenses

- Leases for equipment

- Contractual agreements

TIP

Being organized with these records helps when it comes time for audits and monitoring visits (see Chapter 14). To help keep track of everything, organize all grant-related documents in a hard-copy file, as well as in a computerized system (for more information see Chapters 4, 8, and 9).

Managing Federal Grant Money

For years, federal agencies had in-house rules governing the administration of grants awarded, which were tailored to the type of recipient. These rules were confusing to grant recipients and made managing grants a burdensome task. In 2013, to mitigate confusion, reduce administrative burden and manage risk, the Office of Management and Budget (OMB) joined forces with the Council on Financial Assistance Reform (COFAR) to draft universal administrative procedures and rules. The OMB, which evaluates the effectiveness of all federal programs, publishes and monitors these procedures.

TECHNICAL STUFF

At completion of the project, COFAR was disbanded by the Office of Management and Budget (OMB). However, the universal administrative procedures and rules flowing from this collaboration are still in place.

As a result of that collaboration, all grant recipients must follow the same set of rules, which are contained in 2 Code of Federal Regulations (CFR) Part 200. This guidance is also known as the "Super Circular" or the Uniform Guidance (UG) and can be viewed at www.ecfr.gov/current/title-2/subtitle-A/chapter-II/part-200.

The effective date of those first universal administrative procedures and rules was a year later in December 2014. Per 2 CFR 200.109, the rules and procedures must be reviewed every five years.

The first update was issued on August 13, 2020. One big takeaway from the update is that the reasons for terminating grant awards has expanded to awards that no longer serve program goals or agency priorities (see CFR 200.340).

TIP

To simplify your life, I suggest you download the current PDF to your desktop. The PDF Table of Contents has hot links allowing you to drill down to special sections. The Edit ⇨ Find option works great, too! For example, I entered 200.340 in the pop-up Find box and was taken directly to the Table of Contents section and further to the 200.340 code section discussing terminations.

REMEMBER

Don't get bogged down with the detailed information in CFR 200 or be intimidated by them. You only need to know a few ground rules, most of which will be included in your award letter. If you stick with your approved budget and talk with your program manager about anything that concerns you, you'll be okay.

TIP

In addition to the requirements contained in 2 CFR Part 200, many federal agencies have agency-specific requirements. Most federal agencies offer periodic training about how you should manage your grant. Talk with your program manager about grant management training.

Outlining administrative requirements

If you need a refresher on grant terms and definitions, go to 2 CFR Part 200 Subpart A first for a quick review. Otherwise, follow me to Subpart B through Subpart D, which discuss administrative requirements, cost principles, and audit requirements. Part B is important because it outlines the dance steps Uncle Sam wants you to follow if you want to keep the federal grant money flowing.

There is a lot of information in these three subparts. Overarching, the three subparts (B–D) contain the requirements for grant agreements, management of the federal awarding agency before the grant is made, and the requirement that can be place on nonfederal agencies receiving grants from federal agencies.

Clear as mud? To make it more user-friendly, here are some of the highlights:

>> **Required versus best practice:** Addressed in Part B, throughout the CFR you see guidance labeled *must* and some labeled *should.* There is no wiggle room if a requirement is classified as *must* — follow these requirements exactly as stated. *Should* indicates that what follows is a recommended rather than required approach.

>> **Pre-federal award requirements:** Addressed in Part C, pre-federal requirements include planning, design, and public notice of the federal assistance program. It also includes general eligibility requirements and the merit review process.

>> **Post-federal award requirements:** Contained in Part D, this section explains financial and program management, including performance measurement and internal controls.

Determining costs

Subpart E discusses Cost Principles and is used by all federal agencies to determine the cost of work performed by nonprofit organizations and information about cost treatment and consistency of applying rules to determine whether costs should be charged to a grant. You can look here to read the detailed do's and don'ts concerning what to buy and not buy. Your grant auditor will check to see whether all your costs are in compliance with generally accepted accounting principles (GAAP) and the cost principles outlined in Subpart E.

This subpart walks you through important cost fundamentals. For example, the nonprofit receiving the grant must efficiently and effectively administer the grant award and manage the grant award in accordance with any terms or conditions set by the federal funding agency. Federal grant recipients also must have written procedures in place for applying cost principles under the reasonable, allocable, allowable, and unallowable concepts. Here's an explanation of each:

>> **Reasonable cost:** A reasonable cost is what an average, unrelated person would pay under the same circumstances. In other words, just because Uncle Sam is paying that doesn't mean you buy the most expensive items. Treat the grant like your personal cash and exercise good judgment. This is also referred to as the "prudent person" standard.

>> **Allocable cost:** An allocable cost is chargeable or assignable to a grant because the expense is incurred specifically for the grant, benefits both the grant and other work, or is necessary to the nonprofit's operations.

>> **Allowable cost:** Costs are allocated in accordance with the relative program benefit received. However, the cost must also pass other tests (for example, it must be allocable, reasonable, necessary, and consistently applied). Some examples are reasonable employee compensation and the associated fringe benefits, equipment, materials, and supplies purchased in performance of the program tied to the grant.

>> **Unallowable cost:** Well, you guessed it! These are costs that are not reasonable or allocable or specifically excluded from the grant's list of permissible costs. Some examples are entertainment, marketing, and lobbying costs.

WARNING

Just because your salary is paid out of the grant doesn't mean you can set it at any amount. Anyone paid out of a grant should be paid a reasonable salary based on the market and location. The Department of Labor has information on its website about how much positions pay, based on location. Before you accept a contract to hire someone or set your own salary, take a look at the following website to make sure the wages are reasonable for your area: www.dol.gov/general/topic/wages.

Understanding audit requirements

Finally, Subpart F covers audit requirements. I can't overstress the importance of accountability when spending Uncle Sam's money. A good practice is to dot every *i* and cross every *t* by following the rules. An audit of your grant files should prove that you're a good manager and you can be trusted to do what's right.

You're required to keep track of everything related to your grant by keeping copies of all grant documents. Your grant auditor and/or monitor will want to see what you bought and how much you paid for it. The audit will verify whether you followed administrative requirements and cost principles (see the preceding two sections for more on these).

As you're spending federal money that comes out of the U.S. Treasury, the federal government wants to make sure you're spending it for the intended purpose and that you're following the rules and guidelines. If you don't follow the rules in this subpart, you may face one of the following consequences:

>> **Suspension:** Classified as an exclusion, if your agency is suspended you lose your rights to get a grant, typically for 12 months. Suspension is normally the first step in legal proceedings against your nonprofit. All suspensions reflect on SAM.gov.

>> **Debarments:** Also an exclusion, if your organization is debarred, it loses its right to serve the community, normally for three years. SAM.gov publishes your name as ineligible.

>> **Sanctions:** If you fail to follow the rules or don't take corrective actions when requested by the federal grantor agency, the government may impose a sanction by charging you fines and penalties and make you pay back the money you misspent.

>> **Restrictions:** If you face restrictions, the feds are going to watch closely how you spend every dime.

>> **Federal prosecution:** The worse scenario for breaking the rules is to be prosecuted and sent to jail.

By the way, only a few nonprofits make the debarment list. The list is very short, but as a grant recipient, you shouldn't do business with anyone on the list. Ask your federal grant manger for a copy of the Excluded Parties List or go to https://sam.gov/content/exclusions to find out more.

Not knowing the rules doesn't exempt nonprofit organizations from stiff penalties for abusing taxpayers' dollars. It's imperative that you keep adequate records — for three years after the grant period(s) — as to how each dollar was spent. Every invoice, bill, voucher, and check written should be copied to the grant files.

Working Through the Details of Your Grant Agreement

Grants are similar in many ways. They all have reporting requirements that can make your head spin. But after you understand the requirements, it's like learning to ride a bike. After all the dust has cleared — that is, the applicable federal agency finishes its review process — the award process begins. Yes!

This kicks off with receiving your *notice of award* (NoA), which defines the grant agreement relationship between the federal agency and your organization. The NoA is your official, legally binding award issuance and may vary slightly from agency to agency.

Your program director will receive an email with a downloadable file about your grant award. In the letter, you'll find important information about the terms of your grant award. Think of the terms as the rules of the grant game. You can't play the game if you don't know the rules.

The NoA includes

- >> Recipient information, including your name, address, UEI, and other contact information

- >> Budget summary, including the budget period, which is normally 12 months

- >> Awards numbers, including your unique federal award identification number

- >> Award data listing the award calculation, direct and indirect costs, federal share, and summary totals by year

- >> Terms and conditions explaining the laws and regulations associated with the grant

>> Special terms and conditions, which list any program-specific management you must abide by

>> Payment information giving you the instructions on how to access your grant funds using the Payment Management System (PMS)

TIP

Wondering what an NoA looks like? You can access the Substance Abuse and Mental Health Services Administrative agency's sample NoA via a PDF file at www.samhsa.gov/grants/grants-management/notice-award-noa. That link also provides information about amending the NoA if necessary and how to access standard terms and conditions by year. As of the publication of this book, 2016 through 2022 standard terms and conditions are available. If you have the time, it may be interesting to see the variance year over year.

The following sections help you work through the details of your grant agreement. Following the rules is easy when you understand them.

Summarizing the grant budget

The grant budget, sometimes also called the award data, summarizes the budget the government expects you to follow to manage your grant. It indicates costs and revenues linked to grant activities, helps you monitor and control grant funds, and provides a clear indication of grant performance.

The award calculation summary indicates how much money has been allocated to each category. Your NoA may have different costs, but the typical summary includes the following accounts in the following order:

>> Personnel

>> Fringe benefits

>> Travel

>> Equipment

>> Supplies

>> Contractual

>> Construction

>> Direct and indirect costs

>> Other

All costs combined equal your approved budget. The award calculation also includes both the federal and nonprofit share should the federal share not be 100 percent.

Knowing the due dates for financial status reports

As of fiscal year 2021, federal grant recipients file the annual Federal Financial Report (FFR, SF-425) in the PMS. This form is due no later than 90 days after the end of your budget period and your final FFR is due no later than 120 days after the end of the period of performance in the PMS. I cover form SF-425 in greater detail in Chapter 12. Go to https://pms.psc.gov for a sneak peek of this service provider.

Additionally, federal award recipients generally must submit performance and progress reports, the frequency of which ranges from quarterly to annually. The Performance Progress Report (PPR) consists of a cover page and various attachments, such as the coming year's budget or a personnel report, some of which may not be applicable to your nonprofit. This progress reporting shows how you've performed on your mission statement using the federal dollars.

The federal grant-making agencies post grant spending information on USASpending.gov (www.usaspending.gov). These reports are used by Congress to determine whether the grant award is making the expected difference in the lives of the people it aims to help. Head to Chapter 12 for more about completing progress reports.

REMEMBER

Your NoA will contain instructions for submitting performance and progress reports. See www.grants.gov/web/grants/learn-grants/grant-reporting.html for more information about your nonprofit's grant-reporting requirements.

Indicating special conditions

If you receive a grant award, federal agencies may feel it necessary to impose special award conditions. Sometimes a grant applicant may have issues that warrant special conditions placed on them by the awarding agency. If a nonprofit has a history of poor performance, isn't financially stable, or lacks responsibility in management systems, the federal agency may award the nonprofit a grant because the nonprofit is supporting a good cause, but impose special conditions because of the organization's problems.

Your nonprofit will be notified in writing if the federal agency places special conditions on your grant award. The notification explains the special conditions and why your nonprofit is subject to these conditions. You'll also find out what corrective action you can take to lift the special conditions and the time frame for completing any corrective actions.

Keeping the award/project period in mind

Your grant has a beginning date and an ending date, which is called your *project period*. Your project period may range from one to three years. I highly recommend you keep a close eye on the grant project periods. It's important to know how much time you have to spend your money.

WARNING

If you forget to spend the money, it goes back to the federal government. Make sure you don't let a grant expire without using the funds.

Treating program income

Recipients are generally required to hold advances of federal grant funds in interest-bearing accounts. There are three exclusions to this requirement as of the publication of this book:

>> The amount you receive is less than $120,000 annually.

>> Expected interest income is less than $500 per year.

>> Unfavorable bank conditions exist for the interest-bearing account, such as an excessively high minimum balance.

WARNING

Earning more than $500 of interest income can result in your having to pay the money back. The government allows you to keep the first $500 of interest earned on grant money. You report interest earned when you file your grant reports, and interest over $500 will be treated as a grant distribution to you. Always talk with your program manager if you're concerned about program income. Keep in mind that grant amounts and interest income limitations can fluctuate from year to year.

Figuring your indirect cost rate

While running your grant program, you incur both direct and indirect operating costs. Direct costs are those that directly relate to a particular program or award. On the flip side, indirect costs are not easily traced back to a particular program or award. Indirect costs are generally related to facilities (depreciation of property, plant, and equipment, as well as maintenance and repairs) and administrative costs (for example, professional fees or postage). Indirect costs are a necessary part of doing business, and you incur them whether you run one program or many programs.

You may have to submit an indirect cost rate proposal as part of the grant process. The proposal package generally includes audited financial statements, and other supporting documents, such as your general ledger, trial balance, statement of activities, and financial position. Based on the information submitted, the federal agency will give you an indirect cost rate, which is a percentage of all your expenses to operate your nonprofit.

That indirect cost rate provides a reasonable and consistent process for allocating costs not directly associated with a single project or cost objective. Figure 11-2 gives an example of the calculation.

TECHNICAL STUFF

If you're in the mood for another look at the CFR, you'll find the indirect cost rate addressed at 200.414 and in Appendix IV.

Indirect costs	75,000
Modified total direct costs	500,000
Indirect cost-rate percentage	15% (75,000/500,000)
Modified total direct costs = all direct costs reduced by certain exclusions such as the purchase of long-term assets.	

FIGURE 11-2:
Indirect cost rate calculation.

Matching federal and nonprofit shares

Unfortunately, sometimes not all the costs to run a program are paid in full by the grant. Some grants require a match. A *grant* match is when your nonprofit pays a percentage of the total award. I like to think of it as sharing the expense. The NoA indicates the amount the federal agency pays (called the federal share) and what, if any, the nonprofit must match (called the nonprofit share) in Section I.

For example, if you submit a grant application stating it will cost you $100,000 to run your program, the granting agency may want you to pay 10 percent of that amount. Your 10 percent of the cost will be $10,000, and the 90 percent federal share will be $90,000.

TIP

Match requirements are listed in the grant announcement or notice of funding availability. Therefore, you'll know before applying for funding that a match is required. You can account for the nonprofit share of the match when you submit the budget with your application.

Chapter **12**

Tracking and Accounting for Federal Dollars

G o ahead and celebrate! You worked hard, and you received the federal grant. You've been awarded grant funding to establish, develop, and implement a project for your organization. Now you have to manage your grant. Get ready for tons of paperwork, but don't worry — I walk you through the whole process in this chapter. After you find out what really matters, you'll be on your way to managing the federal government's money in your sleep.

Your underlying responsibility is to understand your obligations to the federal government and your awarding agency. After you know what's expected of you, you can follow the directions your awarding agency gives you.

In this chapter, I give you some tips on how to stay on top of your federal grant game. This includes spending the money according to the grant budget, complying with the awarding agency's requirements by submitting all reports on time, and knowing how to close out the grant. If you're thinking that you'll be dealing with lots of paperwork, you're right. After all, you know that everything the government does involves lots of paper. (I focus on federal grants in this chapter; if you're curious about grants from sources other than the federal government, see the "Defining the difference between private and public grants" sidebar in this chapter.) And although state and local governments also issue grant awards, this chapter discusses federal grants only.

DEFINING THE DIFFERENCE BETWEEN PRIVATE AND PUBLIC GRANTS

You need to be aware of a few key differences between the application, review, and management processes of grants offered by private corporations and foundations (commonly referred to as private grants) versus those offered by the government (commonly referred to as public grants). How you track and manage your grants depends on the grant maker's terms. Everything that deals with the government, including its grant process, is very detailed and thorough, and information is easily accessible at Grants.gov. On the other hand, corporate grant makers may not be as organized or as open as the government in terms of grant details. Information about private grants may not be in one central location. Foundations and corporations may choose to advertise grant opportunities on their websites.

Federal government grants are well defined and competitive, and you can request feedback if your grant application isn't funded. The grant process for public grants involves a peer review, in which a panel of at least three individuals reviews your application. This panel scores your application according to a predetermined numbering system that you receive before you turn in your application. This process is the same for every applicant, which ensures a certain level of consistency.

Private grants are a little different. Each awarding entity has the freedom to define its own grant process. Corporations usually have more leniency in the way they award, administer, and manage grants. Corporate funders set the rules and change them as they see fit. For example, a corporation may choose to give your nonprofit a check with no strings attached, or it may have a detailed process you have to follow throughout the duration of your grant.

Many community foundations are a bit more structured than corporations in terms of their grant processes. They often have grants that donors set up for specific purposes. These donors may even stipulate how the grant recipient should use the money. Some of the larger foundations — such as the Bill & Melinda Gates Foundation, the Ford Foundation, the W.K. Kellogg Foundation, and the Mary Reynolds Babcock Foundation — use grant processes similar to those of the government.

Whether your grant has been awarded by a corporation, foundation, or federal government agency, make sure to find out all the rules you need to follow so you don't lose your grant.

Understanding Your Obligation

As a grant recipient, you've agreed to fulfill a need in society, and the federal government has agreed to give you the money to do so. As a grant recipient, you're responsible for

>> **Managing the money:** This part of the job can be fun. It includes

- Ensuring that grant funds are spent according to the grant budget

- Monitoring grant activity and expenses

- Ensuring that grant funds aren't returned to the awarding agency

>> **Handling the paperwork:** I know you don't want to be a paper pusher, but if you're going to spend the government's money, you have to keep track of every detail. Here's what you have to do:

- Prepare and file reports on time

- Maintain detailed documentations and records

>> **Running the program according to your application:** This is likely the most rewarding part of managing the grant. You get to help people improve their lives, which is probably why you got into this field in the first place.

WARNING

If you don't take care of these three aspects according to the grant guidelines, you can lose your funding. How you manage the money, fill out the paperwork, and run your program establishes your organization's reputation with the federal government. If you poorly manage your grant, your awarding agency may give you additional reporting requirements that you have to meet for the duration of your grant. For instance, if you develop a history of poor performance and financial instability, your program manager may require you to present reports more often than quarterly or semiannually (see Chapter 12 for more information).

I cover the money and paperwork aspects of federal grants in the rest of this chapter. I leave the managing of the grant program up to you. I know you can handle it.

Managing Grant Funds

Grant money is another form of income for your nonprofit, but you can't just throw it in the pot with all the other cash donations and other income to do whatever you want to with it. You have to keep track of the grant funds so the awarding agency knows you did what you said you were going to do with the funds and didn't fritter the money away on non-grant purposes.

You must establish a separate financial account for the receipt, spending, and reporting of the grant funds. You can't comingle federal grant funds with funds from other sources. You must also purchase only those items that were approved in your grant application budget and keep the appropriate purchase orders, invoices, or other payment records. If applicable, make sure you seek competitive bids.

Best practices for grant management include the following steps:

>> Read and follow the terms and conditions in your notice of awards (NoA).

>> Comply with any grantor-specific award regulations, policies, and procedures.

>> Register your nonprofit in the Payment Management System (PMS) if required.

>> Submit required payment reports.

>> Submit performance/financial reports on time.

If you have any questions pertaining to your NoA or any of the best practices I list here, contact your grant administrator or grant management specialist. Your NoA includes the relevant contact information. Your administrator/specialist is also the individual who will contact you if your reporting is overdue.

TIP

If you need help setting up a system to help you manage your money, turn to Chapter 4. A good financial management system helps you record and track expenses, maintain records, and balance your grant budget.

In the following sections, you find out how to go about getting the money that's been awarded to you. I also explain how to avoid mismanagement of federal grant funds, including keep your grant money separate from your other income and expenses and reporting requirements.

WARNING

Grant mismanagement can result in returning disallowed funding, a freeze on disbursement until procedures are in place, fines, suspension from receiving future grants, or increased oversight.

Maintaining a separate budget for your grant dollars

When you received your NoA (see Chapter 11), it includes an award calculation. The information in NoA Section I outlines how the federal government expects you to spend the money and may be the same as or very similar to the budget you submitted with your grant application. You're expected to be a wise steward and to exercise good judgment when making decisions about what to buy and how much to pay.

Within your nonprofit, you should keep a separate budget and set up separate accounts in the chart of accounts (see Chapter 5) for your grant transactions. Keeping separate accounts is important when you receive a federal grant because you need to avoid commingling funds, which means mixing grant money with your organization's other sources of income. Commingling of funds is one of the audit findings that can cause you to lose funding. (For more about grant audits, see Chapter 14.)

You need to keep track of what you buy with the grant money so you can prove to your awarding agency and your auditor that you used the money according to the set award calculation. Keeping copies of all paperwork, especially receipts of purchase, pertaining to the grant is a good idea.

You should secure bids for any large or capital improvement expenditures for which grant dollars were approved. An example would be if you're making renovations to a building or acquiring a van or other vehicle for mobile outreach.

WARNING

Pay attention to your grant period, because if you don't spend the money during the specified grant period on approved purchases, you have to return the unspent funds to the awarding agency, and you lose everything you didn't spend.

If you're feeling a bit unsure about how to keep everything separate, you may want to set up a completely separate bank account for your grant money, which you can do at your local bank.

TIP

Someone has to oversee the project's progress and funding. Depending on how much money you received and your other responsibilities, you may want to consider hiring someone to manage the project's funding.

Making changes to your grant

Okay, nothing is written in stone. Things change, people move, prices go up and down; as a result, nothing in the budget is absolute. If you need to make budget changes, contact your grants administrator and ask for a grant adjustment notice (GAN). A GAN gives you written authorization to make changes to your grant agreement. These changes can be actual changes to your budget, extensions of the funding period, or changes in personnel, among others.

If you need to make a change to your budget that requires a GAN, call your grants administrator to discuss the process and request the form. Following up this call with an email to verify the request is always a good idea. After your grants administrator approves the changes, you receive a GAN by mail; add the notice to your grant files. Your grants administrator may also contact you if, based on your reporting, they think you may need an amendment.

REMEMBER

The most common kinds of adjustments are change of scope requests or changes to the budget. Get all approved changes to your grant agreement in writing. Documentation is important for you to have so you can justify all your actions pertaining to the grant.

TIP

Check with your grant administrator to see if the 10 percent rule applies. The 10 percent rule states that you can move up to 10 percent of your budget money (10 percent of the total grant amount) from one budget category to another without prior approval, as long as you don't create a new budget category.

Handling the responsibility of subgrantees

Subgrantees are the organizations that form a partnership with the lead agency, or *grantee*, to apply for the grant. If you're the lead agency, you're responsible for overseeing the financial management of yourself and the subgrantees. You establish this relationship through a subaward of your grant to your subgrantee.

The grantor is the federal agency that awards and establishes a grant agreement with the grantee through the NoA (see Chapter 11 for more on this document). The grantee may have partners that it included in the grant budget as subgrantees.

Subgrantees answer directly to the grantee and seldom have any direct contact with the grantor. The grantee establishes a grant agreement with the subgrantee similar to the agreement that the grantor has with the grantee. The grantee authorizes all payments submitted for reimbursement to the grantor and makes drawdowns from the grantor for both themselves and the subgrantees.

Subgrantees send their reporting data to the prime awardee. And if the subgrant is $25,000 or more the subgrantees must have their data shared by the prime awardee through the FFATA Subaward Reporting System (FSRS). Go to www.fsrs.gov to find more about FSRS, including users guides and training materials.

The grantee submits all reporting requirements to the grantor. The grantee places reporting requirements on the subgrantee. The grantee is responsible for overseeing not only the actions of its nonprofit but also the actions of the subgrantees.

Creating the grant agreement for subgrantees

Whether you call it an agreement or a contract, you need to have something in writing that states the terms of your agreement with the subgrantees — how much money you'll allocate, to whom you'll allocate the money, what the money should be used for, and when you'll allocate it.

TIP

You can find a PDF subgrantee agreement at https://nonprofitdocuments.law. stanford.edu/grants-and-subgrants/subgrant-agreement. It probably won't be 100 percent applicable to your nonprofit, but it gives you a starting point. You should also consult an attorney for subgrantee grant agreements.

The authorized representative of your organization signs the agreement. Your authorized representative is the person responsible for the overall management of your grant, usually your organization's director. Keep in mind that your executive director doesn't have to administer or manage the program, but they are responsible for it. Also, the agreement should state when financial and progress reports are due from your subgrantees (see the "Reporting Requirements" section in this chapter for more about these reports).

Generally, grantees give subgrantees a deadline of two weeks before the reports are due to the grantor. As the lead agency or grantee, your financial reports are generally due 45 days after the end of the quarter. Therefore, if you're managing subgrantees, you should give them a deadline of 30 days to submit their financial reports to you.

Additionally, as of October 15, 2015, you're required to file a Federal Funding Accountability and Transparency Act (FFATA) subaward report by the end of the month following the month in which you, as prime contractor, award any subcontract greater than $30,000. Best practices would be to give your subgrantees 15 days to get their progress reports to you. Your subgrantees send information to you, and then you send it, along with your own reports, to the grantor or awarding agency.

Monitoring and verifying subgrantees' reports

As the lead agency, your responsibility is to monitor the reports that the subgrantees submit. Some questions to ask yourself when looking over these bills and documents include the following:

>> Are the expenses the subgrantees submitted to you in the budget?

>> Are the costs associated with the project?

>> Do the subgrantees have an adequate accounting system?

Make sure you keep copies of all the paperwork your subgrantees send you. You may need it later to justify money paid to subgrantees. As the lead agency, you're responsible for managing both your own transactions and those of your subgrant-ees. You answer to the grantor if questions about your subgrantees' expenses arise.

REMEMBER

When a subgrantee submits a claim for reimbursement to you, you need to review the expenses and check to see whether they're in the budget before you approve expenses. If the expenses aren't listed in the subgrantee's budget, you have to deny the claim. The subgrantees try to use grant money to pay for something totally unrelated to the purpose of the project. Always compare the expenses to both the grant budget and the guidelines set in the grant award document.

Drawing Down Federal Dollars

The federal government doesn't send you a check for the total amount of your grant up front. In fact, most federal agencies reimburse you rather than pay you in advance, so as a grant recipient, you have to request the money after you spend it. However, make sure you follow the drawdown instructions in your NoA.

Additionally, many NoAs have the grant funds drawn down in stages. If so, follow the drawdown schedule in your NoA. Best practices dictate you draw down only as much cash as necessary to meet the immediate needs of the project and you pay out funds for grant activities as soon as possible after you make your drawdown.

WARNING

Avoid doing anything that would make the grantor think you're drawing down excessive funds. You may be required to return that surplus — with interest. On the flip side, if you draw down too little money, the grantor may take this as a sign that your project is not actively engaged.

Drawdown instructions are stated in your NoA, which you can discuss with your grant administrator if need be. You may be instructed to use the PMS to draw down grant funds. If so, after you received your notice of grant award, it will post in PMS allowing you start your drawdowns through PMS.

To gain access to PMS you must put in an online request and be approved by the Program Support Center (PSC). The member of your nonprofit who will be using PMS needs to provide information about your nonprofit and their contact and supervisor information, and then select the requested access level required. After reviewing your request for accuracy, it's signed and submitted to PSC. PSC will review the request and, after it's approved, provide your nonprofit a username and a temporary password. For more information about PMS, go to https://pms.psc.gov/.

The Automatic Standard Application for Payments (ASAP) is another platform your grantor may use to process your grant payment requests. If your grantor uses ASAP, they send you an invitation to enroll in ASAP. The enrollment process is similar to PMS, whereby you provide information about your nonprofit and contact information. To find out more about ASAP, go to www.fiscal.treasury.gov/ASAP.

Inside your award package, you may also find forms to set up electronic transfers from the U.S. Treasury to your bank account. You need to fill out these forms and send them to the awarding agency. You'll include your bank routing number, the name of your bank, your account number, the contact person — all the information you use when you authorize an electronic transfer during your nonprofit's normal course of business. You may also have to submit information authorizing your bank to process the drawdown, which authorizes your bank to transfer the funds into your bank account.

TIP

Your grantor may have Electronic Handbooks (EHBs) such as these from the Health Resources and Services Administration (HRSA) that you can access at https://grants.hrsa.gov/EAuthNS/internal/home/EHBHome. Check out your NoA or ask your grant administrator.

REMEMBER

As you request drawdowns throughout the grant period, keep track in your own files of how much money has been drawn and how much money is left to be drawn (for more information on tracking your records, turn to the "Tracking the electronic transfer" section in this chapter). Make sure your records coincide with the numbers in your grant budget.

Transferring grant money

Look in your NoA for specific instructions on how to draw down funds. At present, PMS has several payment options including ACH (electronic bank-to-bank transfers) and Fedwire (fund transfers accomplished via your Federal Reserve Bank). Your nonprofit also must submit a Form SF-1199A Direct Deposit Sign-Up form. For more information about this form go to https://pms.psc.gov/grant-recipients/banking-add-change.html.

Your granting agency may request you submit SF-270 Request for Advance or Reimbursement. You can view this form in the form's repository at www.grants.gov/web/grants/forms.html. See the "Preparing the required financial status reports" section later in this chapter for instructions on how to navigate this page and pull down the form and its instructions to your desktop.

The SF-270 is a two-page form with numbered and lettered fields you fill in. After completing the form, you send it to the address in your NoA. Here's a line-by-line walk-through to completing this form:

>> **Line 1: Type of Payment Requested:**

  a. Your options are Advance, Reimbursement, or both. If you're requesting an advance, the request is cash based — that is, you're laying out the cash now for a cost approved in your grant application.

  b. Final or Partial.

>> **Line 2: Basis of Request:** Cash or Accrual (see Chapter 1, if need be, to refresh your memory on the difference between the two).

>> **Line 3: Federal Sponsoring Agency:** Essentially your grantor.

>> **Line 4: Federal Grant or Other Identifying Number:** Each grant awarded has a grant ID number, which the federal agency giving you the money assigns to you.

>> **Line 5: Partial Payment Request Number:** Enter if applicable.

>> **Line 6: Employer identification number:** Your employer identification number (EIN) is the identifying number the IRS assigns to you for tax purposes.

>> **Line 7: Recipient's Account Number or Identifying Number:** Write your nonprofit's self-identifying number (only if it has one).

>> **Line 8: Period Covered by this Request:** Write the beginning date of the request in the From box and the ending date of the request in the To box.

>> **Line 9: Recipient Organization:** Write the name of your nonprofit and its complete address.

>> **Line 10: Payee:** If you're being paid by check, write where the check should be sent if different from the address on line 9.

>> **Line 11: Computation of Amount of Reimbursements/Advances Requested:** Fill out the four columns as applicable providing details about your separate cost breakdowns.

>> **Line 12: Alternate Computation for Advances Only:** If applicable, write in your estimated cash outlays during the period, less your grant balance and amount requested.

>> **Line 13: Certification:** Your nonprofit-authorized certifying official signs the form and fills in their name, address, and phone number.

After you complete the drawdown steps contained in your NoA and set up your bank account to receive money from the government's account, you can start requesting drawdowns. You'll generally need the following information to request a drawdown:

>> **Grant ID number:** Each grant awarded has a grant ID number, which the federal agency giving you the money assigns to you.

>> **EIN:** Your EIN is the identifying number the IRS assigns to you for tax purposes.

>> **Amount of money requested:** You need to know exactly how much money you're requesting. Keep invoices and bills to justify your requests.

>> **Time period the money was used:** You need to know during which period your organization spent the money. For example, the period covered by this request can be a week, month, or quarter.

REMEMBER

Documentation is very important when working with a large agency like the federal government. Keeping copies of all transactions and communications, especially the drawdowns you've requested and received, is essential to proper documentation. Doing so also helps you track and monitor your grant balances. So, if you choose the telephone method, create your own records of the transactions you make.

Tracking the electronic transfer

One way to track electronic transfers is to create a spreadsheet of every drawdown requested. In this spreadsheet, you want to record the date of the request, the time of the request, the amount requested, and the time period covered (flip to Chapter 4 for pointers on creating a spreadsheet). Updating your spreadsheets at least on a monthly basis is a good idea. Waiting longer than one month can cause you to get behind and lose track of what's what. These up-to-date spreadsheets help you when you have to fill out your quarterly financial reports. See the "Reporting Requirements" section for more about filling out your financial reports.

In addition to the spreadsheet, you should print out and create a hard-copy file of every transaction you request. This file needs to coincide with your budget balance for the grant.

TIP

If you want assurance that you and your award agency have the same balances, you can request a grant summary from your grant administrator. A grant summary is a printout of all your grant transactions according to the awarding agency's records. You can double-check your records against the government's records anytime you need to.

Knowing when to request a drawdown

If your budget is tight, you need to carefully track how much time the U.S. Treasury can take to move the money to your bank account. In today's age of electronics, things can be transmitted instantly, but sometimes the government doesn't move that fast. So, you need to pay attention to the timing.

WARNING

Sometimes the last five days of the month are the busiest for the federal agency because everybody is trying to close out the month and process payments. For this reason, you shouldn't wait until the last week of the month to request a money transfer. If you do wait until the end of the month to request your grant money, expect to wait a little longer to receive it. Like banks, the U.S. Treasury isn't open every day. Most agencies tell you that moving money takes five working days, but sometimes you have to wait a little longer.

How long processing a payment request takes depends on whether your nonprofit is the grantee or the subgrantee. If you're the subgrantee, you have to wait for the grantee to receive payment from the grantor before you receive your money. How fast the grantee receives payment depends on the accounting procedures your awarding agency has in place. For instance, if your awarding agency is a large state agency that has a separate finance department, you may find that the department takes more time to process the reimbursement than does a smaller agency with fewer requests.

Reporting Requirements

Everyone has to report to someone, and that's especially true when you're spending Uncle Sam's money. After disbursing funds, a grants management officer at your nonprofit's funding agency monitors your reporting compliance. After reading your grant agreement and/or award letter, you should know how many reports you have to submit and when you need to submit them.

TECHNICAL STUFF

In addition to monitoring your reporting compliance, the grantor agency may perform on-site visits with your nonprofit program director or perform grant audits. See Chapter 14 for more information about the grant auditing process.

There are nine standard grant reporting forms, most of which are probably not going to be applicable to your nonprofit:

>> SF-270, Request for Advance or Reimbursement

>> SF-271, Outlay Report and Request for Reimbursement for Construction Programs

- » SF-425, Federal Financial Report
- » SF-425A, Federal Financial Report Attachment
- » SF-428, Tangible Personal Property
- » SF-429, Real Property Status Report
- » Research Performance Progress Report (RPPR)
- » SF-LLL, Disclosure of Lobbying Activities
- » SF-SAC, Data Collection Form for Single Audits

The next sections of this chapter walk you through the two post-award financial reporting forms that most likely will be applicable to your nonprofit: SF-425 and the SF-425A. I also provide a description of when you would use the other six forms (I discuss Form SF-270 earlier in this chapter).

WARNING

You must file applicable reports on time. The consequences of not filing your reports on time can be detrimental to your organization. If you stop the flow of paperwork, the federal government stops the flow of money. Therefore, if you don't submit reports, you don't receive your money. Mark your calendar, send yourself reminders, do whatever you need to do to remember what's due and when.

Preparing the required financial status reports

The most important report you have to submit to your federal grantor is the Federal Financial Report (FFR), which you complete using Standard Form 425 (SF-425). The FFR tells your grantor how much you've spent in the current quarter versus prior quarters and how much you have left in your budget. To access the forms repository to see all forms and specifically SF-425, go to www.grants.gov/web/grants/forms.html. Scroll down the page until you get to Forms Repository; click the Post-Award Reporting Forms link. Then scroll down to the middle of this page to find links to download both the form and instructions. Figure 12-1 has a partial view of the web page.

Filling out SF-425

After you download the SF-425 from the Forms Repository, print it so you can easily follow along with the following instructions. Each item on the form has a number or letter, which makes explaining it rather easy. The top portion of the form (numbers 1 through 9) covers information that identifies the federal agency, nonprofit organization, funding period, payment accounting method, and period (month or quarter, for example) covered by the financial report.

Agency Owner	▲ Form Name	Adobe Form	Form Schema	Form Items Description	Form Instructions
Grants.gov	Disclosure of Lobbying Activities (SF-LLL)	PDF	Schema	FID	Instructions
Grants.gov	Federal Financial Report (SF-425)	PDF	Schema	FID	Instructions
Grants.gov	Federal Financial Report Attachment (SF-425A)	PDF	Schema	FID	Instructions
Grants.gov	INSTRUCTIONS FOR THE SF-429 Real Property Status Report	PDF	Schema	FID	
Grants.gov	SF-270 Request for Advance or Reimbursement	PDF	Schema	FID	Instructions
Grants.gov	SF-271 Outlay Report and Request for Reimbursement for Construction Programs	PDF	Schema	FID	Instructions
Grants.gov	SF-429 Real Property Status Report (Cover Page)	PDF	Schema	FID	Instructions
Grants.gov	SF-429-A Real Property Status Report ATTACHMENT A (General Reporting)	PDF	Schema	FID	Instructions
Grants.gov	SF-429-B Real Property Status Report ATTACHMENT B (Request to Acquire, Improve or Furnish)	PDF	Schema	FID	Instructions
Grants.gov	SF-429-C Real Property Status Report ATTACHMENT C (Disposition or Encumbrance Request)	PDF	Schema	FID	Instructions
Grants.gov	Tangible Personal Property Report - Annual Report - SF-428-A	PDF	Schema	FID	Instructions
Grants.gov	Tangible Personal Property Report - Disposition Request/Report - SF-428-C	PDF	Schema	FID	Instructions
Grants.gov	Tangible Personal Property Report - Final Report - SF-428-B	PDF	Schema	FID	Instructions
Grants.gov	Tangible Personal Property Report - SF-428	PDF	Schema	FID	Instructions
Grants.gov	Tangible Personal Property Report - Supplemental Sheet - SF-428-S	PDF	Schema	FID	Instructions

FIGURE 12-1: Post-Award Forms Repository.

The following steps explain the items on the SF-425 and what to do for each one:

>> **Line 1: Federal Agency and Organizational Element to Which Report Is Submitted:** Enter the name of the federal agency that awarded the grant.

>> **Line 2: Federal Grant or Other Identifying Number Assigned by Federal Agency:** Write the grant number assigned by the federal agency, which you can find in your grant award package.

>> **Line 3: Recipient Organization (name and complete address, including zip code):** Write the name of your nonprofit and its complete address.

>> **Line 4: UEI and Employer Identification Number:** Enter your unique entity identifier (UEI) one line 4a and write your nonprofit's federal employer identification number (FEIN or EIN) on line 4b.

>> **Recipient Account Number or Identifying Number:** Write your nonprofit's self-identifying number (if it has one).

TIP

The recipient account number is a self-designated number you use in your nonprofit. If you're managing several projects and need to separate them, you should assign each project an account number to help you. You can leave this line blank if it doesn't apply to you.

>> **Line 6: Report Type:** Check which is applicable: quarterly, semiannual, annual, or final.

>> **Line 7: Basis of Accounting:** Check either the Cash box or the Accrual box, depending on which method of accounting you use.

If you account for transactions when cash changes hands or use your checkbook as your primary accounting system, check the Cash box. If you record transactions when they take place, regardless of whether any cash has exchanged hands, check the Accrual box. (See Chapter 2 for more about the cash and accrual methods of accounting.)

>> **Line 8: Project/Grant Period:** Write the beginning date of the grant in the From box and the ending date of the grant in the To box.

Make necessary adjustments for any grant extensions you've received.

TIP

If you need an extension, request it at least three months before the grant closing date. Most federal programs run a little behind schedule at the beginning, so extensions are common. Most federal agencies are willing to grant up to a one-year extension.

>> **Line 9: Reporting Period End Date:** Write the dates of the period you're covering with this report in the To and From boxes. For quarterly, semiannual, and annual interim reports, enter 3/31, 6/30, 9/30 or 12/31. If it's the final FFS, the reporting end date is the end date of the project or grant period.

>> **Transactions:** This section of the SF-425 has lines labeled a through o broken out into four sections: Federal Cash, Federal Expenditures and Unobligated Balance, Recipient Share, and Program Income.

- **Section 1, Federal Cash:** The cumulative cash received, disbursed, and ending balance as of the reporting date. If this is the first report, this amount is zero.

- **Section 2, Federal Expenditures and Unobligated Balance:** The total federal funds authorized, the amount spent on a cash basis, the obligations incurred by your nonprofit but not yet paid.

- **Section 3, Recipient Share:** All matching and cost sharing your recipients and third parties provide to meet the level required by your grant.

- **Section 4, Program Income:** All program income earned and expended.

>> **Indirect Expense:** This rate, commonly called an indirect cost rate, is a cost rate that helps cover some overhead administrative costs. Check with your program manager to get an allowance to pay indirect expenses. (See Chapter 18 for more about indirect cost rates.) This section of the SF-425 has alphabetic columns labeled as follows:

a. **Type:** Enter whether your indirect expense is provisional (based on other criteria being met as outlined in NoA), predetermined (defined in your NoA), final (you're done!), or fixed (defined per your NoA).

b. **Rate:** This is pulled from your grant application and NoA.

c. **Period From and To:** Enter the beginning and ending dates for the rate.

d. **Base:** The amount of your base used in rate calculation.

e. Amount Charged: Your indirect costs charged during the period. The formula is Rate × Base.

f. Federal Share: This is the federal share of the Amount Charged.

g. Totals: Enter totals for d (Base), e (Amount Charged), and f (Federal Share).

>> **Line 12: Remarks:** This box is usually not applicable. However, if your awarding agency has asked for any additional explanations, provide them here.

>> **Certification:** Be sure to acquire the correct signature on the SF-475. Auditors will write you up if your Financial Status Reports (FSRs) aren't signed, so make sure your director signs them. The signature certifies that the report is correct and that grant money has been spent according to guidelines.

TIP

Find complete instructions for form SF-425 at the form's repository (refer to Figure 12-1).

Learning when to use SF-425a

Use this form when you're reporting for multiple grants. Your nonprofit may never have to use SF-425a.

There are five sections, which ask for the same basic information as the first five sections in SF-425. Section 5 has an option to add additional rows by selecting Add Additional Row. There is a section to provide a total, which if you're using an electronic version of the form, should autofill based on info you enter in other sections.

Submitting SF-425

Double-check your NoA, but generally, FSRs are submitted quarterly and at the close of the grant. Please note that the due date is 30 days after the end of the quarter, so for quarter-ending months with 31 days, the due date is the 30th not the 31st.

At the end of a project, two reports are due: a report for financial quarterly activities and a final report. Usually these two reports have the same financial information. The only difference is that you check Yes on the final report.

Check your NoA to see how to transmit the form to the grantor. If your grantor is using the PMS, you'll most likely upload the form to that portal. Ditto if your grantor uses a system such as ASAP or eRA Commons (used by some federal agencies). Alternatively, you may be provided with instructions on how to mail, email, or fax the form to the agency.

Unless otherwise noted in your NoA, FSRs are due according to the following table:

Reporting Quarter	Due Date
January 1–March 31	April 30
April 1–June 30	July 30
July 1–September 30	October 30
October 1–December 31	January 30

Explaining other post-award forms

At this point, I've walked you through three of the nine post-award reporting forms. Before we move out of this section of the chapter, I provide a brief explanation of the other six post-award reporting forms. Going in order of form number:

» **SF-271, Outlay Report and Request for Reimbursement for Construction Programs:** Use this form if your nonprofit is requesting funds for administrative, architectural, engineering, and inspection costs for construction related projects.

» **SF-428, Tangible Personal Property:** There are several versions of this form to report purchases of tangible property, such as office furniture and fixtures. Choose which version you use based on the type of reporting. For example, SF-428-A is your annual reporting form and SF-428-B is the final reporting report. See the instructions on the form's repository for more information about each.

» **SF-429, Real Property Status Report:** There are several versions of this form to report purchases of real property such as land and buildings. Choose which version you use based on the type of reporting. For example, SF-429-A is for general reporting and SF-429-B is used to request to acquire, improve, or furnish real property. Depending on the project, you might use SF-271 in conjunction with SF-419.

» **Research Performance Progress Report (RPPR):** This form is used by some grantees to provide performance measurement information to the grantor. Not available on the form repository, you'll secure if need be, from your grantor.

» **SF-LLL, Disclosure of Lobbying Activities:** More than likely not an issue for your nonprofit, use this form to identify the type of covered federal action for which lobbying activity is and/or has been secured to influence the outcome of a covered federal action.

>> **SF-SAC, Data Collection Form for Single Audits:** This form is also not available on the form repository. If included as an auditee, you must submit Form SF-SAC and the Single Audit reporting package within 30 days after receipt of the auditor's report(s) or nine months after the end of their audit period — whichever comes first. Your grantor will provide this form if need be. See Chapter 14 for more information about grant audits.

Reporting your progress

Your awarding agency wants to know how you're doing with your grant project, so periodically you have to submit a progress report. The progress report, which comes in many forms, states the status of achievements in accomplishing project goals. The progress report indicates the status of the following:

>> Equipment purchases

>> Number of people served

>> Amount of money spent

>> Plans for spending the grant money

>> Overall status of the grant project

Some reports include corrective actions or plans to resolve problems. After all, the program may not run according to schedule. The progress report provides you with a place where you can explain program problems and ask for technical assistance from the grantor.

Some federal agencies have their own reports, so check your NoA and discuss with your federal program manager where to find copies of progress reports. You submit most progress reports online, and you can download them from your awarding agency's website.

Required performance measures vary between each type of grant and can vary from year to year for the same type of grant. I recommend you start the progress report process before beginning your grant application. After you read and understand the grant solicitation, make a note to yourself what types of performance measures you'll be asked to provide should you be awarded the grant. Then think about how you're going to capture the performance measurements. Another big deal is the frequency and due dates of the performance measurements reports and what additional information will be requested when submitting the reports.

Completing your progress report

Filling out progress reports is fairly straightforward. Different agencies may use different reporting forms, but you'll be asked for the same type of information including basic information about your nonprofit, your project, the period covered and a narrative section. The narrative section is where you provide specific details about your project's progress within the last period. Finally at the end, you put your contact information and sign certifying that the report is correct and complete.

Talk to your program manager about how much information you need to include in this report. Basically, your awarding agency wants to know numbers: how many people you served through your program, how many people participated, how many people directly benefited from your program, and so on. These numbers provide outcome measurements, which help the awarding agency decide your project's overall efficacy so far.

TIP

It's best to use brief sentences that get to the point on these progress reports. Your awarding agency won't be impressed with a novel about your program — your report customer wants only relevant information. If accurate and true, I suggest that you state the facts in numbers and percentages that indicate a reasonable amount of progress.

Include a commentary on all your grant goals and objectives. Discuss what goals and objectives were met, highlighting your nonprofit's success. If not, discuss unexpected hindrances and challenges. Make sure to compare performance measures from the beginning to the end of the grant cycle.

Refer back to your award letter and grant agreement for specific instructions about how often your program manager wants to know your status. Usually, progress reports cover a six-month period. Keep in mind, though, that some agencies may require progress reports on a different schedule, or they may ask for additional information (not covered in the progress report) about your project.

Pay attention to any special conditions listed in your award document. Special conditions deviate from the norm. For example, your awarding agency may want you to submit progress reports on a monthly or quarterly basis instead of semiannually. Read your award documents and follow the instructions the awarding agency gave you. For example, National Institutes of Health (NIH) progress reports are required at least annually to document recipient accomplishments and compliance with the terms of the award.

Submitting your progress report

Most grantees submit their progress reports online. If so, you have to set up a password and user ID to send your progress report online. Your awarding agency gives you all the instructions you need to submit your report.

Progress reports are due 30 days after the end of the reporting period. Progress reports typically cover six months, usually from January through June and from July through December. Therefore, a report is due no later than July 30 for the period covering January 1 to June 30, and January 30 for the period covering July 1 to December 31. Look at your award letter to see exactly when your awarding agency wants you to submit all reports.

In addition to the semiannual progress reports, you have to do a final report at the closeout of the grant, which is due 90 days after the end date of the grant. See the next section for more information about closing out your grant.

REMEMBER

Some agencies may still allow you to send progress reports by mail or fax. Keep in mind, though, that your program is just one of many programs overseen by the federal government. Sometimes paperwork gets lost in the shuffle. Keep copies of everything you send or receive concerning your grant program, especially your financial and progress reports.

Closing Out a Grant

Closeout of a grant occurs when the awarding agency determines that all applicable administrative actions and all required programmatic work under the grant have been completed, with the possible exception of the final audit (see Chapter 14). The closeout process completes the grant agreement between the awarding agency and you, the grant recipient. This process can take several months.

In order to complete a closeout, your nonprofit must submit the final financial and programmatic reports. Usually, you're required to submit a final form in the SF series and a final performance progress report to close out the grant. You must submit these reports within 90 days after the expiration or termination date of the grant award. And yes, even if you've already submitted a quarterly report, you still need to submit a final report with the same information.

The awarding agency will review these reports to ensure compliance with all the grant terms and conditions, as well as to make sure you spent all the funds appropriately. The federal awarding agency has to confirm that your nonprofit completed all the required grant work and all the applicable administrative tasks. Until this is complete, you're still responsible for fulfilling all the terms of the grant.

If your organization acquired any property using grant funding, the closeout step is making sure to handle this property exactly as the grant stipulates, which includes completing the appropriate reports on this property. After the grant period has ended, the awarding agency may allow you to keep property purchased with the grant. Deposition of property varies among different agencies. You want to talk to your federal program manager about how to handle any property and equipment purchased with grant money. Your program manager can help you follow your agency's property disposition procedures.

After a grant is closed out, your awarding agency sends you a GAN indicating that your grant has expired. This notice also indicates whether all funding was spent or whether some of the money was returned to the U.S. Treasury.

You're typically required to keep all records pertaining to grant activities for three years after the expiration of the project. Keep the following records:

>> Application

>> Award documents

>> Canceled checks

>> Correspondence

>> Deposit slips

>> FSRs (SF-425)

>> GANs

>> Invoices

>> Paid bills

>> Performance progress reports

>> Sales slips

>> Supporting documentations

Chapter **13**

Staying in Nonprofit Compliance

Knowing the rules of engagement for your nonprofit is similar to following the laws to drive your car. If you understand and obey traffic laws, register your vehicle, and renew your driver's license, you keep your driving privileges. The same is true for operating your nonprofit: As long as you comply with federal and state laws, you keep your nonprofit status.

To do this, you need to know exactly what the Internal Revenue Service (IRS) expects of you and what your state officials require of you. The core requirements of maintaining nonprofit status come from the IRS. Then you have to comply with the state statutes regarding your nonprofit's operation.

A preponderance of nonprofits keep their books under the accrual method of accounting, preparing their financial statements using generally accepted accounting principles (GAAP), which are accounting standards set by the Financial Accounting Standards Board (FASB). Tax return preparation follows the Internal Revenue Code (IRC), which varies from GAAP.

If you don't keep up with accounting standards and rules, complying with federal and state laws can cause you some grief. However, if you have a firm grasp of federal and state laws and the accounting standards, you can sort through the red tape and know what you need to do to stay in compliance. This chapter helps you determine how to comply with federal and state laws and accounting rules to keep your nonprofit in good standing.

Understanding Why Being Compliant Is Important for Your Nonprofit

Your nonprofit must be compliant with applicable regulations and federal tax code so it can continue fulfilling its mission. Demonstrating that you're following legal, regulatory, and financial reporting guidelines builds trust with your community and encourages funding.

As your main regulator, the IRS has the authority to give and take away your nonprofit status. So, you want to keep the IRS happy while also staying in compliance with the appropriate federal and state laws and accounting standards. As you build and manage your nonprofit, keep in mind the following two reasons for demonstrating compliance:

>> **To keep your nonprofit status active:** Failure to comply with federal laws can cause you to lose your federal tax-free status. Because you're managing other people's money and you've been given a tax waiver from the IRS, you must follow the rules to keep your status active.

>> **To keep your reputation of being a good steward:** Following the dos and don'ts keeps your community's opinion of your nonprofit in good standing. This, in turn, feeds donor confidence.

As long as you continue to provide the services you promised, stay within the purpose of organizing your nonprofit, and submit paperwork to the government in a timely fashion, you'll be okay. This chapter delves into these rules and explains in further detail what you should and shouldn't do.

In addition to federal rules, you need to comply with your state laws. These laws vary from state to state. Check out the section "Registering with the proper state authority," later in this chapter, for what your state requires of you.

Staying in Compliance

Merely knowing federal and state law governing your nonprofit isn't enough to stay in compliance. You and your staff have to take the necessary steps to make sure nothing slips between the cracks. Although keeping track and staying within those specifications can be stressful at times, your organization's nonprofit status depends on it. It may not be a fun job, but someone has to do it!

The following sections address the four main components your nonprofit must adhere to in order to stay in good standing. Keep reading for specific hands-on advice you can follow so your agency doesn't lose its nonprofit status.

Registering with the proper state authority

The first step to ensure that your nonprofit stays compliant is to register it with the appropriate state authority. Each state has its own guidelines about how you should register, manage, and maintain nonprofit organizations. Some states require nonprofits to register with the secretary of state's office, state department of revenue, and/or state attorney general's office. Some states offer benefits similar to the IRS by granting a sales tax exemption.

TIP

To find your state laws, visit www.501c3.org/state-nonprofit-guide, or call your state attorney general's office or secretary of state to get more information about your state's requirements.

Accounting for nonprofit activities

If your nonprofit requires an independent auditor's report, compliance generally means you need to present your nonprofit's financial activities in accordance with the standards established by the FASB. As of July 1, 2009, the FASB Accounting Standards Codification (ASC) became the single source of nongovernmental, authoritative GAAP in the United States. GAAP (see Chapter 1) offer guidance and a list of rules about how to account for nonprofit activities.

TIP

At present, GAAP is the same for public, nonpublic, and nonprofit organizations.

You may be wondering if the Securities and Exchange Commission (SEC) has nonprofit rules you must follow. The quick answer is no. The SEC has the statutory authority to set accounting standards for publicly held companies but historically has relied on private-sector bodies to set those standards.

TECHNICAL STUFF

A *publicly held company's* shares are freely traded on a public stock exchange. Although it may seem counterintuitive that a nonprofit could trade its net assets, accounting standards for public entities apply to a nonprofit if the nonprofit qualifies as a public entity. This is an advanced financial accounting topic that probably won't apply to smaller or new nonprofits. However, it's a great topic to add to your questions for your accountant.

Because presenting this how-to information is quite involved, more detail is included in the section "Finding Out about Accounting Standards" later in this chapter. I also present journal entries prepared for common nonprofit transactions in chapters 8 and 9.

Hiring professional help

At the end of your accounting year, it may be necessary to have an independent audit of your financial statements to stay compliant with grant and other contributor requirements. As a result, you need to hire an independent certified public accountant (CPA) to perform this audit. The independent CPA has an involved set of procedures set by generally accepted auditing standards (GAAS) for evaluating your financial records to verify whether they comply with GAAP and properly reflect your activities. At the end of the audit, the CPA will issue an opinion as to whether your financial statements are materially correct. Learn more about the auditing process in Chapter 14.

REMEMBER

You can hire a bookkeeper, accountant, or internal auditor for day-to-day bookkeeping, accounting, and internal controls, but only an external CPA or CPA firm can perform an independent audit of your financial statements. To cut costs, you could keep a CPA on retainer only, to stay abreast of new rules governing your nonprofit. See the section "Selecting an audit committee to hire an independent CPA," later in this chapter, for more about choosing an independent CPA. Also, check out Chapter 1 for more specific information you can follow when hiring professional help.

Abiding by IRS statutes

Another important process to follow to ensure that your nonprofit stays in compliance is to adhere to IRS statutes. To do so, you need to file an annual report to the IRS about your nonprofit's activities. Individuals and for-profit corporations pay federal income taxes by filing an annual income tax return, but nonprofits file an informational, generally tax-free form. Nonprofits file one of the forms in the IRS 990 series, Return of Organization Exempt from Income Tax. (Chapter 16 has step-by-step instructions for filing Form 990.)

WARNING

The IRS requires financial information about all organizations given tax-exempt status to make sure they're in compliance with their mission statements and don't have excessive unrelated business taxable income. If you file your organization's annual return late, the organization may have to pay a penalty. If you forget to file your organization's annual return for three years in a row, your organization can lose its nonprofit status. To reinstate your organization's tax-exempt status with the IRS, you'll have to file the necessary paperwork and pay a fee. So, make sure you don't make that mistake. For more information, go to www.irs.gov/charities-and-nonprofits.

Finding Out about Accounting Standards

Your nonprofit must have relevant, reliable, and meaningful financial data to ensure that accounting books and records are materially correct. External financial reports issued by your nonprofit should be prepared following guidance from the FASB, GAAP, and, depending on the circumstances, the Sarbanes–Oxley Act (SOX) as well. Did someone spill a can of alphabet soup?

So, what do all these letters mean? FASB is the authoritative body of accounting and reporting standards. GAAP provide the specific rules dictating how financial accountants must organize the information on the financial statements. As if these standards weren't enough, SOX was enacted as federal law mandating certain practices in financial recordkeeping and reporting that apply to all U.S. publicly traded companies, their boards, and their management, as well as public accounting firms.

The rest of this chapter takes a closer look at these three sets of regulations, whether they apply to your nonprofit, and what you need to do to ensure that your nonprofit is in compliance with them.

Following FASB standards

FASB sets financial accounting and reporting standards for your nonprofit via the adoption of the FASB ASC in 2009. However, keep in mind that the ASC didn't change GAAP by rewriting all the accounting rules and reporting standards. Instead, the ASC organizes GAAP in a more user-friendly fashion, placing a consistent format across the board for all GAAP topics. This section focuses on a few ASC sections that are common to all nonprofits, large and small.

TIP

FASB allows free, limited access to the ASC. To check it out, go to https://asc. fasb.org. Click Access the Basic View. Accept the terms and conditions to be taken to the codification basic view page. If you access the left-hand menu bar, you can select Industry and go to Section 958 for Nonprofits.

ASC 958-205-05, Not-for-Profit Entities: Presentation of Financial Statements

This ASC addresses the following financial statements required to be prepared by all nonprofits:

>> **Statement of activities (see Chapter 17):** This document shows how your nonprofit's net assets have increased or decreased.

- >> **Statement of financial position (see Chapter 18):** This statement sums up your organization's overall financial picture.

- >> **Statement of cash flows (see Chapter 19):** This form shows how your nonprofit's cash position has changed.

- >> **Statement of functional expense (see Chapter 20):** This statement is required for all nonprofits. Your statement of functional expense reports expenses by their function and nature. Your statement of functional expense can be its own financial statement, or you can include the information on your statement of activities or in the notes to the financial statements.

ASC 958-205-55, Not-for-Profit Entities: Implementation Guidance and Illustration

This ASC provides handy examples for how the statement of financial position, statement of activities, statement of cash flows and notes to the financial statements should be prepared. It also provides examples of notes to the financial statements and addresses the two groups of net assets: net assets without donor restrictions (which are *not* subject to donor restrictions) and net assets with donor restrictions (which *are* subject to donor restrictions).

If the nonprofit board votes to restrict an asset, that asset is also classified as net assets subject to donor restrictions.

ASC 958-605-25-5A, Not-for-Profit Entities: Revenue Recognition – Contributions

This ASC provides guidance for classifying assets as either with or without donor restrictions. For the nonprofit to deem an asset as having donor-imposed restrictions, both of the following conditions must be satisfied:

- >> The donor-imposed condition must have one or more barriers to overcome before the recipient is entitled to the asset transferred or promised.

- >> There must exist a right of return to the contributor or a right of release of the promisor from its obligation to contribute the asset.

ASC 958-360-35, Not-for-Profit Entities: Depreciation

This ASC requires all nonprofits to recognize depreciation in the financial statements and to disclose the depreciation expense, the balances of major classes of depreciable assets, the accumulated depreciation at balance sheet date, and a description of the depreciation method used.

Using GAAP

GAAP lay the ground rules for accounting and reporting standards. All financial accountants use GAAP when accounting for, preparing, and presenting financial information. Think of GAAP as a uniform way to analyze and record financial activities.

GAAP allow you to fairly evaluate and compare numbers, creating a level playing field so all nonprofits play by the same rules. That means the way you present your financial position is materially the same way another similar nonprofit using GAAP evaluates its position.

REMEMBER

Most GAAP-based financial statements are presented using the accrual basis of accounting, which deals with the recognition of transactions. For example, all transactions are recorded on the books when they occur, no matter when cash actually exchanges hands. (See Chapter 1 for more information about the accrual basis of accounting and examples of GAAP-basis journal entries in chapters 8 and 9.)

To ensure that you stay in compliance and protect your nonprofit's status, here are some accounting principles you should be aware of:

» **Accrual principle:** This is the concept that all accounting transactions record in the accounting period when they take place, not during the accounting period when the cash actually changes hands. This is to make sure that your financial statements reflect what actually occurred in the period.

» **Conservatism principle:** Under this principle, you record expenses and liabilities as soon as practical. A classic example of this is at the end of the year, when employees have worked up to December 31 but won't get paid for this work until January. You need to account for this accrued expense in the period you incur the expense (see chapters 8 and 9 for more info about accruals). On the flip side, revenue and assets record when it's certain they'll occur (for example, after you receive a donation rather than an unsubstantiated promise from an individual to support your cause).

» **Consistency principle:** When you pick a method to account for your accounting transactions, you stick with it. Changing it up midstream causes old financial statements to be skewed when comparing them to current financial statements. One great example is the method used to depreciate assets, which I discuss in Chapter 2.

» **Cost principle:** The *cost principle* requires assets to be recorded in the books at their cost. This is the price paid in exchange for the asset. This cost is commonly referred to as the *historical cost* or *original cost* because it doesn't change. It doesn't matter if the asset's current value goes up (appreciates) or goes down (depreciates); the value recorded on the statement of financial position remains the same, according to the cost principle.

- >> **Economic entity principle:** The economic entity principle deals with the separate legal entity concept, which means that if you incorporate, your nonprofit is a separate legal entity from you and/or the owners. The biggest advantage to incorporating is to protect your board and staff from personal legal liabilities, such as lawsuits. If the nonprofit is separate from you, then it, not you, is generally responsible for its debts and any charges of misconduct.

  Of course, being a separate business entity doesn't mean that you can't be sued. Anyone can file a lawsuit, so the ultimate protection is to acquire board of directors, management, and officers' insurance.

WARNING

- >> **Full-disclosure principle:** The *full-disclosure principle* requires that all situations, circumstances, and events relevant to your nonprofit's financial statements and necessary for understanding the financial statements have to be discussed. For example, changes made to accounting methods, inventory valuation, and pending lawsuits must be disclosed in the notes to the financial statements. Follow the FASB guidance for required disclosures, keeping in mind that any event out of the ordinary or material to your financial condition should be noted or disclosed in the financial statements. See Chapter 21 for more information about notes to the financial statements.

- >> **Matching principle:** The *matching principle* requires donations and revenues received and expenses incurred to be recorded in the same period you receive or incur them. In other words, you should recognize expenses in the period you incur the expense. For example, if your December utilities expense is $400, you record the $400 as a liability and expense in December, even though you don't pay the utility bill until the following year.

  You should match contributions received with expenses incurred in the same time period on the statement of activities. If someone makes a $50 donation to pay a volunteer, you should match that donation with the volunteer expense in the same time period, unless there are restrictions.

- >> **Materiality principle:** With respect to materiality, everything is relative. What may be material for *your* nonprofit may not be material for another. Stated very broadly, you must consider the potential for the information to alter the decision making of any users of your financial statements. Materiality is another great topic to add to your list of questions for your accountant.

- >> **Reliability principle:** This principle states that you record transactions only when proved. A good example of this is receiving an invoice from a vendor, providing verification that a good or service was received by the vendor for a specific amount of money to be paid by your nonprofit.

- >> **Revenue recognition principle:** Generally, this concept means revenue is recognized only when substantially earned. In the case of donations to a nonprofit, the *revenue-recognition principle* requires that when you receive donations, you must recognize them as revenue when they become unconditional. *Unconditional* means the donor has placed no restrictions on use of the donation, so your organization is free to spend the donation as it sees fit in the fulfillment of its mission statement.

TIP

Conditional contributions and restricted contributions are often confused because restrictions can be conditions, but not all conditions are restrictions. Let's say a donor offers you a potential gift of $10,000, but they won't give it to you unless your organization can raise *x* dollars or meet some other criteria. If you meet the condition, you get the money with no strings attached; it's then recognized as an unrestricted contribution. However, the donor may say you can have $10,000 for your capital campaign to be spent to purchase a building if you raise *x* dollars. If you raise the money, the gift becomes unconditional, but it's restricted to being spent only to purchase a building, and so it's recorded as a restricted contribution. When spent on bricks and mortar, the restriction is met, and it becomes unrestricted.

For more information about restricted and conditional contributions, see Chapter 17.

TIP

In addition to the accounting principles you must also be objective. For example, you determine and verify the value of all donated items in an unbiased manner.

To fairly represent your true financial condition, you have to give donated items an impartial value. When valuing assets donated to your organization, you should ask a qualified, unrelated third party (like an appraiser), who has no interest in the outcome, to give an objective view. To determine a donated asset's value, the following sources can also be of value:

>> Sticker price or purchase invoice

>> Sales invoice

>> Property deeds

>> Transfer of title

>> Kelly Blue Book value

>> Banker or creditor

REMEMBER

Sometimes, even after digging into GAAP via the ASC and with a sprinkling of objectivity thrown in, you may reckon there is more than one way to handle an accounting transaction. In that case, review the accounting principles to see if one treatment more closely matches the general accounting intent.

Sorting out the Sarbanes–Oxley Act

In response to public outcry after Enron, Global Crossing, and WorldCom (and the subsequent billions of dollars of investor losses), Maryland Senator Paul Sarbanes and Ohio Representative Michael Oxley worked together on protective measures to stop the fraudulent practices of accounting firms and their clients across the nation. These protective measures resulted in the Sarbanes-Oxley Act of 2002, commonly referred to as *SOX*.

SOX isn't exactly light reading, and it only applies to publicly traded companies — those registered with the SEC. However, many nonprofits have adopted provisions of SOX that help improve the management and financial reporting of their organizations. In light of the 2002 United Way of the National Capital Area scandal — where a former CEO defrauded the nonprofit to the tune of $497,000 — nonprofits are striving to become more transparent and accountable to their constituents.

Following are two SOX sections your nonprofit may be interested in adopting (even though it isn't required to).

Selecting an audit committee to hire an independent CPA

SOX Section 301 – Public Company Audit Committees mandates that audit committees be directly responsible for the appointment, compensation, and oversight of the engagement of the company's independent auditor and ensure that auditors are independent of their audit clients. An audit committee is also responsible for overseeing the financial reporting and disclosure process. The committee, which consists of at least three independent members of your board, with at least one being a financial expert, oversees the work of both the internal and external auditors. Individual board members aren't part of the organization's management team or paid management consultants; their only compensation is for being a board member.

REMEMBER

The terms *independent auditor* and *independent CPA* are interchangeable.

Internal auditors are employees of the nonprofit, and their job is setting up strategic processes to ensure that the objectives of the board are fulfilled by the nonprofit. *External auditors* are independent CPAs required to report to the audit committee prior to and during the audit of the financial statements.

External auditors must be independent in fact and appearance, have adequate training and experience, and exercise due diligence during all phases of the audit. *Due diligence* means the external auditor plans and adequately supervises and reviews any professional activities for which the external auditor is responsible.

The *general standards on auditor independence* outline what your audit committee should consider when choosing whether to enter into a relationship with or service provided by an auditor. You should make sure the external auditor is independent and objective, doesn't perform certain non-auditing services, and is prohibited from forming certain relationships with your nonprofit.

Being *independent* means the external auditor has no special relationship with or financial interest in your nonprofit that would cause them to disregard evidence and facts. *Objectivity* means the external auditor is impartial and honest and avoids any conflicts of interest with your nonprofit.

The external auditor is prohibited from providing the following non-audit services to an audit client, including its affiliates:

>> Bookkeeping

>> Designing and implementing financial information systems

>> Appraisal or valuation services, fairness opinions, or contribution-in-kind reports

>> Actuarial services

>> Internal audit outsourcing services

>> Management functions of human resources

>> Broker-dealer, investment advisor, or investment banking services

>> Legal services and expert services unrelated to the audit

>> Any other service the nonprofit's board determines, by regulation, to be impermissible

REMEMBER

The purpose of all these guidelines is to make sure your financial statements fairly represent your financial position. To avoid a biased opinion, it's important that your auditor is totally independent and has no other deals with you that may possibly sway their professional opinion of your organization.

Prohibited relationships are also an important point to remember under SOX. They're relationships between you and/or your nonprofit and the firm, CPA, or auditor who will offer an opinion about your financial statements.

The following are general rules about prohibited relationships deemed to affect independence and should be addressed by the CPA in their engagement letter. An *engagement letter* solidifies the audit arrangement by detailing the duties and obligations for both the nonprofit client and the CPA. In addition, every state in which the CPA is licensed will have numerous and perhaps unique ethical and code-of-conduct rules by which the CPA must abide.

>> **Employment relationships:** You have to wait at least one year before you can hire certain individuals who were formerly employed by your auditor in a financial reporting oversight role. The audit committee should consider whether hiring someone who was employed by the audit firm will affect the audit firm's independence.

>> **Contingent fees:** Audit committees must not approve engagements that pay an independent auditor based on the outcome of the audit results. In other words, your external auditor gives a professional opinion based on your records and reports, not on how much or how you pay them. The fee for the audit is always included in the engagement letter.

>> **Direct or material indirect business relationships:** Auditors and their firms can't form direct or material indirect relationships with the nonprofit, its officers, its directors, or its major donors. *Direct business relationships* refer to relationships where something tangible or of value (such as an investment) is involved between you and the auditor. For example, a relationship where the auditor has an investment in your organization would not be good. *Material indirect business relationships* are relationships where you may have some other business dealings with a family member or affiliate of the CPA firm or auditor, whereby ownership is more than 5 percent.

>> **Certain financial relationships:** Certain financial relationships between your nonprofit and the independent auditor are prohibited. These include creditor/debtor, banking, broker-dealer, and insurance interests, as well as interests in investment companies.

REMEMBER

To avoid any potential problems, set up an audit committee, be cautious when selecting an auditing firm, and disclose all accounting policies and practices to your audit committee. Above all, make sure your auditor is independent. The auditor has an exhaustive checklist they run through before accepting a nonprofit as a client, but the onus is on the nonprofit to honestly answer questions while the CPA firm is researching your fitness to be taken on as a new client.

Requiring a signed financial statement

SOX Section 302 – Corporate Responsibility for Financial Reports shifts the responsibility for the financial statements to the chief executive officer (CEO) and chief financial officer (CFO). It requires that they review all financial reports. They must report any deficiencies in internal control, report fraud committed by the management or any employee closely involved in setting internal controls, and indicate any material changes. This means the CEO and CFO certify via signature that the financial report does not contain any misrepresentations and the information in the financial report is fairly presented.

REMEMBER

Although signing off on a nonprofit's financial statements isn't legally required, doing so indicates management takes responsibility for the statements.

TIP

For more information about SOX that is updated through 2022, go to www.sarbanes-oxley-101.com.

IN THIS CHAPTER

» **Understanding why audits are important**

» **Discussing the reasons for getting an audit**

» **Grasping the annual audit process**

» **Knowing the types of grant audits**

» **Finding out about IRS examinations**

Chapter **14**

Preparing for an Audit

A s the executive director or manager of a nonprofit, you probably already know that audits are a part of business. An audit doesn't mean that you're doing anything wrong. It's simply an evaluation of what's taken place. An auditor looks at events to determine the degree to which the information presented corresponds with established guidelines. After completing the audit, the auditor prepares a report with the details of his findings. Audits are done to verify whether you're doing what you're supposed to do.

Audits come in many forms. This chapter discusses two types of audits: grant audits and financial statement audits. A grant audit takes a look at your grant documents and budgets to verify that your nonprofit is properly using grant money. A financial statement audit assesses if your financial statements are materially correct and are presented in accordance with generally accepted accounting principles (GAAP). The last section of this chapter also discusses Internal Revenue Service (IRS) examinations.

Understanding the Audit Purpose and Need

There are three major reasons why your nonprofit may decide to secure an independent audit. The first is that grant applications may require you to submit audited financial statements in order to be eligible for funding. Additionally, audited financial statements show your donors that you're committed to financial transparency and accountability. Finally, having these statements gives the users of your financial statements more confidence in the financial figures because they've been examined by an independent, objective third party.

The goal of a financial statement audit is that the independent certified public accountant (CPA) forms an opinion regarding whether your financial statements are free from material errors and fairly presented in accordance with U.S. generally accepted accounting principles (GAAP). At the end of the financial statement audit, you receive an opinion from the independent CPA regarding how much reliance users can place on the financial statements.

When your nonprofit receives federal money in the form of a grant award, oversight via a grant audit determines whether your organization performed and complied with the terms of the federally funded grant. Basically, Uncle Sam wants to make sure you're following the rules and being a good steward of federal funds.

Explaining the difference between an independent and grant audit

There can be quite a difference between grant audits and financial statement audits conducted by an independent CPA. Grant awards meeting specific criteria must comply with Uniform Grant Guidance (UGG) auditing requirements found in Subpart F of the Super Circular. For example, If your nonprofit receives federal grant awards and expends $750,000 (or more) of the award in a fiscal year, you're required to have an independent compliance audit referred to as a *single audit*. Single audits are substantially more detailed than regular independent audits are.

TIP

The Super Circular is also known as 2 CFR Part 200 and can be found at www.ecfr. gov/current/title-2/subtitle-A/chapter-II/part-200. You can download a PDF version with hot links for easy review.

Audits by an independent CPA hired by your nonprofit are performed using generally accepted auditing standards (GAAS) and GAAP to guide analysis. When the independent CPA has finished their audit, the process is wrapped up through the issuance of an unqualified report, qualified report, disclaimer report, or adverse report.

Independent audits

When I speak about audited financial statements, I'm referring to the work product resulting from the independent examination of the nonprofit's financial records by a licensed CPA. This examination looks at your nonprofit's system of internal controls, financial records, accounting transactions, and practices.

An audit of your financial statements by an independent CPA is conducted following GAAS. These standards are the product of the Auditing Standards Board (ASB), which is a senior technical committee of the American Institute of Certified Public Accountants (AICPA). Ten GAAS make up the independent CPA's minimum standards of performance.

The first three GAAS are general standards addressing whether the CPA has both adequate training and proficiency to conduct an audit of your nonprofit. They also address whether the CPA is independent in both fact and appearance and that the CPA has to exercise due professional care in performing their auditing tasks.

The next three GAAS govern how the CPA does their job. The audit work has to be adequately planned and all assistants must be properly supervised. The CPA has to get an understanding of your nonprofit and your internal control procedures. The evidence gathered during the audit must be sufficient and competent enough to support the figures on your nonprofit's financial statements (see chapter 17, 18, and 19).

The final four GAAS concern standards of reporting. The CPA evaluates whether the financial statements were prepared using GAAP and if the principles were consistently applied for all financial reporting. The CPA also looks at notes to the financial statements to make sure they're adequate disclosures (see Chapter 21). Finally, the CPA has to include an opinion as to whether the financial statements present fairly in all material respects the financial position of your nonprofit.

Grant audits

The Single Audit Act (which applies when $750,000 or more in grant awards are expended in a fiscal year) requires auditors of nonprofits receiving government awards use generally accepted governmental auditing standards (GAGAS), also known as the Yellow Book, to perform their audits and produce their reports. The Yellow Book outlines the requirements for audit reports, professional qualifications for auditors, and audit firm quality management.

REMEMBER

Even if not required to follow GAGAS, many auditors voluntarily follow GAGAS because it provides a reliable, trustworthy road map for audit work.

Audits conducted in accordance with GASAS are consistent with GAAS but broader in scope. For example, the Yellow Book has a lower threshold for misstatements because of government public accountability.

TIP

You can find out more about the Yellow Book at www.gao.gov/yellowbook and download the 2018 Yellow Book with 2021 Technical Updates at www.gao.gov/products/gao-21-368g. As of this writing, 2023 revisions are still in process.

The purpose of the grant audit is to assess and evaluate your nonprofit's progress. Each federal agency has program managers who are your primary points of contact. Your program manager monitors and oversees your progress by communicating with you. They'll occasionally pay you a personal visit to assess your progress. Before they arrive, your program manager will notify you of plans for an onsite visit and tell you which documents will be evaluated.

Some programs have very detailed monitoring guidelines. The applicable federal agency determines the scope and depth of the monitoring visit. If your program manager believes you're having problems managing the grant, some corrective actions will be suggested.

In addition to program managers, federal agencies have program officers, who perform grant audits by visiting your site and doing a thorough evaluation of your grant files. Program officers are auditors who work for the federal agency that awarded you the grant.

The federal agency that gave you the grant will decide when you're audited or paid a visit. Just rest assured, you'll be notified in advance of the visit and have plenty of time to get everything in order.

TECHNICAL STUFF

There are three types of GAGAS engagements: financial audits (which I discuss in this chapter), performance audits, and attestation engagements. Performance audits are as the name implies: Analysis is done by the CPA to make recommendations for improving your program performance. Attestation engagements look at a broad range of financial and nonfinancial data based on the particular needs of the nonprofit.

Introducing internal and external auditors

Before you go any further in this chapter, I want to make sure you understand the difference between internal and external auditors. *Internal auditors* are employees of your nonprofit. *External auditors* are independent of your nonprofit.

Your internal auditor's job is to make sure your nonprofit runs efficiently and effectively. They perform financial, internal control and compliance audits for your nonprofit. For example, these employees help set internal controls and perform self-assessments on how well the internal controls are working.

REMEMBER

Internal controls are policies and procedures set in place to safeguard the nonprofit by minimizing risks and also tell employees how to do their job. For example, a strong internal control would not allow one employee to handle many aspects of a related task.

Your independent external auditor works with your internal auditor to understand your nonprofit's internal controls and determines whether the internal auditors are competent. Strong internal controls enforced by qualified internal auditors may allow your external auditor to place more reliance on the veracity of the financial statements. This, in turn, allows the external auditor to tailor and perhaps limit some audit procedures.

Obtaining a financial statement opinion

At the end of a financial statement audit, your nonprofit receives an audit report. The audit report begins with a letter. This letter, following a standard format, is addressed to your nonprofit and signed by the CPA firm who conducted the audit. The standard format consists of four paragraphs with the auditing firm's opinion, basis for opinion, responsibilities of management for the financial statements and internal controls, and auditor's responsibilities. If necessary, the standard format expands to include an Other Matters section. A nonprofit's Other Matters section might include something like the following:

> Other Matters
>
> Our audit was conducted for the purpose of forming an opinion on the financial statements as a whole. The schedule of expenditures of federal awards, as required by Title 2 U.S. Code of Federal Regulations (CFR) Part 200, Uniform Administrative Requirements is the responsibility of management and was derived from and relates directly to the underlying accounting and other records used to prepare the financial statements. The information has been prepared in accordance with auditing standards generally accepted in the United States of America. In our opinion, the information is fairly stated, in all material respects, in relation to the financial statements as a whole.
>
> Other Reporting Required by Government Auditing Standards
>
> In accordance with Government Auditing Standards, our report dated March 10, 2024, provides our evaluation of Jay & Top Community Cat Project's internal control over financial reporting and on our tests of its compliance with certain provisions

of laws, regulations, grant agreements and other matters. The purpose of that report is solely to describe the scope of our testing of internal control over financial reporting and compliance and the results of that testing, and not to provide an opinion on the effectiveness of Jay & Top Community Cat Project's internal control over financial reporting or on compliance.

Following the letter are the financial statements, notes to the financial statements and any other information the independent CPA deems necessary to include in the audit report. See the "Gathering final evidence and issuing the report" section later in this chapter for more about the different types of independent opinions.

Receiving grant audit findings

When your auditor is finished with the grant audit, they issue an audit report, which tells your organization the results of the audit. The audit report is the final stage of the audit process, and it communicates audit findings. Audit findings are what the auditor discovers after careful evaluation and comparison of your grant activities to the rules and standards. When you get your audit findings depends on how long it takes the auditor to prepare it. As with all things government related, it can take a while.

As a general rule, auditors are required to report any questionable costs totaling $10,000 or more for known or likely noncompliance issues. This threshold amount can change from one year to the next. Make sure to check your notice of award (NoA) for the current threshold. The report includes the method used to calculate the questionable costs and the facts supporting the identified deficiency. Government threshold and tolerance for audit findings are stringent. If the program officer discovers anything that indicates you haven't handled the grant money according to the guidelines, you may have to pay back the funds.

The type of report your nonprofit receives depends on the type of review or GAGAS engagement. For example, a desk review will produce an entirely different report than a GAGAS financial audit, attestation-level examination, or performance audit. You can find more about desk reviews and GAGAS engagements in the "Identifying the Types of Grant Audits" section later in this chapter.

REMEMBER

All state, local, or tribal governments; nonprofit organizations; educational institutions; and hospitals that receive grant money must comply with auditing rules handed down by the federal government. All nonprofits should undergo some type of audit. What type of audit you need depends on whether you receive more or less than $750,000 of grant money in a year — those nonprofits receiving $750,000 or more are subject to single audit procedures conducted according to the GAGAS guidelines.

Walking Through the Independent Audit Process

To fully explain this topic I would need to write a book (which, in fact, I have!). So, the purpose of this section of the chapter is to give you enough information to have a basic understanding of the steps your independent auditor must go through. This is important because your nonprofit management and staff work closely with the auditor providing oral and written testimony relating to and requested during the independent audit.

Selecting an independent CPA is a function of your audit committee (see Chapter 13). In a nutshell, your audit committee is responsible for board financial and accounting oversight. The committee, which consists of at least three independent members of your board, with at least one being a financial expert with recent financial experience, oversees the work of both the internal and external auditors.

REMEMBER

Your independent CPA conducting the audit doesn't prepare the financial statements. The fair preparation and presentation of financial data is the responsibility of management, as is the design, implementation, and maintenance of internal controls.

Planning and design

Your potential independent CPA has a lot of due diligence to complete before they accept your nonprofit as a client. The CPA conducts general research about your nonprofit and will schedule an initial interview to discuss what services you require and how and whether the CPA can fulfil your goals. If you've had independent audits in the past with another CPA, you'll also be asked for that CPA's contact info.

After the initial interview, there are other pre-acceptance steps such as interviewing the prior auditor (if one exists) and establishing whether the CPA feels they can be independent in fact and appearance. The CPA also performs steps to judge your integrity and may not be thrilled about entering into an engagement with your nonprofit if your management appears to be inept. This is because, if there isn't a knowledgeable financial person supervising the preparation of the financial statements, chances are, the financial statements aren't reflective of appropriate accounting principles, which might make the audit unfeasible.

If you come to a meeting of the minds, the CPA prepares an engagement letter solidifying the audit arrangement. It serves as a contract detailing the design of the audit, duties, and obligations for both your nonprofit and the CPA firm.

Calculating audit risk

To kick off the audit, your CPA assesses the risk that they won't catch a major misstatement on the financial statements. Your CPA looks at inherent risk, which is the likelihood of an inaccurate audit conclusion based on the nature of your business. The CPA also looks at control risk determining if your nonprofit's internal control procedures aren't sufficient to detect or prevent mistakes. Another risk CPAs consider is detection risk, which is the risk that the CPA won't detect material errors in your financial statements.

After considering all aspects of risk, your CPA prepares risk factor workpapers. These workpapers determine what type of audit evidence needs to be gathered to test and verify your financial statement assertions.

Doing analysis

Whew, that's a lot of work on the part of your independent CPA before they get to the nitty-gritty of determining sample size, collecting, and documenting audit evidence. Your CPA has voluminous procedures and required documentation. In order for the CPA to do their job, at a minimum you'll be asked for your general ledger, journals, invoices from suppliers, substantiation for donor contributions, employee time cards, and other payroll information. The CPA will analyze account balances for existence, completeness, valuation, occurrence, accuracy, allocation, rights, obligations, and schedule employee interviews to discuss the bookkeeping and accounting processes.

Gathering final evidence and issuing the report

One of the last steps in the independent audit process is the CPA performing their final due diligence. The biggie on this is testing events taking place after the balance sheet date. So, if the audit engagement is for the calendar year ending December 31, 2023, the CPA looks at certain things going on in your nonprofit up to the date of the audit report, which will probably be months after the balance sheet date.

For example, you may be breathing a sigh of relief because an adverse event like a fire or employee lawsuit occurred after the balance sheet date of the financial year under audit. However, based on the nature of the event, your CPA may have to address it as part of the audit report as pro forma financial information — that is, how the financial statement would've looked had the event taken place before the balance sheet date.

After all this is done, your CPA will issue the audit report. The report is amazingly short given all the effort that goes into a financial statement audit. There are four types of report opinions:

» **Unqualified:** What your nonprofit is aiming for. It means that your financial statements represent fairly, in all material respects, your nonprofit's financial position as of the date of the balance sheet. This holy grail states that, in the auditor's opinion, the financial statements under audit and the changes in net assets and their cash flows are in accordance with accounting principles generally accepted in the United States.

» **Qualified:** You receive a qualified report when your CPA has a scope limitation or a material departure from GAAP, but the rest of the financial statement assertions were audited to the CPA's satisfaction under GAAS. Here's an example of a qualified opinion:

> Basis for Qualified Opinion: As discussed in Note 5 to the financial statements, no uncollectible allowance has been provided for donor accounts receivable. Therefore, a provision of $X should be made for the year ending December 31, 2023. Accordingly, net assets and accounts receivable should be reduced by $X.

> Qualified Opinion

> In our opinion, except for the effects of the matter described in the Basis for Qualified Opinion, the financial statements give a true and fair view, in all material respects in accordance with accounting principles generally accepted in the United States of America.

TIP

An example of a scope limitation would be if the CPA couldn't sufficiently test because you lacked sufficient, competent substantiation. For instance, say you gave your auditor a list of donors, but the contact information was missing, so the auditor couldn't verify the donors' gifts. Everything else presented was in accordance with GAAP. Therefore, the auditor will state in the report that your financial statements were presented fairly, with the exception of the donors' gifts, which couldn't be audited.

» **Disclaimer:** If the CPA wasn't able to issue an opinion because they weren't able to gather sufficient evidence, the CPA will issue a disclaimer report. This most often happens if the nonprofit can't or doesn't provide the records the CPA requests or the CPA thinks you're hiding something. Here's an example of a disclaimer added to the report:

> DISCLAIMER We were not appointed as auditors of the company until after the balance sheet date of December 31, 2023. Bank statement reconciliations and the response secured from donor confirmation letters show numerous errors in donor accounts receivable. As of the date of our report, management was still in the process of correcting the errors.

As a result of these errors, we were unable to determine whether any adjustments might have been found necessary in respect of recorded or unrecorded donor accounts receivable, and the elements making up the statement of activities and financial position.

» **Adverse:** Yup, not good. You receive this type of report when the GAAP departures are so widespread that the CPA can't say the financial statements are presented fairly in accordance with GAAP. Here's an example of an adverse opinion:

Adverse Opinion

In our opinion, because of the significance of the matter discussed in the Basis for Adverse Opinion section of our report, the accompanying financial statements does not present fairly the financial position of the nonprofit at December 31, 2023, and of its statement of cash flows for the year ended in accordance with accounting principles generally accepted in the United States of America.

Identifying the Types of Grant Audits

You'll find out you're due for an audit by letter. The letter includes details about the type of audit engagement and who will perform it. The letter also gives you details about what you need to do to prepare your nonprofit. Sometimes you may have to present information about your grant's progress; this can be something as simple as a Microsoft PowerPoint presentation.

When the time for the audit arrives, your auditor will meet with your executive director and the executive staff that manages the grant before and after the auditor evaluates your grant files. During the first meeting, the auditor introduces themselves, talks about what will take place, and gives a general overview of how long the audit may take. During the closing meeting, the auditor lets you know that the audit is complete, and the findings will be mailed after the report is complete. No results or findings are discussed during this closing meeting.

How long the audit takes depends on how much grant money you've received and if you have a good grant management system that allows you to quickly locate the paperwork and files the auditor wants to see. Some audits may take only a couple of hours, while others may take up to a week to complete.

Just like nonprofits vary in their purpose and scope, so do audits. Audits can range from a short phone call, to a single audit or an audit in which a representative from the Government Accounting Office (GAO) shows up with a fine-tooth comb to review your records. If you've broken out in a sweat thinking about that latter type of audit, you're right to do so. It's the most serious type, so you want to do everything you can to avoid it.

The Government Performance and Results Act (GPRA) states that federal agencies must show how the money they spend actually furthers their mission, goals, and objectives. The government measures the success of each grant program through quantitative outcomes measures. GPRA evaluates whether the grant program accomplished its objectives as stated in the project narrative you submitted when you applied for the grant. For more information about the GPRA go to www.performance.gov/about/performance-framework.

The following sections give you the lowdown on the four types of grant audits: desk audits, site visits, single audits, and inspector general audits.

Conducting a desk audit

Desk reviews are the simplest kind of grant audit and are an evaluation of your nonprofit's administration capacity with a focus on your accounting system and cash and general management. Your program manager calls you with a series of questions about your grant. The program manager will request written documentation, which is reviewed and analyzed at the reviewer's site. After the desk review has been completed a report to senior management will be issued describing any issues identified during the review. A corrective action plan (CAP) may be required to remedy any identified deficiencies.

TIP

Answer the questions honestly, submit requested documentation in a timely fashion, and it's over! This audit can take anywhere from 5 to 30 minutes or perhaps longer, depending on the nature of the questions. Of course, you're given a heads-up on what to expect from your program manager beforehand.

Be prepared to answer questions about your federal programs. You may get questions such as

>> How much grant money have you spent and what is your present balance?

>> Have you expended $750,000 of grant funds within the current year?

>> Have you made necessary corrective action steps from the desk audit/ monitoring site visit?

>> What, if any, problems are you experiencing while implementing the grant project?

Based on your answers during the desk audit, your program manager may schedule a monitoring site visit (see the next section). Your program manager wants to help you be successful in implementing your grant. To ensure your success, they'll periodically visit you to check on things.

REMEMBER

Subgrantees are usually subject to desk audits. Subgrantees are the agencies that partnered with you to get the grant. (See chapters 11 and 12 for more information about the relationship between grantor, grantee, and subgrantees.)

TIP

In some cases, desk reviews are scheduled in advance of a site visit.

Setting up the site visit

Your program manager may skip the desk audit (see the preceding section) and schedule a monitoring site visit. During this type of audit, an evaluation is made of all grant-supported activities to determine the progress you've made toward achieving project objectives; to verify your compliance with the terms, conditions, and purpose of the grant; and to identify technical assistance needs.

The monitoring site visit is conducted at the location of your nonprofit. It involves reviewing written policies and procedures, scrutinizing documents, touring your facility, and interviewing employees. The purpose is to both check on you and offer technical assistance. The results of the monitoring site visit are in the form of a written report to senior management.

REMEMBER

Your monitoring site visit will be scheduled at a good time for you and your federal program manager. The monitor doesn't just show up at your door. This gives you ample time to make sure everything is in order. After the program manager leaves, you'll receive a CAP about how to fix any problems the monitor finds. (Refer to the "Following the corrective action plan" section, later in this chapter, for more about the CAP.)

A program monitoring site visit may be casual and as brief as one hour or it can be more formal and last a couple of days. The length of the visit is based on whether you're experiencing problems managing your program's progress, spending the grant money, or managing a large sum of grant money. If you're managing several million dollars with several partners, your program manager will evaluate your project and meet you and your partners in person.

Your program manager will oversee the day-to-day operations of your grant-supported activities, but they're not going to get too detailed about how your entire management system operates. If deemed necessary, your federal agency may send a grant program officer (GPO) to assist in the site visit. The GPO is responsible for the programmatic and technical aspects of the grant and works with other grant management staff on post-award administration, including review of progress reports, participation in site visits, and other activities.

Sometimes one person may show up, or a team may come in and audit your files in one day. The complexity of the audit and how long it takes depend on how much money is handled. When this team is scheduled to pay you a visit is left up to your program manager and the federal agency that awarded the grant. During this auditing site visit, your program officer checks out the following:

>> Program compliance

>> Subgrantee monitoring

>> Financial system (internal control system)

>> Procurement system (policy and procedures)

>> Travel system (policy and procedures)

>> Personnel system (time and attendance reports)

>> Property management or inventory system

>> Project performance (Government Performance and Results Act)

>> Financial status, progress, and closeout reports

TIP

Make sure you tag all equipment purchased with a unit cost of $5,000 or more with grant money and give it an inventory control ID number that clearly indicates that the equipment was purchased with grant money. Not only do you have to look out for yourself, but you're responsible for any other agencies that partnered with you to get the grant. If you receive federal money that you're sharing with other agencies, follow up with your partners and make sure that any equipment they've purchased isn't sitting in a box.

REMEMBER

Desk audits and site visits are a fantastic chance for two-way communication between yourself and the grantor. As a plus, technical assistance provided by the grantor is also a means for you to make sure you're complying with the award agreement.

Gearing up for oversight audits

This section discusses both the single audit and the inspector general audit. The single audit is a rigorous, organization-wide audit of an entity that expends $750,000 or more in federal awards during the entity's fiscal year. It's not great to be informed your nonprofit is subject to an inspector general audit; they only take place if your awarding agency thinks you're in major trouble.

Single audits

As a result of the uniform guidance in CR 200, all nonfederal government agencies and nonprofit organizations that expend $750,000 or more in federal awards in a given fiscal year are required to obtain a single audit. Your nonprofit is responsible for securing and paying the independent CPA firm. You can use a reasonable amount of grant funds to pay for the audit.

The process to secure an independent auditor to conduct the single audit is relatively the same as outlined in the "Walking Through the Independent Audit Process" section, earlier in this chapter, with the following additional requirements:

» Your audit committee develops a statement of work (SOW) outlining objectives and a timeline for the audit.

» A request for proposal (RFP) using the guidance in 2 CFR 200 Subpart F details auditor selection requirements, including securing a copy of the auditor's peer review.

» Auditor solicitations are made via the RFP and evaluated; ultimately, a written recommendation report is sent to your audit committee, which approves the auditor.

This audit is performed annually for years your nonprofit meets the $750,000 criteria. Its objective is to provide assurance to the federal government regarding the management and use of federal funds by grant recipients. It encompasses both financial and compliance components. After completion, results of the single audit must be submitted to the Federal Audit Clearinghouse (FAC) along with a data collection form.

During the single audit, the auditor evaluates the following:

TIP

» Are your nonprofit financial statements presented fairly and accurately and in accordance with federal cost principles?

Examples of federal cost principles are if the expense is allowed under the grant and if direct and indirect costs are handled correctly.

» Do you have an adequate internal control structure implemented, monitored, and maintained?

» Is your nonprofit in compliance with any special government regulations/laws applicable to your specific federal grant? For example, is your nonprofit engaging in any unallowed activities? Does it have effective cash management procedures in place and is it correctly monitoring cash transactions?

» Are expended funds in accordance with the grant award and any federal law or regulation having a material effect on the expended funds?

Sub-recipient monitoring is another biggie. If your nonprofit has sub-recipients, you must diligently track sub-recipient activities and spending.

Inspector general audits

The Office of Inspector General (OIG) is responsible for promoting effective management and accountability in the federal government through independent evaluations and audits that identify problems and provide solutions. An OIG audit takes place when a federal inspector conducts an independent audit and investigation on behalf of Congress and the executive branch of the federal government.

An OIG audit is the Federal Bureau of Investigation (FBI) of audits. Your nonprofit gets an inspector general audit only when you're in major trouble. "Major trouble" can include suspicions of fraud, waste, abuse, and misconduct. If the desk audit reveals some problems and the site visit indicates that you have significant material differences, then the OIG investigates the case. This type of audit is very serious.

The purpose of an inspector general audit is to evaluate whether your nonprofit has spent the government's money for its intended purposes, has accurately accounted for it, and has adequate controls in place that comply with laws and regulations.

If you face an inspector general audit, you most likely have been accused of some wrongdoing. This accusation may have been the result of your not responding to corrective actions advised by your program manager or program officers, or a concerned citizen may have reported you. If an investigation reveals the accusations to be true, you'll probably have to pay back the money, and you may be hit with heavy penalties and ordered to serve jail time.

Getting Ready for the Auditor

If you've ever put your house on the market, you know how people come in and look in closets, open cabinets, pull out drawers, and see the truth (which you may not be very comfortable with). Well, your auditor will look through everything to make sure your nonprofit is following the rules. The auditor performs three general tasks:

>> **Look for improper payments.** All grants have rules about how to allocate expenses, what you can buy, and what you shouldn't buy. These are called *cost principles.* Your auditor will look for improper payments and determine whether costs were allowable according to cost principles.

>> **Look at internal controls.** To ensure your organization has taken steps to protect its assets, the grant auditor determines whether you've established internal controls, or checks and balances. You have to follow the rules about administering the grant program. The auditor checks your use of internal controls to make sure you're following the rules.

>> **Assess the risk factor.** Based on your purchasing, accounting, and inventory systems, your auditor will assess the risk for problems. It doesn't take a rocket scientist to detect trouble, especially if your accounting system is inadequate and you're not keeping up with things.

For your organization to have a successful audit, you need to make sure the program manager can access all requested records. The following sections explain the importance of getting your books in order, preparing other important documentation, and presenting the grant expenses that you've kept track of so your audit can go off without a hitch.

Preparing the books and records for audit review

In order for your program manager to monitor your grant's progress, you need to make sure your records are available. Get all your records in order so when the grant program manager comes knocking, they have everything they need at their fingertips. They'll tell you what will be examined. Of course, one thing can lead to another, so I suggest that you only give them what they ask for.

TIP

Be sure to make and keep copies of everything pertaining to the grant, including financial and progress reports (see Chapter 12), to make the program manager's job easier. Keeping good records is important because you want the audit to move like clockwork. If your program manager has a difficult time making sense of your documentation, you may prolong the audit process.

For every grant you receive, you should keep the following in a hard-copy file:

>> Copy of the grant application

>> Copy of all letters and correspondence (including emails)

>> Copy of the grant award document

>> Copy of the grant budget

>> Copy of all grant adjustment notices (including subgrantees)

>> Copy of all receipts, invoices, bills, and canceled checks

>> Copy of the grant employees' payroll information

>> Copy of time and attendance reports

Your program manager will look at these records to make sure you're in compliance with the intended purposes for the grant award.

REMEMBER

If you have well-organized and adequate records of all grant activities, you're sure to breeze through the grant audit process. The only thing an audit does is verify that you've followed the grant guidelines. It's virtually impossible to verify what you've done without documentation.

Your grant program officer will want to see records that verify how and when your organization was structured. In addition, the officer will ask for documents about your financial structure, personnel policies, and procedures. Make sure you have the following papers readily available:

>> **IRS letter of determination:** Your IRS letter of determination is the letter you received when you established your nonprofit. It indicates that your organization is exempt from federal corporate income taxes. It contains important information regarding the basis for your exemption and the requirements associated with maintaining it.

>> **Articles of incorporation and organizational bylaws:** The articles of incorporation and bylaws are documents you set up when you started your organization. If you've made any amendments to your bylaws, make sure to attach those to your original bylaws.

>> **Names and addresses of board members:** An up-to-date list of your current board members may be needed for an evaluation of members' political affiliations. (*Remember:* There isn't supposed to be any undue influence made by anyone to get grant money.) It's best to have information about the other boards your members sit on and where your members are employed available just in case you're asked for it. Contact information, including email addresses and phone numbers, for board members may be required. The best solution is to have résumés of all board members on file.

>> **Organization operating budget:** Your program officer probably will want to see your operating budget for the current or upcoming program year. This organizational budget differs from the grant project budget. It allows the auditor to put the grant money in a larger context and see the big picture. They can use this budget to determine how much you're relying on grant funding to run your programs. (See Chapter 8 for more on operating budgets.)

>> **Indirect cost rate:** The auditor will need a copy of your organization's indirect cost rate (if you have one) to verify that the correct percentages have been allocated to the grant. (Your indirect cost rate assigns a percentage of your general overhead and administrative expenses to the grant. See Chapter 18 for more info about this.)

>> **Financial statements:** Your program officer will want to review your financial statements and Form 990s to determine whether you're financially stable. If you're over your head in debt, your organization may not be the best invest-ment of grant dollars. On the other hand, if you're stable financially, it proves that the government made a good choice in selecting you to receive grant money. Check out the chapters in Part 4 for how to create these statements.

Having all these documents and information at your fingertips when the auditor arrives saves time, and it shows that you're organized and a good recordkeeper.

Tracking all grant expenses

The federal government has given your organization money, and it expects you to use it properly. To prove that you spent the money in accordance with the govern-ment's expectations, you need to track all expenses back to the invoice and to the request for bid for any significant cost or expense such as major renovations or equipment purchases (check your NoA for specifics). A request for bid advertises that you need professional services or plan to purchase something from an outside vendor. Be careful with requests for bids because your program manager will want to verify that it was handled correctly.

For every federal dollar you spend, you should keep the receipt and anything else pertaining to the purchase. When your program manager shows up at your office, they're not just going to take your word that you paid certain amounts for certain items out of your grant budget. You have to have documentation to support every transaction.

Your program manager should be able to take a charge allocated to grant funds and track it back to the request for bid. Copies of checks written, and rebate checks should correspond to purchases. Your grant manager will want to see how you account for grant expenditures and how you keep them separate by account num-bers from your regular normal nonprofit expenses. (See Chapter 11 for more on keeping grant expenses separate from other expenses.)

You need to pay particular attention to employee salaries paid from grant money. Your accounting system should have accounting codes that separate and allocate grant employees' pay to a designated grant account. You may want to set up a spreadsheet that shows that you keep up with employees paid by the grant. (See Chapter 4 for information about using spreadsheets.)

TIP

Time and attendance reports should be recorded and kept on file for every employee paid by the grant. These reports should be signed by the employee's immediate supervisor. One of the most common audit findings is the lack of time and attendance reports. (See Chapter 18 for more about payroll reports.)

WARNING

Before you destroy any grant files, contact your program manager. All records of grant activities should be kept on file for three years after the closeout of the grant period unless an investigation is underway. If you're under investigation, you'll need to keep the records until after the investigation is over.

Showing proper cash management

During the audit, the program manager checks your nonprofit's cash management. In fact, having excess cash on hand is a common audit finding. A good system of cash management helps determine how much cash is needed to take care of immediate needs.

As a director or manager of a small- to medium-size nonprofit, you need to have a system of cash management because having excess cash in your bank account is a sign of poor cash management. This section helps you reduce the amount of cash on hand and discusses the importance of protecting the money in-house.

Minimizing cash on hand

The key to drawing down federal grant dollars from the U.S. Treasury is to not have more money in your checking account than you need (see Chapter 12 for more on drawing down grant money). Your auditor will review all drawdowns to determine whether you're properly managing federal dollars by keeping the money on hand for a minimum amount of time.

Most people don't have excess cash in their personal checking accounts. The same should go for your nonprofit and its grant money. Your grant money should not lie in your bank account long enough to draw substantial amounts of interest. The main reason: The federal government is giving you this grant money to use on your programs and services, not to sit in your checking account. The money requested from the U.S. Treasury should pass through your checking account quickly.

You need to remember three things about having cash on hand:

>> **Up to $250 per year may be kept for administrative expenses.**
Administrative expenses are the costs to oversee the administration of a project, such as the time spent processing payments. As with all things grant related, verify this with your program manager.

>> **Interest earned on federal fund balances in excess of $500 is required to be returned to the federal agency.** Earning more than $500 of interest income can result in your having to pay back the money. The government allows you to keep the first $500 of interest earned on grant money. You're not supposed to hold the money in your bank account for extended periods of time during which it can collect interest.

You report interest earned when you file your grant reports, and interest over $500 will be treated as a grant distribution to you. Always talk with your program manager if you're concerned about program income. If you earn interest, you should report it to your program manager and make them aware of why it happened.

>> **Don't use the grant money for anything other than to support the program for which the money is intended.** You can't borrow money from the grant funds to pay for things and then put it back. It's not excess cash.

Keep in mind that expense and interest income limitations can fluctuate year to year. Always check your NoA for the current limitations and discuss any questions with your program manager.

Segregating duties through internal controls

Internal controls provide reasonable assurance that the spending of grant money complies with laws and regulations. In plain language, this would be called a system of checks and balances. As the director or manager, you need to make sure your nonprofit has internal controls in place to protect the organization's finances and assets.

Your auditor will review your entire management system and look at the internal controls you've established. No audit is complete without checking for protective measures that safeguard you from possible theft or embezzlement. Your accounting, procurement, personnel, property, and travel systems are all interrelated, so your auditor will check the adequacies of these areas.

I suggest you implement the following internal controls in your organization to protect not only the grant money you receive, but also all donations and assets you have:

>> **Have your in-house project manager (not to be confused with the program manager from the federal agency that issued your grant) be the person who authorizes payments and charges against the grant budget.**

>> **Segregate duties within your organization.** The person who writes checks shouldn't be the same person who balances the books. Furthermore, the person counting the money shouldn't make deposits, approve payments, and request money from the federal government. This is why some companies have separate accounts receivables and accounts payables departments. Separating duties safeguards your money.

>> **Require two signatures on all checks over a certain amount.** You can also have your bank call you for checks over a set amount. Decisions about these amounts depend on your accounting activities and size of your overall budget. For example, if your organization seldom writes a check for more than $500, you may want to place restrictions on all checks written above this amount. Discuss this with your board if you're not sure what amount to use.

>> **Have internal auditors on staff.** You save time and money when people inside your organization make sure that you're properly accounting for expenditures and check to see that you're in compliance.

REMEMBER

Keeping a close watch on your money can protect you from theft or embezzlement. A weak internal control system opens up the possibility that your nonprofit will be stolen from.

WARNING

Make sure you don't supplant any grant money. To *supplant* grant money means to use grant money for something that's already in your budget. Grant funds should be used to supplement — not supplant. For example, if you receive a donation to hire a new secretary, but you use grant money to pay the secretary's salary, you've supplanted grant funds. If you're unsure about how to allocate expenses to your grant, ask your program manager about training opportunities offered by the federal agency.

Receiving the Report of Audit Findings

When the auditor is finished with the grant audit, they issue a grant audit report, which tells your organization the results of the audit. The audit report is the final stage of the audit process, and it communicates audit findings. Audit findings are what the auditor discovers after careful evaluation and comparison of your grant activities to the rules, standards, and circulars. When you get your audit findings depends on how long it takes the auditor to prepare it. As with all things government related, it can take a while.

Auditors are required to report any large, unusual questionable costs for known or likely noncompliance issues. The report includes the method used to calculate the questionable costs and the facts supporting the identified deficiency. Government threshold and tolerance for audit findings are stringent. If the program officer discovers anything that indicates you haven't handled the grant money according to the guidelines, you'll be made to pay back the funds.

The following sections give you the lowdown on how audit findings are classified and how to take corrective action to ensure your nonprofit gets back on your program manager and program officer's good side.

Classifying the audit finding

Anytime something is wrong in a court of law, juries, judges, and prosecutors consider the intent behind the misconduct. This is true with audit findings as well. If your auditor finds something wrong with your federal grant records, they'll specify how the mistake came to be, using one of the following terms:

>> **Error:** This is when you unintentionally fail to comply with laws, regulations, or terms and conditions of a grant agreement, or you unintentionally omit amounts or disclosures in financial statements.

>> **Irregularity:** An irregularity is an intentional misstatement or omission on a financial statement.

>> **Illegal act:** This is an outright violation of laws or regulations. Whether an act is illegal may have to await a final decision by a court of law.

>> **Improper conduct:** An agency employee, contractor, supplier, or recipient is said to have exhibited improper conduct when they perform their duties in a manner that contributes to the abuse or waste of grant money, but that isn't a criminal violation.

>> **Abuse:** Abuse is defined as conducting a government program in a manner that doesn't meet the public's expectations for prudent behavior, but that doesn't violate any law, regulation, agreement, or contract.

>> **Fraud:** You've committed fraud if you're found guilty of an illegal act that involves obtaining something of value through willful misrepresentation.

>> **Waste:** This is when you overspend on items that can be purchased for less.

>> **Noncompliance:** Your agency is found to be in noncompliance when you deviate from the laws and regulations governing the administration of grant funds.

These classifications are listed in your audit report according to the dollar value of the findings.

Following the corrective action plan

After your grant program manager leaves, you'll receive a written report of problems to fix. You'll have to respond with the steps you'll take to correct problems. These steps are called your CAP.

Some common findings included on a CAP are the need to monitor subgrantees and to establish segregation of duties. As a grant recipient, you need to take the actions specified in the CAP. If you need help, contact your grant program manager for suggestions or technical support. Your program manager will ask for a report from you that explains how the corrective measures are being implemented.

REMEMBER

It's in your best interest to respond promptly to the CAP. The consequences of not responding can be detrimental to your current funding and all future funding. If you fail to follow your CAP, you're not cooperating with the terms of the grant agreement, and this makes it difficult for all parties involved.

Discussing an IRS Examination

Based on various criteria set by IRS algorithms, your nonprofit may be notified that it has been selected for an examination of either the Form 990 (see Chapter 16) or your payroll tax returns (see Chapter 15). Just as with your personal taxes, your nonprofit may be selected for an examination at random. You may also be audited if someone reports you to the IRS for questionable activity or the IRS has some indication that you're no longer operating as a nonprofit.

Notice that I call this an examination and not an audit. Examination or "being picked up for exam" is how the IRS agents refer to their Internal Revenue Code (IRC) compliance checks. The Tax Exempt and Government Entities (TE/GE) division of the IRS conducts nonprofit compliance exams. Review the TE/GE Internal Revenue Manual (IRM) information on how these examinations are conducted at www.irs.gov/irm/part1/irm_01-001-023. Depending on what IRS procedures are in place at the time, an examination of your payroll tax returns may be conducted by an employment tax (ET) agent rather than one from the TE/GE.

REMEMBER

The IRS will ask for a copy of an independent audit report to assist in their examination. However, the IRS will never require you to get an independent auditor to audit your financial statements.

The IRS always initiates a compliance examination via a letter not a phone call. If you get an exam letter from the IRS, call the accounting firm that prepared your return. Get help because you don't want to face Uncle Sam alone. Even if you're savvy enough to read the fine print and work through the red tape, I still advise you to seek professional help from a CPA or your tax return preparer.

When you're asked for substantiation, provide it to the best of your ability in a timely fashion. If you can't find something the IRS is asking for, discuss alternative methods of substantiation with your examiner. Don't fabricate or prevaricate. IRS agents with more than two years of experience have heard and seen it all and are very good at detecting when oral testimony doesn't appear logical or written testimony is made up. Newer agents will have an on-the-job instructor (OJI) shadowing them, who have years of experience allowing the same ability to sniff out falsehoods.

WARNING

During the course of the examination, if the IRS agent sees badges of fraud, they'll discuss this with a fraud expert who may recommend referral to the IRS Criminal Investigations (CI) division.

IN THIS CHAPTER

» **Creating payroll accounts for employees**

» **Calculating federal, state, and local taxes**

» **Paying quarterly payroll taxes**

» **Submitting IRS payroll requirements**

» **Reporting info about contract employees**

Chapter **15**

Accounting for Payroll and Payroll Taxes

You're the executive director or manager at a small- to medium-size nonprofit, so you may assume that because of your organization's nonprofit status, you don't have to pay any taxes. After all, your status means your organization generally owes no corporate income taxes. However, you're still responsible for withholding federal and state payroll taxes for your employees.

As an employer, you're required to remit state and federal payroll taxes on behalf of your employees and any employer portion as well. If you previously ran payroll in the for-profit sector, the good news is accounting for payroll and payroll taxes for nonprofit employees is quite similar.

It's easy to set up your organization's payroll accounting yourself. Or if you prefer, you can hire part-time help, use a payroll service, or buy prepackaged software. Regardless of the method you choose, you're responsible for accounting for payroll, taking out and matching the right amount of taxes, and submitting taxes with the required paperwork on time.

This chapter shows you how to account for your payroll taxes and all other deductions for the federal, state, and local governments. After reading this chapter, you'll know how to file the necessary paperwork, where to send forms, and when to file forms so you stay current with your paperwork — not to mention keep your nonprofit status.

REMEMBER

As an employer, you need to concern yourself with establishing and paying a fair rate of pay and submitting payroll tax payments on time. Some issues, such as minimum wage, have already been decided for you.

TIP

Go to www.irs.gov/forms-instructions to access all the forms mentioned in this chapter. You'll also find instructions there for using those forms and other helpful information.

Setting Up Payroll Accounts for Nonprofit Employees

Before you can pay federal and state payroll taxes for your employees, you need to make sure you have the proper records and documentation. To do so, establish payroll accounts for your employees by creating a file for each employee. These files can be either electronic or hard copies, depending on your preference. If you use computer software to set up your payroll, your computer walks you through this process. Only your personnel clerk, bookkeeper, accountant, supervisor, and executive director should have access to payroll files. You should keep these files under lock and key because of the private information they contain.

Federal law requires all employers to keep records of total wages and hours worked by employees, but it doesn't specify how to keep these records. A great place to keep track of hours and wages is in your employee personnel files, which you can create on an employee's first day. Set up a file for each employee with the following information:

>> Employee's name, Social Security number, home address, job title, gender, and birth date

>> Workweek hours and dates

>> Total hours worked each workday

>> Total daily or weekly regular time earnings

>> Regular hourly pay rate

» Total overtime pay for the workweek

» Deductions from wages

» Additions to wages

» Pay date and pay period

Make sure you include Form W-4, Employee's Withholding Allowance Certificate, in the paperwork you give your new employees to fill out on their first day of work. Form W-4 indicates filing status, exemptions, and any extra taxes to be taken out of an employee's salary. The purpose of Form W-4 is to tell you how much federal income tax to withhold from your employee's paycheck. For more information about the Form W-4, visit www.irs.gov/forms-pubs/about-form-w-4.

Federal law requires that every U.S. employer complete Form I-9, Employment Eligibility Verification. This form helps you verify your employee's identity and employment authorization. For more information about your I-9 filing requirements, forms, and instructions, visit www.uscis.gov/i-9-central.

TIP

Retaining employee time sheets can help you justify why you paid what to whom to assure both the government and your employees that you're adhering to federal employer–employee guidelines. The Department of Labor oversees these federal guidelines concerning employer and employee relationships. The Department of Labor enforces laws established by the Fair Labor Standards Act, which ensures that employees receive fair wages and overtime pay. The act also requires employers to allocate and pay payroll deductions in a timely manner.

Deducting the Right Amount of Taxes

When I first opened my certified public accountant (CPA) firm, one of my least favorite tasks was calculating the 941 deposit amount in time to make sure the deposit got to the bank on the depositing schedule. Back then all my clients were once-a-month depositors required to make the prior month's payroll tax deposit by the 15th of the following month. For example, the payroll tax deposit for April is made by May 15, which is still the current depositing requirement for monthly depositors.

There was always a timing issue as I had to wait until roughly the 8th of the month to pick up both the client's check stubs and the bank statement to figure the deposit, fill out the 941 deposit slip, and get it back to the client in time for them to make the payroll tax deposit at their bank by close of business on the 15th.

One thing the IRS did to make payroll departments and my payroll accounting life easier was overhaul the depositing method. Eliminating the mad dashes to the bank, the IRS now requires the use of the Electronic Federal Tax Payment System (EFTPS) to make payroll tax deposits. You find out how to do this in the "Accessing the EFTPS to make tax deposits" section later in this chapter.

Of course, an important part of the equation is knowing how much of your employee's gross wages should be withheld and what additional amount you should deposit. The actual journey from gross to net payroll is a simple mathematical calculation. It requires you to understand how to figure gross payroll, know what your obligations are to deduct and match Federal Insurance Contributions Act (FICA) tax and correctly reduce gross payroll by any other employee-requested deductions.

Your first step is understanding federal and state withholding tax. Don't worry. You don't have to be a math whiz to do so. The IRS and state governments offer you tax tables to tell you how much to deduct for federal and state taxes. The following two sections walks you through the employee and employer side of the Form W-4 used to calculate federal withholding tax.

Receiving Form W-4 from the employee

You calculate the amount of federal income tax to withhold from each employee based on a federal income tax table, which considers the information your employees put on the Employee's Withholding Certificate Form W-4 they fill out on their first day of work. This information includes how many dependents they want to claim, what their filing status is (single/married filing separately, married/qualifying surviving spouse, head of household), and if they want extra money taken out of their paychecks.

Form W-4 has four steps (Steps 2 through 4 are filled out if applicable):

1. **Enter personal information.**
2. **Note multiple jobs or working spouse.**
3. **Claim exemptions or other credits.**
4. **List other adjustments.**

It is not your responsibility to monitor what filing status your employee checks off because the selection is only the employee's anticipated filing status. For example, a married person can opt to have deductions taken out at the higher single rate.

The employee's goal is to have the correct amount of federal withholding tax deducted from their gross wages each pay period. That's why the employee can also opt to have an additional amount deducted from their gross pay over and above that from the tables. Additionally, employees meeting the criteria to be exempt from withholding can write "Exempt" at the bottom of the form to have no federal withholding deduction.

REMEMBER

Existing employees do not have to submit a new Form W-4 each year if their withholding requirement or tax circumstances are the same as the prior year. New employees must fill out and return Form W-4. If they do not, employers must withhold using the default rule, which is single filing status with no other adjustments.

The current Form W-4 has instructions attached guiding your employee how to correctly fill out the form (see www.irs.gov/pub/irs-pdf/fw4.pdf). For more information, you can also direct your employee to the following video: www.tax.gov/Individual/Resources/UnderstandingTheNewFormW-4. There is also an online tax-withholding estimator your employees may find helpful at www.irs.gov/individuals/tax-withholding-estimator.

TECHNICAL STUFF

If it has been a few years since you ran payroll, you'll notice the Form W-4 dramatically changed in 2021. I find it not as employer user-friendly as the Form W-4 that was in use for decades. Not to worry, I walk you through using the updated Form W-4 in the "Using Form W-4 as the employer" section of this chapter.

Using Form W-4 as the employer

After receiving the Form W-4 from your employee, you may be wondering, "Okay, what's next? How do I use the information on the form?" Well, if you're figuring payroll manually or using an automated payroll system, your next step is to IRS Publication 15-T, *Federal Income Tax Withholding Methods*. Outside the scope of this chapter, there is a bunch of information in this publication that may or may not be applicable to your nonprofit, such as paying nonresident aliens or foreign estates. Consult with your accountant or CPA if you have questions about the publication or special circumstances that you don't know how to handle.

At present, this publication is just under 70 pages long. I recommend you download a PDF version of the publication by going to www.irs.gov/pub/irs-pdf/p15t.pdf. The download has hot links so you can easily jump to relevant sections.

For this chapter, let's assume you're using a manual payroll system (don't worry, I discuss automated payroll systems in Chapter 9), and you have a Form W-4 from 2020 or later. Click the hot link for Section 4 or just scroll through the pages until you get to Section 4. This brings you to Worksheet 4, the Percentage Method Tables, Step 1 through Step 4, which I briefly walk through below:

>> **Step 1: Enter and adjust the employee's wage amount for the current pay period.** Figure 15-1 show the adjusted wage amount if the employee's weekly wages are $1,000 and the employee enters $200 on Form W-4 Step 4(a).

>> **Step 2: Figure the tentative withholding amount.** The employee selects the Single/Married Filing Separately option and doesn't check any boxes in Step 2 of Form W-4. Keep in mind that Publication 15-T Section 4 lists the withholding rate schedules after Worksheet 4. Figure 15-2 shows the tentative withholding amount calculation.

>> **Step 3: Account for tax credits.** On Form W-4, the employee claims two qualifying children dependents at $2,000 each for a total for $4,000. Figure 15-3 shows the tax credit calculation.

>> **Step 4: Figure the final amount to withhold.** In addition to being paid by your nonprofit, the employee also has a part-time side gig and requests an additional $100 deduction on Form W-4 Step 4(c) to cover that income as well. The amount to withhold from this employee's wages this period is $107.38 ($7.38 + $100).

1a	Employee's total taxable wages this pay period	1,000.00
1b	Number of pay periods in the year	52
1c	Amount from employee's Form W-4 Step 4(a)	200.00
1d	Divide 1c by 1b	3.85
1e	Add 1a and 1d	1,003.85
1f	Amount from employee's Form W-4 Step 4(b)	0.00
1g	Divide 1f by 1b	0.00
1h	Adjusted Wage Amount	1,003.85

FIGURE 15-1: Percentage method Step 1.

2a	Standard withholding rate from the single rate table, weekly pay period	478.00
2b	Column C amount	21.20
2c	Column D percentage	12%
2d	Subtract 2a from 1h ($1,003.85- $478)	525.85
2e	Multiply 2d by 2c	63.10
2f	Add 2b + 2e for Tentative Withholding Amount	84.30

FIGURE 15-2: Percentage method Step 2.

FIGURE 15-3:
Percentage
method Step 3.

3a	Form W-4 Step 3 amount	4,000.00
3b	3a divided by 52 (weekly payroll)	76.92
3c	Subtract 3b from 2f (84.30 - 76.92)	7.38

REMEMBER

Don't forget to get the current Publication 15-T at the beginning of each year so you have the current tax tables for the year you're calculating payroll. The laws change constantly, so the tables that you used last year aren't valid this year. This section discusses federal withholding tax only. Contact your state department of revenue for state information.

Deducting FICA

In addition to withholding tax, you have the obligation to deduct and match FICA tax. The FICA tax rate is broken up between Social Security and Medicare and can fluctuate year to year based on updated legislation.

As of the publication date of this book, the FICA tax rate is 15.3 percent in total, with half deducted from your employee's gross wages and half paid by your non-profit. There are exceptions to this general rule, which I discuss later in this chapter in the "Calculating Specific FICA Payroll Taxes and Deductions" section.

When figuring out how much to deduct and pay in federal payroll taxes for each employee, gross wages is your starting point and an important factor to consider. However, it's not the only one. The next section highlights the areas you need to consider when determining how much to pay in federal payroll taxes.

Considering salaries and wages

Payroll is the process of paying employees for services performed. It includes not only salaries, wages, and commissions but employee benefits as well. One major employee benefit is the portion of health insurance paid by the employer.

Before you figure the salaries and wages part of the payroll process, you need to know the IRS's two main classifications of employees. These classifications may significantly affect your employee's gross payroll amount.

Governed by the Fair Labor Standards Act, the two types of employees are as follows:

>> **Exempt:** These employees are paid a set salary and generally don't qualify for overtime pay.

>> **Nonexempt:** These employees are paid an hourly rate and do qualify for overtime pay.

You can find out more about the Fair Labor Standards Act and make sure you're in compliance at www.dol.gov/agencies/whd/flsa.

REMEMBER

According to federal law, nonexempt workers are entitled to a minimum wage of at least $7.25 per hour. Many states also have minimum wage laws. If an employee is subject to both the state and federal minimum wage laws, the employee is entitled to the higher of the two minimum wages.

Adding in overtime and cash advances

When calculating how much tax to deduct from your employees' paychecks, you need to consider two important areas other than salary: overtime and cash advances. *Overtime* is the amount of time an employee (generally nonexempt) works beyond normal working hours. According to federal law, employers must pay workers overtime pay at a rate of at least one and a half times their regular pay rate when the workers work more than 40 hours in a given workweek.

AN AUTOMATIC WAY TO GIVE AND RECEIVE

Some donors give organizations contributions via authorized payroll deductions, which are deductions right from their paychecks. They're like money in your bank account because you receive the money in a systematic way around the same time after each pay period. Donors choose which paychecks you receive donations from. For example, some donors allow you to take deductions out of their second checks if they're paid twice a month.

Larger nonprofits have been using authorized payroll deductions for years. For example, United Way takes authorized payroll deductions right out of its donors' payroll checks. Doing so works well for both the people giving and the organization receiving because it spreads the donations out over longer periods of time for the donors, and gives the recipient — United Way, in this example — a solid projection of expected revenues.

For example, if an employee works 48 hours in a workweek and is paid $15 per hour, the employee is entitled to $22.50 per hour for each hour of overtime ($15 × 1.5). The employee's regular pay for 40 hours is $600. For eight hours of overtime, the pay rate is $22.50 × 8, which equals $180. This employee is entitled to $600 plus $180 for a total of $780.

TIP

For questions about overtime pay, call the Wage and Hour Division of the Department of Labor at 866-487-9243.

Your nonprofit may periodically allow an employee's request for a cash advance. *Cash advances* are loans that the employer gives to an employee that will be repaid from the employee's future pay. Giving cash advances to your nonprofit employees is a subject for board discussion and approval.

If you do decide to give cash advances, don't confuse advances and wages. Advances aren't taxed; they're loans. The employee's wages are taxed. The employer withholds the amount advanced to an employee from the employee's gross pay as repayment of the advance. Before you decide to give cash advances, be sure to check with your board of directors and CPA.

FRINGE BENEFITS AND THE IRS

The IRS doesn't concern itself with regulating what fringe benefits employers provide to employees. You're generally not obligated to provide fringe benefits to your employees under federal law. However, check with your CPA, because you may need to familiarize yourself with state laws that do affect these benefits.

Common fringe benefits include the following:

- Paid sick and vacation leave

- Holiday pay

- Providing on-site day-care services

- Health insurance

- Company cars and employee personal use of a company car

- Retirement plans

- Immediate payment of final wages to terminated employees instead of waiting for the normal payroll cycle

(continued)

(continued)

The IRS's only concern is that you properly remit any taxes due on the fringe benefits. For example, employee personal use of a company car is usually added to the employee's gross wages and subject to payroll tax. Paid sick, vacation, and holiday pay are included in the employee's gross wages in the applicable payroll cycle and subject to tax the same as regular wages. This is a good topic to discuss with your CPA when setting up your nonprofit.

Calculating Specific FICA Payroll Taxes and Deductions

Earlier in this chapter in the "Deducting the Right Amount of Taxes" section, I walk you through an example of figuring federal withholding tax using the employee's Form W-4. Your second step in the journey from gross to net payroll is figuring the FICA tax deduction.

FICA is a federal payroll tax that both employees and employers have to pay. The funds collected from FICA are used to fund Social Security and Medicare retirement benefits and to provide for disabled workers and children/qualifying spouses of deceased workers.

The FICA rate was 15.3 percent for many years, but in recent years it has fluctuated. As of this writing, it's back to 15.3 percent. This is important information you should check at the beginning of each year in Circular E, which is also known as Publication 15 and is found at www.irs.gov/publications/p15.

Of that 15.3 percent, you withhold 7.65 percent of employee's gross wage (subject to threshold limits) for FICA. As the employer, you must match this by paying the same 7.65 percent.

Now what about that threshold limit I mention earlier? To understand the threshold limit, you also have to understand how the 15.3 percent is allocated. Of the 15.3 percent, 12.4 percent (6.2 percent each for the employee and employer) funds Social Security, with the remaining 2.9 percent (1.45 percent each for the employee and employer) funding Medicare.

As of this writing, the Social Security threshold is $160,200. That means that when your employee is paid $160,200 or above in the calendar year, you no longer deduct or match the 6.2 percent. Medicare has no threshold. Both you and the employee are responsible for the 1.45 percent regardless of how much the employee makes.

Running through a basic payroll FICA tax calculation, let's say you have an employee who grosses $500 during the pay period and their total year to date is under the $160,200 threshold. You — as the employer — have to pay $38.25 (7.65 percent × $500) for FICA taxes. Your employee has the same $38.25 withheld from their gross wages.

The Social Security Administration (SSA) through the IRS calculates FICA taxes at the same rate on regular pay, overtime pay, and bonus pay. When you have to remit payroll taxes to the IRS depends on the amount of payroll taxes your nonprofit collects — that is, how much money you're obligated to remit to the IRS in the form of payroll taxes in a given week, month, or quarter.

The current guidelines for when to remit payroll taxes to the IRS are found in Section 11 of Publication 15. Smaller nonprofits normally deposit on a monthly schedule. Medium and larger nonprofits should add when to deposit payroll taxes to the list of questions they have for their accountants.

On a monthly schedule you must remit payroll taxes by the 15th of the following month. So, if your payroll tax liability on August 31 is $1,500, the $1,500 must be remitted to the IRS by September 15.

See the following section, "Paying Quarterly Payroll Taxes with Form 941 and Electronic Funds Transfer," for more information about making payroll tax deposits for FICA and federal withholding tax.

Members of religious groups who meet certain criteria can apply to be exempt from participating in the Social Security program. If you're employed by a group granted exemption and you're paid more than $100 per year, you're considered self-employed. This means you pay your own FICA tax at the 15.3 percent rate. This is done via Schedule SE, which you file with your Form 1040. If you're new to the self-employment/Schedule SE game, talk about this with a tax specialist to get the correct information about your depositing and filing requirements.

REMEMBER

Here's some good news regarding paying taxes on federal unemployment benefits under the Federal Unemployment Tax Act (FUTA): You don't pay FUTA tax if your organization holds an IRC Section 501(c)(3) exemption status under IRC Section 501. To verify your exemption, take a look at your letter of determination from the IRS to find out how the IRS classified your nonprofit status and under which code it established your nonprofit status.

Paying Quarterly Payroll Taxes with Form 941 and Electronic Funds Transfer

Quarterly payroll taxes are taxes that your nonprofit owes to the IRS for that which you have withheld from your employee's gross pay and your matching portion of FICA. As an employer, you're responsible for matching the employee's FICA, which is generally 7.65 percent of gross wages (don't forget about the Social Security threshold I mention earlier in this chapter).

The employee portion of the payroll taxes is called the *trust-fund portion*. The trust-fund portion is not an expense to your nonprofit. You're merely safeguarding the trust-fund portion until it's time to make your payroll tax deposit.

WARNING

It's very important to make your payments to the federal government on time. The IRS takes this very seriously. There is nothing more certain to lead to hefty IRS late payment penalties than failing to deposit your payroll taxes in a timely manner.

There is a whole section later in this chapter walking you through how to make your payroll tax deposits electronically. For now, let's discuss the payroll tax form you must file quarterly.

You file Form 941, Employer's Quarterly Federal Tax Return, to report your quarterly wages and payroll taxes to the IRS. Total taxes on Form 941 should generally reconcile to your electronic tax deposits. See the "Accessing the EFTPS to make tax deposits" section later in this chapter for more information about electronic funds transfers.

Form 941 includes the following information:

>> Wages you've paid

>> Tips your employees received

- » Federal income taxes you've withheld

- » Employer's and employee's shares of Social Security and Medicare taxes

- » Advance earned income tax credit (EITC) payments

- » Adjustments for prior quarterly payroll taxes

WARNING

We can't stress enough how important paying these quarterly taxes is. If you fall behind, catching up can be extremely difficult. If you do fall behind on payroll taxes, talk with your tax accountant about what steps to take. You may want to go to your local bank and borrow the money. The penalties and interest on IRS outstanding debts is quite possibly higher than any credit card on the market.

The following sections walk you through Form 941 and electronic funds transfer. You'll also find out how to file the forms and where to send them and your payment.

TIP

Create a file with copies of all the forms, checks, and everything else you send to the IRS. Sometimes the IRS makes mistakes. Plus, you need to keep up with what you've paid.

Completing Form 941

As an employer, you withhold federal taxes from your employees for the federal government. Form 941 is your explanation to the IRS of how much you've deducted from your employees' paychecks and held for the federal government in federal income taxes, Social Security, and Medicare taxes.

According to the IRS, preparing, copying, assembling, and sending Form 941 takes just two hours of your time every three months. If using automated accounting software, the program will prepare Form 941 for you. Although accounting software greatly reduces the time needed to process the form, you should always check an automated form for accuracy — especially the deposit amounts.

TIP

To save time when preparing the form manually, you can save a copy of the online form on your computer so each quarter you need to fill in only the information that has changed since the prior quarter.

Over the years this form has morphed from a simple two-page form to the current six-page version — some of which is reserved for future use. As some of the six pages will not be applicable to your nonprofit, the following discusses the commonly filled-out portions, starting with page one of six:

1. **Fill in the top portion of the form.**

   Fill in your employer identification number (EIN), the name of your organization, your business address, and the reporting quarter.

2. **Complete Part 1, Page 1.**

Part 1 is the meat of the form. Answer the questions about how many employees you have, how much they've earned, how much federal income tax you've withheld, taxable Social Security and Medicare, and tax due. If working through this part by yourself is difficult, consider contracting out your payroll services to a bookkeeper, accountant, or payroll service.

3. **Complete Part 1, Page 2.**

Page 2 determines your tax liability for the quarter, asks for the deposited amount, and calculates if there is a balance due, if there is an overpayment, or if total tax due is the same as deposits.

4. **Complete Part 2.**

Line 16 spells out if you have to list your tax liability for each of the three months in the quarter. If so, using this info, the IRS determines if you made timely deposits each month and will send you a penalty/interest statement if you didn't deposit on time. If you need help, you may want to hire an accountant.

5. **Complete Part 3.**

Part 3 asks specific questions about your business, which you leave blank if not applicable.

6. **Complete Part 4.**

Part 4 asks whether you authorize someone else to discuss your 941 taxes with the IRS. If you have a payroll service or outside accountant prepare the form, I recommend giving authorization to the preparer.

7. **Complete Part 5.**

Provide your signature, printed name, date, and daytime phone number. If you hired an accountant to prepare the form for the nonprofit, have them supply this information as well.

8. **If you have a balance due, detach and fill out Form 941-V.**

Prepare a check for the balance due. Include Form 941-V and payment when you mail Form 941.

Filing Form 941

After you complete Form 941, you need to file it with the IRS, and if you haven't made tax deposits or you still have a balance due, you need to make a tax payment with the 941. Because Form 941 is only a report, you need to submit a payment voucher — Form 941-V — if you're submitting a payment with your quarterly report.

If you're a new nonprofit with no previous tax payment history, you're generally required to deposit monthly via the EFTPS. Monthly deposits are due by the 15th of the following month. For example, you have to deposit taxes from paydays taking place during December by January 15. After you've established a payment history, the IRS can project what your future payments are likely to be. Based on this projection, the IRS will notify the nonprofit if there is a change in depositing frequency. Larger nonprofits may have to deposit more frequently on a weekly or semiweekly schedule.

If your nonprofit owes less than $2,500 in payroll taxes, you may be able to pay the payroll taxes quarterly with a timely filed Form 941, enclosing your check and payment voucher 941-V. To make sure your nonprofit meets that criterion, read the instructions on Form 941, page 5, and discuss any questions about this with your accountant.

TIP

You may be able to bypass the quarterly Form 941 and report yearly using Form 944, Employer's Annual Federal Tax Return. You can do this only if the IRS notifies you in writing that it's okay to do so. Go to www.irs.gov/newsroom/employ ers-should-you-file-form-944-or-941 for more information about switching from Form 941 to Form 944.

Refer to Table 15-1 to find out when your quarterly Form 941 is due.

TABLE 15-1   ## Due Dates for Quarterly Filing of Form 941

For the Quarter	Quarter Ends	Form 941 Due Date
January, February, March	March 31	April 30
April, May, June	June 30	July 31
July, August, September	September 30	October 31
October, November, December	December 31	January 31

WARNING

Don't wait to send a payment with Form 941 unless you're certain you qualify for the quarterly payment schedule. If you owe more than $2,500 and wait to pay it when you file your Form 941 at the end of the quarterly reporting period, you'll have made a late payment and you may have to pay a penalty.

TIP

If your nonprofit has a *fiscal year-end* (the last day of any month other than December) you still report payroll via Form 941 on a calendar-year basis. That follows through to the W-2s, which still have to be issued reflecting payroll transactions for January through December by January 31 of the following year.

When paying your payroll taxes with Form 941, write a check or money order payable to the United States Treasury. Where you send your payment and Form 941 depends on where you live and if you're mailing the form with or without a payment. Go to www.irs.gov/filing/where-to-file-your-taxes-for-form-941 to find the mailing address.

Accessing the EFTPS to make tax deposits

The IRS has made paying your payroll taxes a fairly easy task through the EFTPS. The EFTPS is free, easy to sign up for, and after you get started, it's a breeze to make your payroll tax deposit. Plus, you can use the EFTPS to deposit any federal taxes — not just payroll.

To get started with the EFTPS, have your EIN and banking information available. Go to www.eftps.gov and select Enrollment from the menu at the top of the page. If your nonprofit is less than a year old, you were automatically pre-enrolled in the EFTPS when you applied for your EIN and should've already received a pre-enrollment PIN in the mail. Find your pre-enrollment PIN and call 800-555-3453 to activate your enrollment.

If you remember receiving a pre-enrollment PIN but can't find it, call 888-434-7338 to have it given to you over the phone. If you didn't receive a pre-enrollment PIN or you want to create a new EFTPS enrollment, just follow the enrollment steps on the screens. After submitting your information, you receive a PIN in the mail in about a week.

After receipt of your PIN, go back into the EFTPS website, select Log In on the menu at the top of the page, fill in the fields, and click Need a Password. Follow the instructions to create your new internet password, and you'll be all set to make your payroll tax deposit at the Payments menu option.

If you don't want to use the EFTPS, ask your bank if it's possible to make your deposits using ACH Credit or same-day wire payments. Another option is using the EFTPS voice response system at 800-555-3453 to make payments.

TIP

After years of making payments using the EFTPS for myself and clients, I can't think of a reason not to use it. Many times I've been traveling out of my local area and, mid-trip, remembered I need to make a federal deposit, either personally or for my business. Five minutes on my laptop on the road and done. You can schedule payments in advance as well.

Completing End-of-Year Forms

At the end of the year, you'll need to fill out Forms W-2 and W-3 to report your employee's payroll information to the SSA. The IRS and SSA talk to each other. If you file Form 941 with the IRS and either didn't submit your W-3/W-2s to the SSA or the forms were never received by SSA, you'll eventually get a letter from the SSA asking you to send copies.

It's extremely important that employee wages are correctly reported to the SSA. Retirement and social benefits hinge on the number of credits the employee earns by employment and the associated salary history. And, of course, on the flip side, if you file W-2s with the SSA but haven't correctly submitted your Form 941s and paid the tax in full, you'll be getting a letter from the IRS with a follow-up contact from IRS collections.

The following section gives you an overview of these two forms and what you have to do with each one.

Filling out the W-2

Form W-2 is the Wage and Tax Statement for a given calendar year. Employees usually receive three copies. The employee files one copy with their federal return (Copy B) and one copy with their state return (Copy 2). The employee keeps the third copy (Copy C) in their personal records. Form W-2 summarizes all wages and tax deductions for a given year.

You find the following information on a W-2:

>> Employer's federal identification number

>> Employer's name, address, and zip code

>> Employee's Social Security number

>> Employee's name, address, and zip code

>> Taxable wages, tips, and other compensation

>> Federal income tax withheld

>> Social Security wages and tips

>> Social Security tax withheld

>> Medicare wages and tips

>> Medicare tax withheld

>> State of employment

>> Employer's state identification number

>> State wages, tips, and other compensation

>> State income tax withheld

Form W-2 consists of the following copies:

>> **Copy A:** Sent by the employer to the SSA.

>> **Copy 1:** Sent by the employer to the state, city, or local tax department if required.

>> **Copy B:** Filed by the employee with the employee's federal tax return.

>> **Copy C:** Kept by the employee in the employee's records.

>> **Copy 2:** Filed by the employee with the employee's state, city, or local income taxes.

>> **Copy D:** Kept by the employer in the employer's records.

As an employer, you need to fill out a W-2 for each employee. After you've completed all your W-2s, you need to fill out a Form W-3, too. See the next section for more about Form W-3.

Filling out the W-3

Form W-3 is the Transmittal of Wage and Tax Statements, which the employer has to submit to the SSA. The Wage and Tax Statements are your W-2s; the W-3 transmits them. Your W-3 totals and reports the amounts for all the W-2s it transmits, so both the W-3 and W-2s are filed with the SSA.

REMEMBER

Form W-3 provides a complete summary of all W-2s attached. Do not cut, fold, or staple forms in the W-3/W-2 package.

WARNING

The SSA is very picky about the physical state of Forms W-3 and W-2 when they arrive via the mail. It only accepts the original red/white form. So, if you download and try to submit the online version, you may be charged a $50 penalty if they can't scan your form.

Knowing where to send the W-2s and W-3s

After you complete these two forms, be sure to send Copy A (red/white) of all Form W-2s along with the red/white Form W-3 by regular mail to the SSA by the due date (the last day of January of the following year) to the following address:

Social Security Administration
Data Operations Center
Wilkes-Barre, PA 18769-0001

You can also file these forms electronically at the SSA's Employer W-2 Filing Instructions and Information web page at www.ssa.gov/employer. You can also create versions of W-2/W-3 at this web page that can be filed with the SSA and printed for your employees and your records.

For any tax year, you have to file Copy A of Form W-2 and Form W-3 with the SSA by January 31 for the previous year. The due dates may change from year to year by a day or two, allowing for weekends and holidays. The correct due date for each year is printed on Form W-3.

REMEMBER

Be sure to distribute the W-2s to your employees. You may also have to mail forms to your state tax department.

TIP

Keeping up with your paperwork is important because the IRS matches the amounts reported on your quarterly payroll taxes (Form 941) with the W-2 amounts totaled on Form W-3. If you do make a mistake when figuring your taxes, you can amend your forms and make corrections by using Form 941-X. For more information about making corrections on Form 941-X, go to www.irs.gov/forms-pubs/about-form-941-x.

To find out more about ordering official IRS Form W-2 and Form W-3, go to the IRS Online Ordering For Information Returns and Employer Returns at www.irs.gov/businesses/online-ordering-for-information-returns-and-employer-returns. If you have no questions about the process, you can go directly to ordering at https://apps.irs.gov/app/taxmat/information-employer-returns.

Accounting for Contract Employees Using Form 1099-NEC

To finish this chapter, I want to briefly discuss those individuals who may do work for your nonprofit but aren't treated like an employee receiving a W-2 at the end of the year. I'm not going into all the hoopla of worker classification as either an independent contractor or employee. Worker classification between the two is outside the scope of this chapter and is a topic for discussion with your CPA.

TIP

You can find out more about worker classification by going to the U.S. Department of Labor website at www.dol.gov/newsroom/releases/whd/whd20210106 or the IRS website at www.irs.gov/businesses/small-businesses-self-employed/independent-contractor-self-employed-or-employee.

I want to make you aware of your reporting obligation for any workers you've correctly classified as independent contractors. The reporting is quite easy — at year-end, you issue a Form 1099-NEC (Nonemployee Compensation) to any individual paid at least $600 during the calendar year for services rendered.

Form 1099-NEC asks for the payer and recipient's information, such as name, address, and tax identification number (TIN). Enter the amount paid to the individual in Box 1. In the unlikely event federal withholding tax was deducted from payments to the independent contractor, enter that amount in Box 4. Fill in Boxes 5 through 7 for any state reporting.

Issue Copy B of the form to the recipient by January 31 of the year following payment. Attach any 1099-NECs you issue to transmittal Form 1096, which is filled out in a manner similar to the W-3. Mail that package to the IRS by January 31 as well. For more information about Forms 1099-NEC and 1096 go to www.irs.gov/instructions/i1099mec.

Chapter **16**

Doing the Accounting for Tax Form 990

Your nonprofit organization is tax-exempt, so you're probably wondering why I've included a chapter on filing a tax report. You may be surprised to find out that even though you generally don't have to pay federal income taxes, your organization *does* have to file a return. Internal Revenue Service (IRS) Form 990, Return of Organization Exempt from Income Tax, is an annual information return that most tax-exempt organizations must file. Although this is a topic most people may prefer to ignore, failure to accurately complete this form leads to repercussions none of us wants. The information a tax-exempt organization provides on this form serves as the primary source of information for the public about that particular organization. Therefore, the information you provide on this form becomes the basis for how the public and the government perceive your organization.

Which version of this form your organization needs to complete depends on your organization's gross receipts and total assets. Before getting too worried about this form, read this chapter to find out the steps you need to follow to prepare your information form for the IRS. Wouldn't it be great if you could spend all your time running the programs that benefit our communities? But there's a time for everything. And right now, it's tax time!

REMEMBER

Be prepared for that first phone call or email from a concerned citizen requesting your Form 990. Your Form 990 is considered public record and must be made available to the public upon request. You have to give your Form 990 to whoever requests it with only a minimal charge (equal to the cost of copying the form). To save paper and time, you can post your Form 990 on your website. When someone requests a copy, you can simply tell that person how to locate the form on your website.

TIP

Go to www.irs.gov/forms-instructions to access all the forms mentioned in this chapter. You'll also find instructions for using those forms and other helpful information.

Choosing the Right Tax Form

Your gross receipts and total assets from grants, donations, contracts, and other sources determine which version of Form 990 your organization must file with the IRS. Your organization may be exempt from income tax, but you have to file one of the following three forms:

>> **Form 990-N:** Form 990-N, e-Postcard, is for small nonprofits.

>> **Form 990-EZ:** Form 990-EZ, Short Form Return of Organization Exempt from Income Tax, is for medium-size nonprofits.

>> **Form 990:** Form 990, Return of Organization Exempt from Income Tax, is for large nonprofits.

TIP

The thresholds and limits that determine which version of Form 990 your organization files are subject to change, so make sure you check the IRS's website (www.irs.gov/charities-non-profits/annual-filing-and-forms) for the most up-to-date information.

See Table 16-1 for tax thresholds and limits in place for the last few years through to the publication date of this book.

TABLE 16-1   Tax Thresholds for Form 990

Form to File	Gross Receipts Threshold	Total Assets Limit
990-N (e-Postcard)	Normally less than or equal to $50,000	Total assets information is not a criterion for using this form
990-EZ	More than $50,000 but less than $200,000	Less than $500,000
990	$200,000 or greater	$500,000 or greater

TIP

Total assets is not relevant for Form 990-N (e-Postcard) because it is not one of the eight items for which you fill in information.

Knowing What Happens If You Don't File in a Timely Manner

If you don't file your personal income taxes, you know Uncle Sam gets upset. The same is true for your organization. Although your nonprofit isn't generally required to pay federal taxes, you still need to file Form 990. If you don't file, you put yourself and your organization on Uncle Sam's bad side. Make sure you file Form 990 to avoid any repercussions and dire consequences for your nonprofit.

WARNING

If your nonprofit is filing a Form 990 for a tax year beginning after July 1, 2019, or later, you probably have to file electronically. See the "Submitting Form 990" section later in this chapter. This is nothing new for Form 990-N — it has always been submitted electronically.

What happens when you don't file Form 990 or you send in an incomplete form? You pay the following penalties:

>> **If you file a return late:** Unless you can show that the late filing was the result of a reasonable cause, the IRS charges smaller organizations a penalty of $20 a day, not to exceed the lesser of $10,500 or 5 percent of the gross receipts of the organization for the year. Organizations with annual gross receipts exceeding $1,094,500 are subject to a penalty of $105 for each day they fail to file (with a maximum penalty of $54,500 for any one return). The penalty begins on the due date. Additionally, the organization can lose its exempt status.

>> **If you don't file a complete return or don't furnish correct information:** The IRS sends your organization a letter that includes a fixed time period during which you can resubmit the form. After that period expires, the IRS charges the person who fails to comply a penalty of $10 a day, with a maximum penalty of $5,000 for any one return.

REMEMBER

You only have to provide information about your nonprofit; you generally don't have to include a check with this return.

TIP

The IRS has free StayExempt training courses and other very helpful information to assist with nonprofit tax compliance at www.irs.gov/charities-non-profits/annual-electronic-filing-requirement-for-small-exempt-organizations-form-990-n-e-postcard.

Understanding the Minimal Requirements Using Form 990-N

The IRS created Form 990-N specifically for small, tax-exempt nonprofit organizations that gross less than $50,000 a year. Refer to Table 8-1 in the section "Choosing the Right Tax Form," earlier in this chapter, for more information on the gross receipts you need to use this form. Form 990-N is an electronic notice and quite easy to complete, which is why it's also called the e-Postcard. You need to file this form every year by the 15th day of the fifth month after the end of an exempt organization's tax year. For a calendar year, the deadline is May 15.

For many years, the IRS didn't require small nonprofits that made less than $25,000 a year to submit any paperwork, but things have changed. Don't fret, though. Filling out Form 990-N is quick and simple. Here's what you must provide:

>> Your organization's employer identification number (EIN)

>> Your organization's legal name and mailing address

- Any other names your organization uses

- Your organization's website address (if applicable)

- The name and address of a principal officer of your organization (usually the executive director)

- Your organization's annual tax period

- A confirmation that your organization's annual gross receipts are $50,000 or less

If applicable, indicate whether your organization is going out of business. The IRS needs to know if your nonprofit is no longer operating, because it regulates nonprofits.

The IRS requires that Form 990-N be filed electronically. No paper form is available. To file Form 990-N, you must have access to the internet, but you don't have to download any software. To get into the Form 990-N Electronic Filing System, you create an ID.me account or sign in with an existing ID.me account.

TIP

Having an ID.me account is handy beyond filing Form 990-N. You can use ID.me to go into the IRS system to pull up filing and refund information and transcripts. Transcripts can be especially useful to see what happened with your return. You'll see the date the return was received by the IRS and any subsequent changes or adjustments to your filing.

To create a new ID.me account, go to https://api.id.me/en/registration/new and follow the prompts, which include providing an email address and password. In addition, you'll be guided through an authentication process. I was able to complete the procedure in less than 20 minutes. To avoid getting error messages, use a computer rather than a smartphone or tablet to create your account.

After you have your ID.me account and your tax year is over, you can file electronically by following these steps (keep in mind that you have to wait until the day after the end of your calendar/fiscal year to file — if you use a calendar year, you can start filing on January 1 and must file by May 15):

1. Go to www.irs.gov/charities-non-profits/annual-electronic-filing-requirement-for-small-exempt-organizations-form-990-n-e-postcard and click the Submit Form 990-N (e-Postcard) button.

2. Click Sign in with ID.me.

3. Enter your ID.me email address and password and click Sign In.

    After you sign in, the screen to electronically file your Form 990-N appears.

4. **Create your e-Postcard Profile by clicking Manage E-Postcard Profile.**

   The purpose of this option is to identify yourself as the organization or preparer. A preparer will be able to file the form for more than one organization. A good example of this is a CPA with many nonprofit clients.

5. **If you're filing the form only for your organization, select Exempt Organization, enter your EIN, and follow the remaining prompts to complete your profile.**

6. **After creating your e-Postcard profile, select** Manage Form 990-N Submissions to work on your Form 990-N.

   You can save the in-progress form to return later to finish it, edit it, or delete it to start over again as long as you haven't submitted the form. This is also where you go to make sure your submission has been accepted.

TIP

Download the user guide at www.irs.gov/pub/irs-pdf/p5248.pdf for reference as you work your way through filing. This guide also provides troubleshooting tips and there is a customer account service help line you can call at 877-829-5500 as well.

WARNING

If you don't file Form 990-N on time, the IRS sends you a reminder notice, but the IRS won't assess a penalty for filing it late. However, an organization that fails to file the required Form 990-N (or Form 990 or 990-EZ, for that matter) for three consecutive years automatically loses its tax-exempt status. The revocation of the organization's tax-exempt status doesn't take place until the filing due date of the third year.

Qualifying to Use Form 990-EZ

Form 990-EZ, Short Form Return of Organization Exempt from Income Tax, is the annual information return that many organizations exempt from income taxes have to file with the IRS. To find out if your organization can file Form 990-EZ rather than Form 990, refer to Table 8-1 earlier in this chapter. As its name implies, Form 990-EZ is a less detailed version of Form 990.

All filing organizations must complete the top portion of the form and Parts I through V. The top portion of the form is self-explanatory with simple questions that identify you by name and EIN. Just fill in the blanks.

TIP

Go to www.irs.gov/pub/irs-pdf/f990ez.pdf to see the current Form 990-EZ. Download the PDF to your computer to be able to access question-mark icons to find out more about what you should enter in each line or section of the tax return.

Parts I through V require information about the organization's exempt and other activities, finances, compliance with certain federal tax filings and requirements, and compensation paid to certain people. These five parts, along with the information you need to include in each part, are as follows:

- >> **Part I — Revenue, Expenses, and Changes in Net Assets or Fund Balances:** This part is basically your nonprofit organization's statement of activities. Part I is logically divided into revenues, expenses, and net assets. See Chapter 17 for more information about this statement.

- >> **Part II — Balance Sheets:** This part provides your organization with a simplified version of its statement of financial position (see Chapter 18 for more information on this statement) entering in beginning and ending year balances for certain asset, liability, and net asset accounts.

   You can use the numbers from your statement of financial position to fill in some of the information in this part. Depending on your nonprofit, you may also have to complete Schedule O. Schedule O is a continuation sheet you use to enter any additional information you feel is needed for the IRS to completely understand your return.

TECHNICAL STUFF

   I often use a continuation sheet, which for Forms 1040, 1120, 1120S, or 1065 is called a supplemental schedule when submitting tax returns my firm prepares for clients. Sometimes you'll have to enter something funky on the return that, if explained via a continuation sheet or supplemental schedule, will give the IRS enough information to keep the IRS from having to issue a letter or select the return for examination to find out more.

- >> **Part III — Statement of Program Service Accomplishments:** Here you get to showcase your major accomplishments during the year. In this part, you report organizational and financial accomplishments that relate to your nonprofit's core program areas. Your responses to the questions in this part highlight your accomplishments.

- >> **Part IV — List of Officers, Directors, Trustees, and Key Employees:** In this part, you report the income for your organization's most highly compensated employees. If your organization provides no compensation, you should list the top three officers, such as president or executive director, treasurer, and secretary.

- >> **Part V — Other Information:** In this part, you answer a series of questions according to each question's specific instructions. Understanding all these questions is important because they disclose information about unrelated business income, the person who takes care of your books, and any new activities not reported in the prior year.

Only Section 501(c)(3) organizations have to complete Part VI. The questions in Part VI ask about your political activities, changes to your bylaws, unrelated business income, and other related topics. Because these questions are fairly basic, you can answer them rather easily. For example, one question asks you for a list of officers, directors, trustees, and key employees. All the questions in Part VI are straightforward.

Furthermore, you may need to complete additional schedules depending on the type of your organization and its activities. A schedule is a supplemental form with questions pertaining to a specific subject or topic that the IRS requires you to fill out, depending on your responses on other tax forms. Form 990-EZ requests information regarding specific activities on two schedules:

>> **Schedule A:** If you're a section 501(c)(3) organization (or an organization treated as such) filing Form 990-EZ, you must also complete and file Schedule A. Schedule A requests information regarding your reason for public charity status, information about your public support, and investment income.

>> **Schedule B:** As of April 2022, some states have lifted the requirement to file Schedule B. However, the IRS still requires Schedule B if you receive large gifts falling under specific guidelines. The guidelines are subject to change, so you should check the Schedule B instructions each year. At present, the guidelines cover contributions of the greater of $5,000 or more than 2 percent of revenues you receive from any one contributor.

See the "Submitting Form 990" section later in this chapter for details on what to do with the form after you complete it.

Filing with Form 990

Form 990 is the primary reporting mechanism for all organizations that are exempt from federal income tax. Every exempt organization that doesn't meet the requirements for the shorter Form 990-N or Form 990-EZ has to file Form 990 and must complete the top portion of the form and Parts I through XI. See Table 8-1 earlier in this chapter for the requirements of the three versions of Form 990.

The next sections help you understand how to complete Form 990 and how to submit it.

Walking through Form 990

Form 990 isn't an overly complex form to complete. You can find a lot of the information you need on your nonprofit's financial statements. First, you have to fill out the top portion of the form by following the directions and reporting general information about your organization, such as its name, address, and EIN.

Go to www.irs.gov/pub/irs-prior/f990--2022.pdf to view the most current copy of this form as of this writing. The specific parts of Form 990 are as follows:

>> **Part I — Summary:** This part basically asks you to summarize your organization. It requests details regarding your organization's activities and governance, revenue, expenses, and net assets.

>> **Part II — Signature Block:** This part requires your signature to verify that the information on this form is correct to the best of your knowledge.

>> **Part III — Statement of Program Service Accomplishments:** Simply put, this part is where the organization describes its accomplishments in the services it provides. It requests the amount of grant money and allocations your organization received for the services provided, along with all expenses related to the programs.

>> **Part IV — Checklist of Required Schedules:** This part determines whether you need to complete any schedules in addition to Form 990 itself.

>> **Part V — Statements Regarding Other IRS Filings and Tax Compliance:** This part alerts your organization to other potential federal tax compliance and filing obligations it has.

>> **Part VI — Governance, Management, and Disclosure:** This part contains three sections: governing body and management, policies, and disclosure. These sections pose questions concerning the organization's conflict of interest policies and monitoring system. This part also asks about the review of Form 990 by voting members of the organization's governing board.

>> **Part VII — Compensation of Officers, Directors, Trustees, Key Employees, Highest Compensated Employees, and Independent Contractors:** This part requires the organization to report the calendar-year amounts paid to compensate employees and independent contractors, taken from Form W-2 (see Chapter 15) and Form 1099.

>> **Part VIII — Statement of Revenue:** Just as its title states, this part is where you state all your organization's sources of revenue, including contributions such as grants and gifts, program service revenue, and fundraising revenue (see Chapter 17 for more information about revenue).

>> **Part IX — Statement of Functional Expenses:** This part requires you to list your organization's expenses by category. The expense categories include program service, management, and fundraising (see Chapter 20).

>> **Part X — Balance Sheet:** This part requires you to fill in the information found on your statement of financial position. Refer to your own statement to help you fill out this part (see Chapter 18).

>> **Part XI — Reconciliation of Net Assets:** This part requires you to fill in the information found on your statement of activities. Refer to your own statement to help you fill out this part (see Chapter 17 more information on the statement of activities and net assets).

>> **Part XII — Financial Statements and Reporting:** This part asks questions regarding the organization's accounting methods and financial statement reporting and preparation.

TIP

If you answer "Yes" to Form 990, Part IV, Line 1, you must complete and file Schedule A with your Form 990. The guidelines for if you need to file Schedule B with Form 990 are the same as those for Form 990-EZ and are outlined in the section "Qualifying to Use Form 990-EZ," earlier in this chapter.

Submitting Form 990

Whew! The worst is over. You've completed Form 990 and Schedule A, and Schedule B if required. Now all you have to do is turn it in on time to avoid late fees. Don't get those postage stamps out just yet! There are exceptions, but effective for tax years beginning after July 1, 2019, you must file Form 990 electronically. If you're a Form 990-EZ filer, for tax years ending July 31, 2021, and later, you must file Form 990-EZ electronically as well.

To see if your nonprofit meets the exception criteria, every year review the updated instructions for whichever Form 990 you file. For more information about your e-filing requirements, check out the IRS December 13, 2019 news release at www.irs.gov/newsroom/irs-recent-legislation-requires-tax-exempt-organizations-to-e-file-forms.

REMEMBER

Form 990-N has always been submitted electronically. Form 990 is due by the 15th day of the fifth month after your organization's taxable year ends. If you fail to turn it in on time, you generally have to pay a penalty of $20 a day which is capped at $10,000 or 5 percent of your organization's gross receipts, depending on which amount is lower. The penalty increases to $100 per day, up to a maximum of $50,000, for an organization whose gross receipts exceed $1,000,000. Be sure to review the form for any omitted information so you don't have to pay the fee for incomplete returns (a fee of $10 a day up to $5,000).

Completing Form 990-T (Reporting Unrelated Business Income)

Your nonprofit may be subject to corporate income taxes if you engage in for-profit business enterprises in which you gain unrelated business income. Unrelated business income is any income generated by a business that is *regularly* carried on and *unrelated* to the exempt function of your nonprofit.

The IRS rule states that all nonprofits that have $1,000 or more in gross receipts from an unrelated business transaction must file Form 990-T, Exempt Organization Business Income Tax Return. You have to file Form 990-T to provide the IRS the following information about your nonprofit:

>> **Unrelated business taxable income (UBTI):** If your nonprofit conducts a trade or business that produces income by selling merchandise or providing a service that isn't related to the cause or purpose of your organization, the income generated is considered unrelated business income if the trade or business activity takes place on a regular basis.

>> **Unrelated business income tax liability:** This tax liability is the amount over $500 that your nonprofit owes for unrelated business transactions. This includes all gross income less deductions directly connected with producing the income.

>> **Proxy tax liability:** This deals with notice requirements of nondeductible lobbying and political campaigning activities engaged in by certain membership associations that hold a tax-exempt status such as 501(c)4, 501(c)(5), and 501(c)(6).

TIP

You can find information about Form 990-T online at www.irs.gov/forms-pubs/about-form-990-t, instructions on how to fill out the form at www.irs.gov/instructions/i990t, and the form itself at www.irs.gov/pub/irs-pdf/f990t.pdf.

WARNING

Be careful with activities outside the scope of tax-exempt purposes. These unrelated business transactions can come back to haunt you. Engaging in excessive unrelated business transactions can change the status of your organization from a nonprofit to a for-profit, which means you lose your tax-exempt status. As long as you stay within the scope of the tax-exempt purpose of your nonprofit, though, you don't have anything to worry about. This is another great topic to add to the list of questions you have for your accountant or tax return preparer.

4

Wrapping Up the Books

Create a statement of activities to indicate whether your organization has increased or decreased its net assets.

Put together a statement of financial position to show your organization's solvency versus liquidity.

Assemble a cash flow statement to route cash according to activity.

Write a statement of function expenses to evaluate your expenses based on their functions.

Close your books for the accounting period, including the notes to the financial statements, which summarize any significant changes to accounting methods and all required disclosures.

Chapter **17**

Analyzing the Statement of Activities

R arely do financial disasters happen overnight. Often, when a nonprofit has to close its doors due to lack of funding, the situation probably could have been avoided with proper financial oversight. Usually, the statement of activities contains signs that, if properly evaluated, reveal the likelihood of trouble and ways to avoid disaster. Good financial managers use their statement of activities as planning tools and indicators of future events.

The Financial Accounting Standards Board (FASB) requires nonprofits to report information about all expenses in one location. This can be on the statement of activities, as a note to the financial statements, or on a separate financial statement. See Chapter 13 for more information about the FASB.

Information found on a statement of activities provides

» **A summary of transactions, events, and circumstances that change an organization's net assets:** This ties in both revenue and expenses.

» **Information about the relationship between transactions and events:** This assists in an important nonprofit control relating to program cost identification and classification.

>> **Information on how revenues are used to provide program services:**
Revenue must be spent in a way that is consistent with donor restrictions, limitations, and any regulations by which the nonprofit must abide.

By evaluating your statement of activities on a frequent basis, you know where your resources come from, how and when they flow, and how to set your course. Knowing how you're doing compared to what you've planned can help you make necessary changes. This chapter explains how to come up with the numbers on your statement of activities and how to use those numbers to strategically plan, carefully forecast and track your donations and expenses, and ensure that your nonprofit is compliant with any restrictions or regulatory requirements.

Understanding the Statement of Activities

Your *statement of activities*, which for-profit businesses call an *income statement*, is a summary of all the income you've earned and every expense you've incurred for a particular time period. It also shows whether your net assets or equity has increased or decreased over that time period.

Large corporations evaluate their expenses and often make conscious efforts to downsize; you may need to consider doing the same thing when operating your nonprofit. Choosing what to cut and what to keep requires careful evaluation of your revenue sources, restrictions on those resources, and your expenses. In addition, you can compare planned expenses, just as you compare revenues, to keep your spending on track.

In a nutshell, your statement of activities (see Figure 17-1) indicates whether your nonprofit had a surplus or is operating in a deficit position (a *deficit* is a negative amount that means you've used all your revenues and then some, and it could signal that you're in financial trouble). It also identifies whether you've made any out-of-the-ordinary large purchases or had unexpected revenue, gains, or losses. Basically, the statement of activities indicates whether you've had a good year (ending in the black) or a bad year (ending in the red).

The sample statement of activities in Figure 17-1 reflects the FASB requirement that all income and expenses be allocated either *without donor restrictions* or *with donor restrictions* and is in the multicolumn format, which highlights the classification between with donor restrictions and without donor restrictions.

Jay & Top Community Cat Project
Statement of Activities
For Year Ended December 31, 20XX

	Without Donor Restrictions	With Donor Restrictions	Total
Revenue, gains and other support:			
Contributions	$ 28,693	$ 12,500	$ 41,193
Event Income	33,888		33,888
Investment return, net	450		450
Gain on sale of asset	15,000		15,000
Other	36		36
Net assets released from restrictions:			
Satisfaction of program restrictions	3,245	(3,245)	
Expiration of time restrictions	6,888	(6,888)	-
Total net assets released from restrictions	10,133	(10,133)	-
Total revenue, gains, and other support	88,200	2,367	90,567
Expenses and losses:			-
Program A	15,600		15,600
Program B	8,400		8,400
Management and general	7,300		7,300
Fundraising	25,000		25,000
Total expenses	56,300		56,300
Fire loss on furniture and fixtures	80		80
Total expenses and losses	56,380		56,380
Change in net assets	31,820	2,367	34,187
Net assets January 1, 20XX	1,02,992	65,493	1,68,485
Net assets December 31, 20XX	$ 1,34,812	$ 67,860	$ 2,02,672

Some nonprofits use the single-column format because it's easier to do year-over-year comparative analysis (see Chapter 8 for an example of the comparative analysis). Figure 17-2 shows the single column format. Generally accepted accounting principles (GAAP) allow either format.

You can use your statement of activities to evaluate ways to downsize or cut expenses and increase revenue streams. When created on a monthly or quarterly basis, your statement of activities can be used to

>> Focus on peak periods when contributions are up.

>> Plan for the downtimes when contributions come in slowly.

Jay & Top Community Cat Project
Statement of Activities
For Year Ended December 31, 20XX

Change in without donor restriction net assets:

Revenue, gains and other support:

Contributions	$	28,693
Event Income		33,888
Investment return, net		450
Gain on sale of asset		15,000
Other		36
Net assets released from restrictions:		
Satisfaction of program restrictions		3,245
Expiration of time restrictions		6,888
Total net assets released from restrictions		10,133
Total revenue, gains, and other support		88,200

Expenses and losses:

Program A	15,600
Program B	8,400
Management and general	7,300
Fundraising	25,000
Total expenses	56,300
Fire loss on furniture and fixtures	80
Total expenses and losses	56,380
Increase in without donor restrictions net assets	31,820

Change with donor restrictions net assets:

Contributions		12,500
Net assets released from restrictions		(10,133)
Increase in net assets		34,187
Net assets January 1, 20XX		1,68,485
Net assets December 31, 20XX	$	2,02,672

FIGURE 17-2:
A sample statement of activities using single-column format.

Knowing your peak periods and slow periods can help you plan to sustain your nonprofit during the slow periods.

REMEMBER

Tracking your revenues and expenses on a monthly, quarterly, and annual basis helps you make better decisions about what expenses to keep and what to give up. When revenues decrease, most organizations look for ways to reduce expenses. As a general rule, most nonprofits try to keep administrative costs down to have more funds available for programs.

TIP

Going back to Chapter 5, you need your chart of accounts to set up your statement of activities because the chart of accounts lists your ledger account names and numbers in the same order that they appear in your financial statements.

Before you can fully use this important statement, you need a firm grasp of what the statement of activities shows. The following sections reveal what information is found on this statement.

Booking revenue

You have two types of donations to account for on the statement of activities:

>> **Without donor restrictions:** This money can be used for anything. For example, a donor gives $10,000 to your nonprofit and doesn't specify how you spend the money.

>> **With donor restrictions:** These donations have strings attached or imposed sanctions. For example, the donor may limit how the donated asset can be used by both purpose and time. When your nonprofit receives restricted gifts, you have a legal obligation to comply with the donor's restrictions.

If your board of directors designates a portion of revenue without donor restrictions for a specific purpose, it may be called an *appropriation* or *board-designated support*. Board-designated funds (see Chapter 2 for more information about fund accounting) aren't restricted in the same way as donor-restricted support.

A board can change its mind and remove this self-imposed limit on some resources, but it can't change the limitation placed on resources contributed from an outside donor. *Remember:* Boards are inside the nonprofits and they *designate;* donors are outside your nonprofit and they have the ability to *restrict.*

To classify revenues on your statement of activities, you should list the totals from all accounts from your general ledger beginning with the number 4. These will include individual contributions, grant support, special events, ticket revenue, unrelated business income, in-kind contributions, and all other sources of income, such as gains or investment income earned by your nonprofit, which must be further broken out between those without or with donor restrictions.

Make sure to follow Figure 17-1's revenue section to see how to report all revenue accounts, especially net assets released from restrictions and the subsequent effect on total revenues, gains, and other support.

Recording expense

Your nonprofit incurs program expenses and overhead expenses. Depending on your establishment, you may have program, management and general, and fundraising expenses. You won't forget to include your expenses if you refer to your chart of accounts and your general ledger.

You generally report all expenses on the statement of activities in the Without Donor Restrictions column. After you add up all your expenses (and losses if any exist), subtract the total from Without Donor Restrictions revenues. As a reminder, expenses show up in your chart of accounts coded to the five series of accounts. See Chapter 5 for more information about the chart of accounts.

Classifying gains and losses

Gains and losses come from activities that are incidental to an organization's central activities or from events and circumstances beyond the organization's control. Gains are reported in the revenue section, and losses are reported in the expense section of the statement of activities. Gains increase net assets, and losses decrease net assets. There are two types of gains or losses:

>> **Realized gains and losses essentially come from transactions or events that have occurred.** The economic impact has happened and can be felt. A transaction example is the gain or loss from the sale or disposition of an organization's investments or some other asset it owns. You have a gain when you receive more than the asset's cost or book value and a loss when you receive less than its cost or book value. An event example is a loss from a fire where the fire caused a decrease in value of an asset. See the section "Understanding what this statement doesn't show," later in this chapter, for more information about book value.

>> **Unrealized gains and losses come from the change in fair market value of investments that an organization holds.** Instead of recording investments at cost, GAAP allows you to elect to value investments with a readily determinable fair market value to that fair market value on the financial statements. For example, your nonprofit has *trading securities,* which are held in the short term with the intent to sell for a profit, and you have a readily determinable fair value. You have not sold the trading securities, so there is no realized gain or loss. However, there is readily determinable gain or loss in their value, it just hasn't been realized or felt because the asset hasn't been sold. If you've made the election to record at fair market value, the gain or loss is reported on the statement as unrealized.

TIP

In practice, most nonprofits report investments at fair value. For guidance on reporting investments at fair value, see ASC 825-10-25-4, which you can access at https://asc.fasb.org/Login. (I walk you through the FASB login process in Chapter 13.)

Make sure to follow through Figure 17-1 to see how to report expenses and losses, through the change in net assets and finishing up with the reconciliation from beginning to ending net assets.

Evaluating the Data

You can use your statement of activities to analyze more than just the total revenues earned and expenses incurred for a given period. For example, you can compare the following:

>> Current month revenues and expenses to prior months

>> Current quarterly revenues and expenses to prior quarters

>> Current annual revenue and expenses to prior years

Depending on your scope of services, you can also use your statement of activities to

>> Compare your data to similar organizations

>> Track how economic conditions affect your contributions

>> Evaluate changes in giving trends

>> Position yourself to better focus on organization and program efficiency

>> Identify programs or areas that need your immediate attention

You can also use information found on the statement of activities to figure out what percentage of your revenues come from the following:

>> Individual donors (private)

>> Foundations

>> Corporate sponsors

>> Fundraising

>> Grants

>> Fees for program goods and services provided

See chapters 8, 18, and 19 for ratio analysis instructions.

Knowing where your resources come from can help you to assess your capability of generating future revenues. The following sections cover all these topics.

Analyzing revenues and expenses

The numbers alone on your nonprofit's statement of activities don't have much meaning. You want to analyze and determine the relationship of its parts and how the results affect your nonprofit.

To analyze the numbers on a statement of activities, it's helpful to convert the numbers to percentages, giving you a better idea of what percentage of revenues come from which sources and which categories of expenses are too high. When the dollar amounts are converted into percentages, it shows how significant the components of your statement of activities are. Then when you compare revenues and expenses, you can better understand the relationship between the two. Reducing numbers to a simpler form helps you discover the true relationship of the parts of the statement of activities to the whole.

Take a look at Table 17-1, which shows how much money a hypothetical nonprofit collected.

TABLE 17-1

Revenues Collected for 2023

Source	Amount
Individual donors	$45,000
Corporate sponsors	$25,000
Foundation grants	$85,000
Government grants	$300,000
Fee for services	$45,000
Total revenues collected	**$500,000**

By converting these figures into percentages, you can evaluate the revenues much easier. See Chapter 8 for more information about statement of activities ratio analysis.

To calculate the percentage for each revenue collected, divide the amount by the total revenues collected. For example, take the $45,000 collected from individual donors and divide it by $500,000, which is the total amount of revenues collected ($45,000 ÷ $500,000 = 0.09 or 9 percent). This means that $45,000 is 9 percent of $500,000, so you know that 9 percent of the revenues came from individuals.

Be sure to double-check your math by adding up the percentages. Your total should equal 100 percent.

The result of converting the revenues from each source into a percentage is shown in Table 17-2.

TABLE 17-2

Percentage of Revenues from Sources

Source	Percentage
Individual donors	9%
Corporate sponsors	5%
Foundation grants	17%
Government grants	60%
Fees for services	9%
Total revenues collected	**100%**

Based on these percentages, this organization is relying heavily on grants, to the tune of 77 percent of its revenues (17 percent from foundation grants plus 60 percent from government grants).

Although I wouldn't try to operate a nonprofit organization without grants because they're important to a nonprofit's funding, having this much money coming from grants can be a good or bad thing. If an aggressive grant-writing campaign is ongoing, then it may be okay. But if the nonprofit isn't aggressively seeking new grants, then it's putting itself in a precarious position because grants aren't permanent sources of income. The nonprofit could be in danger of running low on revenues when the grants end.

Evaluating your expenses gives you a better indication of how much money is going to administrative, program, and overhead expenses. For more information on administrative expenses, see Chapter 20.

Determining change in net assets

A complete statement of activities indicates whether you've increased or decreased your net assets over a given period. Subtracting total expenses from revenues equals either a positive number or a negative number:

>> A positive number means you've taken in more revenues than you have expenses. This is excess income — a *surplus* — and you're "in the black."

>> A negative number means your expenses are higher than your revenues. A negative number equals a loss — a *deficit* — which means you're "in the red."

For example, if your total revenues are $100,000 and your total expenses are $95,000, then your change in net assets is a surplus of $5,000. But if your total revenues are $100,000 and your total expenses are $105,000, then your change in net assets is a reduction of $5,000.

REMEMBER

Revenues – Expenses = Change in net assets

In the private sector, stockholders may benefit from a positive difference between revenues and expenses because dividends may be declared and paid from the company's profits. In the nonprofit sector, stakeholders are the beneficiaries (your donors, as well as the people you help), and the money that's left after you've paid your expenses is reinvested in the nonprofit. When all revenues are collected and all expenses are paid, you need to have a surplus to stay afloat. Just because you're a nonprofit doesn't mean you don't need a positive difference between revenues and expenses.

Using the statement to make comparisons

As the world changes, so do your nonprofit's finances. Revenues go up and down; expenses go up (and sometimes down). You can use the data on the statement of activities to compare:

>> Current and historical amounts for your nonprofit

>> Your nonprofit's finances to the finances of other nonprofits in the same industry

Seeing how the numbers compare over time

You can compare numbers on your statement of activities on a monthly, quarterly, or annual basis. Looking back at previous time frames helps you gauge how well you're doing in the current period.

Comparing your current-year data to prior years shows trends and can help your nonprofit focus on important contributors (start with your donors list to see how much was given by whom) and high expenses. Of course, some expenses are probably up because of the changes in the economy, and there may be little that you can do to change that, but you may be able to offset other expenses. Take a look at Table 17-3, which compares current-year revenues and expenses to prior years.

TABLE 17-3   **Comparing Prior-Year Data to Current-Year Data**

	2023	2022	2021	2020	2019
Revenues	$500,000	$475,000	$450,000	$425,000	$400,000
Expenses	$450,000	$450,000	$425,000	$400,000	$390,000
Change in Net Assets	$50,000	$25,000	$25,000	$25,000	$10,000

Table 17-3 shows a comparative list covering five years of revenues and expenses and the change in net assets. If you take what's happening in 2023 and compare it to any other year, it gives you a bit more than just looking at the numbers. For example, consider revenues starting with 2019 and look at what was reported in 2023. If you divided the revenues from any year into 2023, it gives you a percentage of change. The same is true for the expenses.

Looking at the figures, you see the trend of revenues increasing faster than expenses — revenues increased by $100,000 ($500,000 – $400,000) while expenses increased by $60,000 ($450,000 – $390,000) during the same five-year period. It appears that expenses plateau from 2023 to 2022; you'd need to investigate why to see if this is the start of a trend or a single occurrence.

Comparing your nonprofit to other nonprofits

Not a day goes by that the meteorologist doesn't compare today's temperature with last year's temperature, or even last week's for that matter. A comparison of your nonprofit's finances to the finances of other nonprofits gives you something by which to measure and test your progress.

Just as people can find your nonprofit's Form 990, Return of Organization Exempt from Income Tax, on the Internet, you can take a gander at other nonprofits' Form 990s. You can look up your favorite charities and other nonprofits with operating budgets and programs similar to yours. To do so, go to the GuideStar website at www.guidestar.org.

When comparing your nonprofit to others in the industry, you want to compare apples to apples and oranges to oranges; therefore, try to find a nonprofit that is of similar size and with similar programs in your city. That way you're both subject to the same economic conditions and environment. Of course, you first have to be around for a few years before these types of assessments and analyses can be compared.

Another factor to consider when comparing your statement of activities to another agency's statement is the accounting method used by the other organization. For example, if the other nonprofit uses the cash method and you're using the accrual method, then it's not a good comparison. The primary difference in the two methods is timing recognition of revenues and expenses. For more information about these two accounting methods, see Chapter 1.

Understanding what this statement doesn't show

There are limitations to the statement of activities. Even if it's reporting using general accepted accounting principles (GAAP), the statement can reflect estimates and may require its preparer to use professional judgment on the best way to handle a transaction under GAAP or make assumptions about such things as the useful life of an asset. For example, you may have some things of value that you can't accurately measure or report on the statement. These include the following:

>> **Uncollectible accounts and pledges receivable:** These are assets and potential liabilities, and they're reported on the statement of financial position (see Chapter 18). Changes in the estimate of uncollectible receivables affect net assets on the statement of activities, but the total value of the estimate is reported on the statement of financial position.

>> **Accumulated depreciation:** Although you report the depreciation expense for any year on the statement of activities, you report the depreciation expense that has accumulated over the years on the statement of financial position as accumulated depreciation. Accumulated depreciation holds the write-off amount to keep the current value of a fixed asset accurately stated on the books. It reduces the carrying or book value of the fixed asset. (See Chapter 2 for more about depreciation.)

>> **People's loyalty and devotion to your organization:** Even if someone tried to measure these attributes, it would be difficult to put a number on them.

Chapter **18**

Reporting Financial Position

S
ome experts feel that, out of all the financial statements, the statement of financial position is the most important. The statement of financial position provides a quantitative report of your organization's financial health by accounting for your assets, liabilities, and net assets. It demonstrates responsibility and accountability. It also monitors the progress of your organization and its financial condition.

This chapter walks you through this important financial statement and shows you how to use the numbers on your statement of financial position to analyze your nonprofit's financial health.

Grasping What the Statement Says about Your Nonprofit

The *statement of financial position* (which is the equivalent of the for-profit business's *balance sheet*) reveals what your nonprofit owns (the assets) and what it owes (the liabilities) as of a particular date. The difference between your nonprofit's total assets and total liabilities equals your nonprofit's net assets.

Assets – Liabilities = Net assets

A statement of financial position reveals the overall value of your organization at a certain point in time. It shows your organization's *solvency* (its ability to pay its bills) and *liquidity* (how quickly assets can be converted into cash) at a particular point in time.

Internal users (such as board members, accountants, and managers) use the statement of financial position to get information about

- **Your nonprofit's ability to meet its obligations:** This is revealed by the amount of your current assets, which are used to meet your current liabilities. If your current liabilities are greater than the current assets, people will wonder whether you're having cash flow problems, making it difficult to pay your debts.

- **Your organization's net assets (the difference between what's owned and what's owed):** You can find this information at the bottom of the statement of financial position. Net assets represent the net cumulative results of your nonprofit's changes in net assets over the years. You report the change in net assets for any specific period on the statement of activities; you report the ending net assets on the statement of activities on the statement of financial position.

  This statement also helps explain how you acquired some of your assets. You acquire assets either by borrowing money to buy them (liabilities) or by spending your own surplus funds (this amount is represented by net assets).

- **Your agency's progress and ability to continue to provide services:** Simply compare changes in balances from prior periods to the current period.

- **The need for external financing:** You're in this situation when your current assets won't cover current debts, or if your long-term assets can't be converted into cash in time to pay current liabilities.

- **The results of economic activity:** This is revealed by the overall financial results as displayed on the statement of financial position as of a certain date.

You can tell a lot about an organization by viewing how its finances are managed. External users (such as bankers, creditors, and private and public donors) use the statement of financial position to evaluate whether your nonprofit's financial position is stable enough to secure a loan or whether your nonprofit is worthy of their investments. These folks may also take an interest in the same information your internal users look at. Additionally, many grant proposals require you to include a copy of all financial statements, including the statement of financial position, with the proposal.

REMEMBER

Although a statement of financial position may be prepared monthly, quarterly, or annually, it represents a single point in time. So, if you're having a board meeting and your financial condition has improved or declined significantly due to a large donation or an unexpected large expense, you'll definitely want to reveal the good or bad news by giving your board members copies of an updated statement of financial position.

Creating the Statement of Financial Position

The statement tells a story about your position and condition; it's an X-ray of your financial health. It's based on what you own (current and long-term assets), what you owe (current and long-term liabilities), and the difference between the two (net assets).

Start creating your statement of financial position using your chart of accounts to help you identify which accounts should be included. (If you're not sure about your chart of accounts, see Chapter 5.) Before you can create and read your nonprofit's statement of financial position, you need to know what the different numbers mean. Figure 18-1 shows a sample statement prepared using the classified method. As you read this section, follow along in this figure to see what the different numbers mean.

Understanding the statement's structure

The top of your statement of financial position should include the name of your nonprofit, the name of the statement (statement of financial position), and the date of the balances reporting on the statement.

The statement of financial position is like a scale with two sides. It has a top half and a bottom half. The top half shows assets, and the bottom half shows liabilities and net assets; the two halves have to balance, which is why this statement is sometimes called a *balance sheet*.

Figure 18-1 is a classified statement of financial position, which categorizes assets and liabilities as either current or long-term. This is done so you have a more in-depth example of this statement to work through. It makes the analysis in the section "Evaluating the Numbers," later in this chapter, easier to piece together.

Most statements of financial position included as part of an independent auditor's report will be *unclassified*, which means assets and liabilities will list in order of liquidity with no current or long-term subtotals. Additionally, fixed assets/accumulated depreciation are netted. Figure 18-2 shows the asset section only for an unclassified statement of financial position.

Jay & Top Community Cat Project
Statement of Financial Position
December 31, 2023

Assets		
Current Assets		
Cash:		
Operating account		69,000
Money market account		22,193
Total cash		91,193
Contributions receivable		
Unrestricted		7,000
Restricted		65,000
Total contributions receivable		72,000
Long-term assets		
Fixed assets:		
Office equipment	25,000	
Less accumulated depreciation	(21,000)	
Total fixed assets		4,000
Total Assets		**1,67,193**
Liabilities and Net Assets		
Current Liabilities:		
Accounts payable		2,900
Unearned revenue		37,100
Total current liabilities		40,000
Net Assets:		
Without donor restrictions		62,193
With donor restrictions		65,000
Total net assets		1,27,193
Total liabilities and net assets		**1,67,193**

FIGURE 18-1:
A classified statement of financial position.

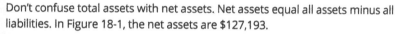

Jay & Top Community Cat Project
Statement of Financial Position
December 31 2023

Assets	
Cash and cash equivalents	91,193
Contributions receivable	72,000
Office equipment (net)	4,000
Total Assets	**1,67,193**

FIGURE 18-2:
The asset section
of an unclassified
statement of
financial position.

Every balance sheet has two main parts:

>> **Assets:** Assets are always shown first on the statement of financial position. Adding all current assets to your fixed assets and other long-term assets gives your total assets. When you've reached your total assets, you've finished half of the statement.

>> **Liabilities and net assets:** In this area, on your statement of financial position, you add your current liabilities to your long-term liabilities to get your total liabilities. Notice in Figure 18-1 that this nonprofit only has current liabilities.

REMEMBER

Don't confuse total assets with net assets. Net assets equal all assets minus all liabilities. In Figure 18-1, the net assets are $127,193.

Underneath net assets, you find net assets without donor restrictions and net assets with donor restrictions. *With donor restrictions* simply means donors have imposed limitations or conditions on gifts that will be met at some future time, whereas *without donor restrictions* means there were no limits or restrictions on the resources and you're free to use them however you'd like.

Jay & Top's statement of financial position in Figure 18-1 shows total net assets of $127,193. The organization's net assets come from $62,193 without donor restrictions and $65,000 with donor restrictions.

To finish the bottom half of the statement of financial position, you add your total liabilities of $40,000 to your total net assets of $127,193 to get your total liabilities and net assets of $167,193. Notice how this is the same amount of total assets at the top half of the Jay & Top's statement of financial position. This is how total assets equals total liabilities plus net assets. You've just completed your statement of financial position!

TIP

A good checkpoint to remember is that total assets will always equal liabilities plus net assets.

Your statement of financial position is unique, and it shows what you own and what you owe. No two organizations will have the exact same statement of financial position. So, don't worry if you don't have every line item (or more) listing on the statement shown in Figure 18-1.

I've covered the basics of the statement of financial position and how it has to always stay in balance. The following sections explain the different parts of the statement of financial position and what information to include in the different fields. Here you can see how to create your nonprofit's statement of financial position.

Classifying assets

Assets are classified on the statement of financial position in the order of their *liquidity*, which means how quickly assets can be converted to cash. This section presents asset categories in the order they should appear on a statement of financial position.

To come up with the figures, you simply add up all the items under each category of assets on the general ledger (see Chapter 6) and take that sum and place it on your statement of financial position.

Current assets

Current assets are those items that can be converted into cash within a year of the date of the statement. Current assets are usually listed in the following order — which generally follows ease of liquidity:

>> **Cash:** Checking and savings account balances (cash is the most liquid asset, so it's listed first) and petty cash.

>> **Marketable securities:** U.S. Treasury bills, certificates of deposit (CDs), stocks, and bonds.

>> **Grants and accounts receivables:** Assets expected to be collected within the year.

Grants and accounts receivables list under long-term assets, if the money will be received more than 12 months after the date of the statement.

>> **Prepaid expenses:** This includes items such as rent and insurance you have paid in advance, and supplies on hand.

Long-term assets

Long-term assets, also referred to as noncurrent assets, are items that you anticipate holding more than 12 months from the date of the statement. Long-term assets consist of the following:

>> **Investments:** Bonds, stocks, and real estate that you don't intend to sell within a year.

>> **Tangible assets:** Any assets you acquire to fulfill your mission purpose and that have a useful life of more than one year from the date of the statement. Common examples are property, plant, and equipment (PP&E) such as land, buildings, equipment, office furniture, and fixtures. Tangible assets are also called *fixed assets*.

>> **Intangibles assets:** Copyrights, patents, trademarks, trade names, customer lists, and other assets that you own. They're called *intangible* because they don't have a physical presence.

>> **Other assets:** Anything that's not classified in the other areas.

Net fixed assets

Net fixed assets report the cost of a depreciable asset minus accumulated depreciation. *Accumulated depreciation* is the total depreciation expense charged to an asset over the years. (See Chapter 2 for more information about depreciation.)

REMEMBER

Assets are recorded on the statement of financial position at their original cost less depreciation. Your depreciation expense is listed on your statement of activities (see Chapter 17), but to show the office equipment at its book value on the statement of financial position, you have to subtract the accumulated depreciation amount from the cost. Figure 18-1 shows office equipment purchased at a price of $25,000 less $21,000 (accumulated depreciation) for a book value of $4,000.

Total assets

Total assets are your current assets plus long-term and net fixed assets. Your total assets include cash in your bank accounts, CDs, accounts receivable, and the value of all equipment and any other long-term assets you have. It's important that you know how much readily available cash you have on hand in order to meet your current obligations on time.

For the statement of financial position in Figure 18-1, the total assets are $167,193. The total current assets are $163,193, and the total fixed assets are $4,000.

Breaking out liabilities and net assets

Knowing your nonprofit's liabilities is important because you need to have assets available to pay your obligations. Have you ever heard someone say, "We're not broke, but our assets are tied up"? This means the organization doesn't have anything it can quickly and easily convert to cash to cover what it owes. You need to have current assets to meet your current liabilities such as accounts payable or salaries payable. Not having current assets available to pay the bills can cause serious cash flow problems for your nonprofit.

Furthermore, by identifying your nonprofit's net assets, you can see pretty quickly how stable your organization is. The difference between your total assets and total liabilities gives a snapshot of your nonprofit's sustainability. Net assets are the same as net worth for a person, and the two are calculated the same way (total assets minus total liabilities).

TIP

In the notes to your financial statements, you should disclose information about the maturity of assets and liabilities and all restrictions on their usage. (See Chapter 21 for more info about notes to the financial statements.)

Current liabilities

Current liabilities represent items that are due within 12 months of the statement date. Your nonprofit should have sufficient current assets to pay the current liabilities as they become due. Some common current liabilities include the following:

>> **Accounts payable:** These include credit card payments or purchases from vendors on credit.

>> **Salaries payable:** This category is for salary expenses incurred but not yet paid at the end of the period.

>> **Payroll taxes payable:** These are payable for state and federal taxes owed on salaries but not yet remitted to the government.

>> **Other unpaid expenses:** These include the cost for items such as rent and utilities your nonprofit has incurred but not yet paid at the end of the period.

>> **Bank loan payable for money borrowed for working capital:** Working capital loans are short-term loans taken to pay immediate items such as salaries payable. Normally, the collateral for working capital loans are accounts or grants receivable expected to be collected in the very near future. Check out the section "Calculating working capital," later in this chapter, to see how to figure your nonprofit's working capital.

TIP

To identify your current liabilities, just take a look at your chart of accounts. Of course, the specific financial information can be found in your general ledger. Just add the totals in your general ledger to get your total current liabilities.

In Figure 18-1, there are two current liabilities — accounts payable and unearned revenue — which total $40,000. Unearned revenue (also known as *deferred revenue*) is payments received in advance before a service or product is earned; for example, a membership fee is paid for a year and only four months have elapsed. The eight months remaining on the membership is unearned revenue.

Long-term liabilities

Having too much debt can be risky business. To determine how much of this risky debt your nonprofit has on its books, look at long-term liabilities on the balance sheet. Long-term liabilities represent obligations due after 12 months from the date of the statement. Some common long-term liabilities are

» Notes payable for mortgages and land payments.

» Equipment payable for vehicles and heavy-duty copy machines.

TIP

To come up with long-term liabilities, add up the amounts for all obligations that you owe that aren't due or payable within a year. These consist of long-term debts such as mortgages and vehicle or heavy machinery loans. In Figure 18-1, Jay & Top has no long-term debts.

Net assets

Net assets represent the difference between your total assets and your total liabilities. Net assets are classified as without donor restrictions or with donor restrictions. If donors choose to restrict their gifts, they set the terms and length of the restrictions.

REMEMBER

Include any information about the nature and amount of donor restrictions as either a part of the statement of financial position or in the notes to the financial statements, which we cover in Chapter 21.

TIP

In the for-profit world, retained earnings represent the net difference between liabilities and assets on the balance sheet. In the nonprofit world, we have net assets.

REMEMBER

Asset accounts (statement of financial position accounts) aren't closed at the end of the accounting year. Statement of financial position accounts are considered real or permanent accounts. The only accounts that are closed are revenue, expense, gains, losses, and income summary accounts, which are referred to as *temporary accounts*.

When preparing financial statements, you always prepare the statement of activities first, because you close the end results of revenues and gains minus expenses and losses to net assets. There is a direct relationship between what happens in the statement of activities and the statement of financial position. Your end results from the statement of activities accounts transfers to your statement of financial position. This is why the statement of activities is the first financial statement prepared. (See Chapter 17 for more about the statement of activities.)

You report your net assets on your statement of financial position. This final piece keeps the statement of financial position (for-profit balance sheet) in balance. You calculate and report the beginning net asset balances, the change in those balances, and the ending net asset balances on the statement of activities. These ending net asset balances also appear underneath liabilities on the statement of financial position.

In the Jay & Top Community Cat Project statement of financial position in Figure 18-1, you see net assets without donor restrictions of $62,193 and net assets with donor restrictions of $65,000, for total net assets of $127,193.

TIP

You can double-check yourself when calculating your net assets by thinking of net assets as the difference between total assets (listed at the top of the balance sheet) and total liabilities. The total assets are $167,193, and the total liabilities are $40,000. Therefore, Jay & Top's total net assets must be $127,193 ($167,193 − $40,000 = $127,193). Also double-check that the net asset balances on the statement of activities agree with the balances on the statement of financial position.

Restricted net assets

Sometimes donors make contributions but place some restrictions on how and/or when the money may be used. These contributions are called *net assets with donor restrictions.* Donors include contributors and makers of certain grants to your non-profit. These donors may restrict the money for a wide variety of functions, including buying a new building, starting a new program, or building an endowment. Your donors will tell you if a gift is restricted when they give it to you. It's your responsibility to honor the terms of the gift and to keep accurate records of how you manage the gift.

You need to report on the statement of financial position or in the notes to the financial statements whether donors have imposed restrictions on contributions. In the statement of financial position in Figure 18-1, you can see that Jay & Top has $65,000 in net assets with donor restrictions.

Borrowing from restricted assets can cause you to lose the entire contribution.

Unrestricted net assets

Net assets without donor restrictions arise from gifts and other revenue that have no restrictions on their use, or from restricted gifts whose restrictions have been met. Unrestricted income is like gold. It has no pre-imposed terms and generally can be used immediately for anything you want.

In the Jay & Top statement of financial position in Figure 18-1, you see net assets without donor restrictions of $62,193.

If your nonprofit receives donated gifts with donor-imposed restrictions that limit their usage to long term, you can't classify them with cash or other assets that are unrestricted. It's important that you separately classify available assets and those intended for future use and not mix the two. Information about the donor-imposed restrictions should be disclosed in the notes to the financial statements, so users of your nonprofit statement of financial position know what's available to you with no restrictions and what's not.

Total liabilities and net assets

To complete the statement, add together the total liabilities and the total net assets. This number must be the same as the total assets line on the top half of your statement of financial position.

In Figure 18-1, Jay & Top has liabilities of $40,000 and net assets of $127,193. When you add the two figures together, you get $167,193, the exact same amount as the total assets. Success!

Evaluating the Numbers

There is more to your statement of financial position than just the numbers or total amount of assets, liabilities, and net assets. Accountants take the numbers from this statement to evaluate how well you're doing. You can do the same: Think of this evaluation of your nonprofit's statement of financial position as a financial checkup.

You can get a sense of whether your organization is in good financial shape just by looking at the lines for total assets and total liabilities and net assets.

If the number on the top half (total assets) of the statement is less than the total liabilities number on the bottom half, you have a problem. How long your problem lasts, or if it worsens, depends on your nonprofit's plans for the future. Some problems are only temporary. For example, you may have experienced unbudgeted increases in expenses. Maybe a water pipe burst, causing you to slip into a different position.

REMEMBER

The statement of financial position date shows the nonprofit's results from the first day of operation to the date on that statement. Going back to Figure 18-1, let's say Jay & Top opened its nonprofit doors on March 1, 2019. Figure 18-1's statement of financial position shows Jay & Top's results from March 1, 2019, to December 31, 2023. Contrast this to the statement of activities, which only shows how the nonprofit is performing for the time frame listing on the top of the report; for example, "for the year ending December 31, 2023" or "for the quarter ending March 31, 2024."

The statement of financial position reveals your organization's ability to pay its bills. It also plays a part in determining what interest rate your lender will charge for credit like working capital or long-term loans. By analyzing current assets and current liabilities, you can figure out how much cash is on hand to pay liabilities. You can study your nonprofit's financial position and get a clear picture of how your nonprofit is doing by using the statement of financial position to compute working capital and analyze your debt-paying ability.

Internal and external users of your balance sheet are interested in evaluating your financial health. Bankers, vendors, investors, donors, board members, constituents, accountants, and executive directors can easily evaluate your financial position by making a few simple computations. They look at your working capital and debt-to-equity ratio to determine whether to lend you money, issue credit cards, or charge higher interest rates.

The following sections show you how to analyze your financial position and compute debt-paying ability and working capital.

Calculating working capital

Working capital is the difference between current assets and current liabilities. Working capital indicates how much money you have available after paying your current liabilities and your ability to cover other obligations that may arise in the future. Creditors use working capital to determine interest rates.

TIP

To figure out your nonprofit's working capital, you subtract the total current liabilities from the total current assets.

Take a look at Figure 18-1. The total current liabilities for the year are $40,000, and the total current assets are $163,193. Subtracting the total current liabilities from the total current assets gives you working capital of $123,193 ($163,193 – $40,000 = $123,193).

REMEMBER

Working capital is the amount you have left after you've paid your bills. If you have excess working capital, it means you can cover your current liabilities and have cash left over for other needs.

Figuring a debt-to-equity ratio

Creditors use the numbers on your statement of financial position to determine what percentage of your total assets is used to pay your liabilities. One of the most commonly used ratios is the debt-to-equity ratio. A *debt-to-equity ratio* is total debts (liabilities) divided by net assets. This ratio gives the users of the statement an idea of how the nonprofit is financed — through debt or through equity. A high number signals that your nonprofit may have wild fluctuations in income or grant/accounts receivable collections and not be able to pay its bills when they're due. The higher the number, the more highly you're leveraged.

Looking at Figure 18-1, Jay & Top has a balance of $127,193 in total net assets with $40,000 in liabilities. To calculate the organization's debt-to-equity ratio, you divide the total liabilities by total net assets. The math comes out to 31 percent ($40,000 ÷ $127,193 = 0.31 or 31 percent). This is a low debt-to-equity ratio and to be expected, because Jay & Top has no long-term debt related to a mortgage or financed equipment purchases.

REMEMBER

Having a low debt-to-equity ratio is a good thing. Anything over 50 percent is considered risky.

Chapter **19**

Eyeing the Statement of Cash Flows

The statement of cash flows is one of the major financial statements required by generally accepted accounting principles (GAAP). This statement reports the inflow of cash to an organization and the outflow of cash from an organization. Cash inflows are cash receipts that come from operating, financing, and investing activities. Cash outflows are cash payments for operating, financing, and investing activities.

The information found on the statement of cash flows gives users an idea about your organization's ability to generate positive future cash flows, its ability to pay debts, and a summary of sources (inflows) and uses (outflows) of cash. The statement of cash flows is a better indicator of this than the statement of activities because the statement of activities can report transactions on the accrual basis not the cash basis. (See Chapter 17 for more about statements of activities.) This chapter explains the importance of the statement of cash flows, how it indicates a nonprofit's ability to pay its debts, and how you can create it and use it to make decisions based on your need for available cash.

Seeing What the Statement of Cash Flows Can Tell You about Your Nonprofit

The *statement of cash flows*, sometimes called the *cash flow statement*, provides important information about your nonprofit. This statement answers questions about your nonprofit with information not found on accrual-based financial statements. It reveals how your organization's growth and expansion were financed. It also identifies cash amounts from operations, selling and acquiring securities, purchasing, selling capital assets, and financing activities with creditors. Your statement of cash flows can cover your monthly, quarterly, and annual cash inflows and outflows.

Cash includes balances in your checking and savings accounts, as well as currency and coins. Cash equivalents include short-term investments that are quickly and easily turned into a known amount of cash and are so near to maturity that changes in interest rates won't affect their value. Examples of these types of investments are Treasury bills, commercial paper, and money-market mutual funds.

TIP

You can improve your cash flow by keeping cash in an interest-bearing account or buying certificates of deposit (CDs).

Using the statement to track cash

The statement of cash flows summarizes where your cash came from and where it went during the period. Donations of cash, checks, credit card contributions, money collected from fundraising, and grants received from all sources are considered cash inflows. Cash outflows are all purchases made with cash, payments for salaries and payroll taxes, and outlays paid with cash during the period.

To have a positive cash flow means that your inflow exceeds your outflow. One major problem most organizations have is the timing of the cash flow. Unfortunately, cash inflows (revenues) may lag behind outflows (expenses), creating a shortage of cash or a negative cash flow.

REMEMBER

Your nonprofit may use a working capital loan to bridge the gap between collecting on receivables and urgent outflows such as salaries and wages. (I discuss working capital loans in Chapter 18.)

This statement shows cash flow divided into three different categories: operating, investing, and financing. This is helpful to board members and other users because it breaks down cash inflows and outflows for the differing types of transactions. Reviewing the statement of cash flows enables users to

- » Understand how an organization obtains and uses cash.

- » Analyze the short-term viability of an organization; it reveals an organization's liquidity or solvency.

- » Evaluate changes in statement of financial position accounts (assets, liabilities, and net assets).

- » Compare current information to prior statements.

- » More accurately predict amounts and timing of future cash flows.

REMEMBER

The statement of cash flows differs from the statement of financial position and statement of activities because it shows the cash flow of activities during the reporting period, meaning that transactions are recorded when cash is received or paid. Other financial statements may reflect the accrual basis of accounting, whereby revenues are matched with expenses in the period earned or incurred, not when cash changes hands.

Making decisions based on the statement

Proper use of a statement of cash flows can help you determine the following:

- » If you need to borrow money
- » When you can make major purchases
- » When you need to consider downsizing

You can use cash flow ratios to get an early warning about potential cash flow problems in your organizations. I explain two important ratios in the section "Analyzing Cash Flow Indicators" later in this chapter.

Understanding How to Create and Use a Statement of Cash Flows

The statement of cash flows generally follows what happens in your organization's checkbook, showing cash deposits and disbursements. The following sections identify the different parts of this statement and explain how to read it so you can fully understand your organization's cash flow status. If you're interested in creating your own statement of cash flows, here's some hands-on direction to get you started.

Use the statement of cash flows alongside your nonprofit's other financial statements (see chapters 17, 18, and 20) to get the total picture of your nonprofit's financial standing.

Getting the statement started

There are two methods for preparing the statement of cash flows: direct or indirect. Both methods classify and report cash receipts and payments from three activities: operating, investing, and financing. Both methods report cash flows from investing and financing activities in exactly the same manner, but they differ in how they report cash flows from operating activities.

>> **Direct:** The direct method operating activities section reports cash receipts and disbursements. Examples of operating cash receipts are donations and grants. Examples of operating disbursements are payments to employees and vendors. Cash receipts less cash disbursements equals net cash provided by operating activities.

>> **Indirect:** The indirect method operating activities section begins with the change in net assets from your statement of activities (see Chapter 17) and makes accrual-to-cash adjustments for revenues and expenses that didn't arise from the receipt or payment of cash during the reporting period. This method focuses on the differences between changes in net assets (net income) and net cash flow from operating activities.

As of this writing, the Financial Accounting Standards Board (FASB) allows nonprofits to use either the direct or the indirect method. Additionally, nonprofits are no longer required to prepare an additional disclosure reconciling the change in net assets to net cash flows from operating activities if using the direct method. The FASB eliminated the additional disclosure to encourage use of the direct method over the indirect method. In practice, many nonprofits use the indirect method because it can be easier to prepare.

Identifying the parts of the statement

To completely grasp the statement of cash flows and what it can tell you about your organization, you need to be able to identify its parts. The statement has three sections:

>> **Cash flows from operating activities** include operating revenues received and operating expenses paid in cash. If it isn't an investing or financing activity, it's an operating activity.

- >> **Cash flows from investing activities** include cash paid for acquiring and cash received from selling securities and/or assets.

- >> **Cash flows from financing activities** includes obtaining cash from creditors, repaying creditors, and receiving donations with long-term donor restrictions.

Figure 19-1 shows an example using the indirect method. See the next section in this chapter, "Doing the math," for an example of the direct method.

Jay & Top Community Cat Project
Statement of Cash Flows
For the Year Ending December 31, 20XX

Cash Flows from Operating Activities:	
Change in net assets	$ 66,423
Adjustments to reconcile change in net assets to net cash used:	
Depreciation	2,580
Increase in contributions receivable	(5,000)
Increase in accounts payable	3,000
Net cash from operating activities	$ 67,003
Cash flows from investing activities:	
Purchase of fixed assets	(2,363)
Proceeds from sale of investment	5,000
Net cash flows from investing activities	2,637
Cash flows from financing activities:	
Proceeds from restricted contributions	12,506
Payments on long-term debt	(8,716)
	3,790
Cash and cash equivalents beginning of year	43,656
Cash and cash equivalents end of year	73,430

Using the indirect method

FIGURE 19-1:
An example of a statement of cash flows using the indirect method.

Doing the math

As Figure 19-1 shows, you use the cash flow amounts from three categories to determine your organization's cash flow. You add the totals for each section to determine your organization's increase or decrease in cash for that period. Here your organization has net cash from operating activities of $67,003, net cash from investing activities of $2,637, and net cash from financing activities of $3,790, to give you a net increase in cash of $73,430.

REMEMBER

Parentheses and dashes are negative numbers.

You also have a beginning cash balance from the previous period that you can use to see how your cash flow has changed over a longer period of time (the beginning cash balance for a period is actually the ending cash balance for the previous period). The difference between the beginning cash balance from the previous period and the ending cash balance from the current period is the net increase or net decrease in cash between the two periods.

Figure 19-2 is an example of how the same information you use to prepare an indirect statement of cash flows shows up on a statement of cash flows prepared using the direct method. Note that net cash balances in each of the three parts and beginning and ending cash are the same regardless of which method you use.

The following sections explains the three sections.

Operating activities

The operating activities section of the statement of cash flows reports how much money was received and disbursed from operating activities.

REMEMBER

If it isn't an investing or financing activity, then it's an operating activity. Non-profits depend on gifts and contributions from individuals, corporations, foundations, and government entities. Some may generate revenue by charging a small fee for the services they provided, but for the most part, they rely heavily on fund-raising activities to raise the necessary funds for operations.

Check out the operating activities part of Figure 19-1. You begin with the change in net assets of $66,423, which is comparable to for-profit net income. Then, all the activity here is reported on the cash basis. Thus, depreciation expense is added back because depreciation expense is not a cash transaction.

You also have a decrease of $5,000 because receivables went up. The contribution is not received but was recorded as income on the accrual-based statement of activities. Liabilities increase by $3,000, resulting in an addition. This is because the expense records on the accrual-based statement of activities, but it has not yet been paid.

FIGURE 19-2:
An example of a statement of cash flows using the direct method.

Investing activities

The investing activities section of the statement of cash flows reveals amounts used to sell or buy securities and to sell or buy property or equipment. Take a look at the cash flow from investing activities in Figure 19-1 (keeping in mind that the investing activities and financing activities sections are the same whether you use the indirect or direct method).

Reflected in this section are the proceeds from an investment you sold and your purchase of fixed assets. In this example, you sold $5,000 of investments and used $2,363 to purchase fixed assets, yielding $2,637 of net cash used by investing activities.

REMEMBER

You get this detailed information from the cash receipts and cash disbursements journals that make up the total amounts posted to the cash account in the general ledger.

REMEMBER

The cash receipts journal records any income your nonprofit receives in the form of cash, such as receiving a check from a donor at a fundraising event. The cash disbursements journal (also known as a *cash payment journal*) records any payment your nonprofit makes using a form of cash, such as writing a check to pay a vendor.

Financing activities

Financing activities include borrowing money, repaying the debt, and receiving gifts with long-term donor-imposed restrictions. Typical long-term credit instruments are mortgages and notes payable. Typical gifts with long-term restrictions are contributions for long-term endowment funds.

You find these amounts in your activity posted to your debt accounts in the general ledger. These numbers were first recorded in either your cash receipts or cash disbursements journal, and then posted to the affected accounts in the general ledger.

Check out the financing activities section in Figure 19-1. The amounts in this section of the statement of cash flows reflect principal payments on the organization's mortgage and the total received from donors' restricted contributions. In this example, the organization repaid $8,716 of principal on its mortgage (long-term debt) and received gifts restricted for endowment of $12,506, resulting in net cash provided by financing activities of $3,790. If you had borrowed some money, you would've reported the amount of cash received here as well.

REMEMBER

Significant noncash investing and financing activity must be disclosed in your financial statement notes (see Chapter 21) or as a supplementary schedule accompanying the statement of cash flows.

Analyzing Cash Flow Indicators

Cash flow ratios are used to evaluate an organization's ability to pay its current liabilities given its current assets. Knowing this number tells you how likely it is that your organization can continue to support itself.

TIP

If you're experiencing problems meeting your current obligations, you need to call an emergency board meeting. Your board can help you remedy this problem. Some cash flow problems are temporary and can be resolved with a short-term loan. If you think your cash flow problems are more significant, you may want to hire a certified public accountant (CPA) to help you foresee future cash flow problems.

Although you can calculate several ratios from the statement of cash flows, this discussion focuses on two of the most important indicators: operating cash flow ratio and free cash flow. The following sections take a closer look at each.

Financial ratios are only meaningful if a reference point is used, such as comparing ratios to historical values and similar organizations. Ratios should be viewed as indicators, and some are limited by different accounting methods.

Calculating the operating cash flow ratio

The operating cash flow (OCF) ratio evaluates whether an organization is generating enough cash to meet its short-term obligations. To calculate the OCF ratio, grab your statement of financial position (see Chapter 18) to get the total current liabilities at the end of the period. Then divide the net cash flow from operating activities (taken from your statement of cash flows) by the current liabilities. Here's the equation:

> Operating cash flow ratio = Net cash flow from operating activities ÷ Current liabilities

For example, Figure 19-1 shows net cash flow from operating activities of $67,003; the total current liabilities are $40,000 (taken from Figure 18-1 in Chapter 18). Dividing $67,003 by $40,000 equals 1.68. This number is the operating cash flow ratio for Jay & Top.

When you calculate a ratio, you measure performance. This result indicates whether an organization can sustain itself. As a general rule, a ratio below 1 indicates potential problems with paying short-term debt. It signals a need to hold a fundraiser, sell some stock, slow down on spending, tap into your reserves, or borrow money. The relevant ratio above 1 is considered safe for most organizations.

Determining free cash flow

Free cash flow (FCF) tells you how much money you have after paying your bills, including paying for investments in capital assets. That is, FCF shows how much money is left after paying the costs to run your nonprofit.

To calculate FCF, you need to grab your statement of cash flows (refer to Figure 19-1). Subtract cash used for purchases of fixed assets (it's in the investing activities section) from net cash flow from operating activities (in the operating activities section). Here's the equation:

> Free cash flow = Net cash flow from operating activities - Cash used for purchases of fixed assets

For example, net cash flow from operating activities is $67,003 and cash used for purchases of fixed assets is $2,363. Subtracting $2,363 from $67,003 equals $64,640.

Many organizations include debt payments made for loans that were taken out to buy fixed assets. If you do this with this example, you also subtract the cash used by principal payments on the mortgage (it's in the financing activities section of the statement of cash flows). This is the amount of cash you have after paying all your operating expenses and your payments for fixed assets. This cash is available for paying other debt and any other investments or expenditures the organization wants to make.

So, for this example, you subtract $2,363 and $8,716 from $67,003, which equals $55,924. This number is excellent. Based on the information provided, Jay & Top is stable and has sufficient funds to meet its financial obligations as of the end of the year.

The lower your amount of FCF, the less money you have to pay for other debts and other nonoperating activities. If it's zero or negative, you might have cash flow problems! FCF indicates amounts of cash available for expansion of programs, facilities, or endowments. Obviously, more is better.

Chapter **20**

Organizing the Statement of Functional Expense

Your statement of functional expense reports expenses by their function and nature. First, expenses are classified by their function, which includes program costs, management and general expenses, and fundraising expenses. Next, expenses are separated into their "natural" classification, such as salaries, rent, utilities, supplies, and depreciation.

All nonprofits must report expenses by nature and function in one of three ways:

» In the notes to the financial statements

» In the statement of activities

» In the statement of functional expense, the topic of this chapter

Nonprofits that have more than one function usually opt for the statement of functional expense.

Prior to 2017, only voluntary health and welfare group organizations were required to include a statement of functional expense. However, the Financial Accounting Standards Board (FASB) issued Accounting Standards Update (ASU) 2016-14, which requires all nonprofits to report the functional and natural relationship between expense categories for fiscal years beginning after December 15, 2017.

This chapter looks at how expenses are divided by function and nature and how to use the numbers to measure efficiency.

Classifying Functional Expense

Your challenges as a nonprofit executive director or manager are to address the needs of your constituents, pay your organization staff, and keep administrative costs down, all while running effective programs. To do so, you can rely on the statement of functional expense. To fully use this statement, you need to know how to classify your organization's expenses.

The functional classification of an expense determines what category the expense belongs in (program services or supporting services). You classify expenses according to function to measure how well you're doing. In other words, you track how much of the donors' money is used to run programs versus being spent on supporting services.

There are two steps to break out your expenses by function and nature:

1. **Understand the difference between program services and supporting services.**

    Program services are what you provide in the way of goods or services that fulfills your nonprofit's mission. *Supporting services* are your management and general, fundraising, and membership development activities.

2. **Have an allocation policy in place for your nonprofit.**

    The *allocation policy* is your methodology for apportioning expenses to functional classifications and can use methods such as employee time sheets or analysis of square footage. Using your allocation policy, the second step is to go over your natural expenses categories and record the allocated expense to the correct fund.

TIP

Classifying and allocating may seem simple enough, but putting this into action the first time can be laborious. For example, to allocate an expense into program services, you have to make sure the expense is directly related to program activities and further allocated to the program that receives that direct benefit. Any expense that is of benefit to the nonprofit as a whole goes to supporting services. This is true even if it appears to relate to a specific program, such as collecting donations.

After you've done all the background work classifying and allocating your expenses, it's time to report the results. Figure 20-1 is a sample statement of functional expense.

REMEMBER

Functional expense classification determines which category the expense relates to. The natural expense classification shows how the funds were spent. For example, a nonprofit will have a "bucket," such as a veterinary care program (a functional expense), and a "sub-classification" (a natural expense), for example for salaries directly related to the mission of the veterinary care program.

Jay & Top Community Cat Project
Statement of Functional Expenses
Year Ending December 31, 20XX

	Salaries, Employee Benefits and Taxes	Professional Fees and Other Expenses	Travel and Staff Development	Grants and Awards	Rent, Telephone, Postage and Supplies	Depreciation and Amortization	Total Expenses
Program services							
Veterinary Care	$ 1,02,000	$ 1,450	$ 8,800	$ 10,400	$ 31,000	$ 350	$ 1,54,000
Shelter Support	57,000	1,450	5,700	9,500	18,500	350	92,500
Total program services	1,59,000	2,900	14,500	19,900	49,500	700	2,46,500
Supporting services							
Managerial and general	24,600	28,285	500		965	650	55,000
Fundraising	10,800	250	700		1,450	300	13,500
Total supporting services	35,400	28,535	1,200	-	2,415	950	68,500
Total expenses	$ 1,94,400	$ 31,435	$ 15,700	$ 19,900	$ 51,915	$ 1,650	$ 3,15,000

FIGURE 20-1: Sample statement of functional expense.

Keeping track of time

Allocating time and matching it with the correct programs aren't mere suggestions when it comes to federal grant programs. It's required that all employees who are paid from grant funds document their time and attendance. If your nonprofit receives any grant money, you're required to use this statement to record in detail your time expense.

The best method to capture this information is by employees preparing time and attendance (T&A) reports that indicate which program to charge. T&A reports are also called *time sheets*. Time sheets indicate how an employee spends their time; they also reflect which program or supporting service may be charged to the employee's salary.

One way to track and allocate employee expense among the categories is by keeping track of how much time is spent doing what. If you make a habit of writing down how you spend your time every day, it removes the guesswork.

If you're like most nonprofits, your agency has three types of workers:

>> Employees who are ineligible for overtime pay (paid on salary)

>> Employees who are eligible for overtime pay (paid hourly)

>> Unpaid volunteers

TIP

You should ask each employee to keep a log of how they spend each hour of their workday. They should also record time off for holidays, weekends, sick days, and vacation time. The T&A report should be filled out to coincide with your nonprofit's pay period, signed, and dated by the employee. Then you or the employee's supervisor should review, sign, and date the report as verification of the employee's time. This report can be used to allocate the employee's personnel expenses to the various functional categories.

Keeping T&A reports yields the following benefits:

>> Helps settle disputes about an employee's pay

>> Creates a paper trail for auditors

>> Verifies how federal dollars are spent

>> Provides a way for management to keep up with employee costs

>> Provides a basis for allocating personnel costs to functional categories

REMEMBER

T&A reports are mandatory for employees paid out of federal grants. Federal grants program managers require these reports because they give accountability and add credibility to how the money has been used. Plus, signed T&A reports provide documentation for audit use.

TIP

Keep completed T&A reports with your grant files. Program managers may ask to see them during a monitoring visit or audit. The time sheet in Figure 20-2 displays how to document and track your time and your employees' time.

TIP

You can also ask volunteers to fill out a T&A report. If a volunteer donates professional services (such as legal or accounting services) that your nonprofit would otherwise have to pay for, you may be able to account for the volunteer's time as an in-kind donation. This is a great topic to add to your questions for your accountant.

SSN: **000-00-0000**   NAME: **Mary Smith**   PERIOD ENDING: **1/15/23**

DIVISION: Executive Division   EMPLOYEE BASE: Montgomery, AL

Month January	1	2	3	4	5	8	9	10	11	12	COMP TIME	TOTAL
Tutoring		2.00	1.00	2.00	3.00	2.00	3.00					13.00
Mentoring		2.00	2.00	1.00	1.00	2.00	3.00					11.00
Fundrasing		3.00	2.00	1.00	1.00	2.00	1.00					10.00
General		1.00	3.00	4.00	3.00	2.00	1.00	8.00	8.00	8.00		38.00
TOTAL DIRECT HOURS		8.00	8.00	8.00	8.00	8.00	8.00	8.00	8.00	8.00	0.00	72.00
ANNUAL LEAVE												0.00
SICK LEAVE												0.00
HOLIDAY LEAVE	8.00											8.00
PERSONAL LEAVE												0.00
MILITARY LEAVE												0.00
COMP LEAVE												0.00
OTHER												0.00
DAILY	8.00	8.00	8.00	8.00	8.00	8.00	8.00	8.00	8.00	8.00	0.00	80.00

Mary Smith   1/15/23   *James Oliver*   1/15/23
EMPLOYEE   DATE   SUPERVISOR   DATE

FIGURE 20-2: A simple time sheet helps you track employees' hours.

Allocating expenses

The expenses listing on your statement of functional expense relate to program services and supporting services, which are ordinary, day-to-day expenses including, but not limited to, salaries, employee benefits, professional fees, travel, scholarships and awards, rent, telephone, supplies, and depreciation. Any of the many expenses your nonprofit incurs may be charged to program costs or supporting services such as management and general costs and/or fundraising costs. You just need to make that determination by identifying the expense by program and then segregating by the expense's natural classification using your allocation methodology.

TIP

Some high-tech devices, such as copiers or printers, can allocate expenses based on actual usage. For example, you can have your copier or printer set up to assign codes to each program and person. Then, each time something is photocopied or printed, the copier or printer matches the expense to the program or person. So, when you're making copies of a fundraising event flyer, your copier can assign the cost of printing to fundraising expenses.

The following sections break down the types of program services and supporting services expenses to help you differentiate between them, so you know how to classify them on your statement of functional expense.

Program expenses

Your programs are used to implement your mission. Program expenses are the costs of goods and services used to fulfill your purpose and to operate your projects. Some common programs are

>> Food pantries and soup kitchens

>> Mentoring programs

>> Tutoring programs

>> Support groups

Of course, many programs benefit people, so these are just a few examples. Program expenses are costs directly related to a program. Common program expenses are

>> Supplies

>> Wages of people working solely or directly for a program

>> Personnel costs related to the program's direct employees

TIP

The total program expense on the statement of functional expense should equal the program expense reported on the statement of activities. The totals for managerial and general expense and fundraising expense should also agree with those amounts reported on the statement of activities.

If an expense is incurred by two or more programs, you divide it using your allocation methodology (see the "Classifying Functional Expense" section earlier in this chapter). For example, consider the cost of labor (salaries, payroll taxes, and fringe benefits). This is usually a high expense for nonprofits. By using T&A reports, you can divide the expense by the hours spent working on each program (see the section "Keeping track of time," earlier in the chapter).

Management and general expenses

The second classification of expenses on the statement of functional expense is supporting services, which includes management and general (M&G) expenses, also referred to as general and administrative expenses. These costs aren't identifiable to any program or fundraising activity. That is, they aren't directly related to an activity, nor are they reasonably allocable to an activity. These expenses represent costs that are shared by all activities and are necessary for the organization's operation. They provide an indirect benefit to your organization as a whole, and you incur them whether you run one or more programs.

Management and general activities include

>> Accounting staff

>> Business management

>> Insurance

>> Legal expenses

>> Payroll taxes

>> Rent/mortgage

>> Salaries

>> Travel

>> Utilities

>> Administrative activities of the organization as a whole

For example, you use a postage machine in your office for day-to-day business. You wouldn't go out and buy a new postage machine just to operate a new program and to keep expenses separate. You use the postage machine as needed for the new program, and you allocate a portion of the phone bill to all programs that benefit from its use. This could be accomplished through meter setup or programming.

Your T&A reports are the best way to allocate expenses for salaries and fringe benefits to the right category. Finally, your operating budget separates program costs from M&G and fundraising costs. (See Chapter 10 for more about operating budgets.)

TIP

If you can't identify the cost as a program or fundraising cost, then it's automatically an M&G cost. Make sure the total M&G on the statement of functional expense matches the M&G amount on the statement of activities.

Fundraising expenses

Supporting services also includes fundraising expenses. The cost of all activities that create support for your nonprofit in the form of gifts, grants, contributions, and services are considered fundraising expenses. Fundraising activities include

- >> Advertising and direct mail campaigns

- >> Maintaining donor mailing lists

- >> Conducting fundraising events, including dinners and dances, concerts and fashion shows, sporting competitions, and auctions

- >> Preparing and handing out fundraising materials

- >> Conducting other activities involved with soliciting contributions from individuals, organizations, foundations, corporations, and government entities

Some fundraising expenses stand out. For example, the cost of a direct mail campaign is easy to allocate to fundraising expenses because you know how much postage was used, how many envelopes were mailed, and how many copies you printed.

You're fully aware of how important fundraising is to your organization. You seek philanthropists who will donate money, goods, services, time, and effort to support your cause. Keeping track of the expenses related to fundraising is important to help you determine whether your efforts at raising money are working and whether you're spending money in the right areas.

WARNING

Some fundraising activities held by some nonprofits may not be considered fundraising events by the IRS. Instead, the IRS could consider them unrelated to your nonprofit's exempt purpose, and if deemed such, the revenue would be taxable unrelated business income. (See Chapter 16 for more information about unrelated business income.)

The following activities can trigger unrelated business income recognition:

- >> Sales of gifts or goods or services unless they're of nominal value (nominal value is generally considered to be less than real or market value)

- >> Sweepstakes, lotteries, or raffles where the names of contributors or other respondents are entered in a drawing for prizes

- >> Raffles or lotteries where prizes have only nominal value

- >> Solicitation campaigns that generate only contributions

If necessary, check with your accountant to verify you're classifying the expenses correctly.

TECHNICAL
STUFF

A new method is emerging to conduct fundraising campaigns over the internet. This new wave is called ePhilanthropy, and it allows you to solicit funds from your website, even while you're sleeping.

Using the Statement of Functional Expense to Calculate Ratios

Potential donors typically like to give money to organizations where they know their money is being spent wisely. They sometimes calculate how much of your total expenses are used for programs versus how much is used for management and general expenses. Let's face it, no one wants to give to an organization and have their gift squandered. You can use the statement of functional expense to show your donors exactly how your nonprofit is spending its money and that you're using your donations to help who you're trying to reach.

To show how you use your funding, you can calculate different ratios that provide insight into your organization's operating performance and financial position such as ratios to measure your nonprofit's organizational efficiency. The total expenses alone don't give a clear picture of your efficiency, but calculating ratios gives the numbers more meaning.

TIP

To calculate a ratio, you divide one number by another number. Ratios indicate the relationship of one thing to another.

REMEMBER

Ratios are only as good as the numbers used to calculate them, so make sure the figures on your statement of functional expense are accurate.

As a general rule, you want to keep your administrative and fundraising costs down and spend donations on their intended purpose of running programs. By figuring the ratios in the following sections, you can show that your donors' contributions aren't being used to pay high salaries and other extravagant expenses. You can ideally advertise that your nonprofit has low administrative and fundraising costs.

Calculating the program spending ratio

The program spending ratio tells you what percentage of your total spending goes toward programs. Having your program expenses broken down by percentages gives the statement of functional expense more meaning. It allows people to get a quick overview of how much of their donations support programs.

To calculate the program spending ratio, you divide total program expenses by total expenses. Refer to Figure 20-1 to see the two types of program services — veterinary care and shelter support — for this example.

The total allocated to the veterinary care program is $154,000. The total program expense for the shelter support program is $92,500. The total program expense is $246,500.

The total expenses for the year are $315,000. The program spending ratio is 78 percent ($246,500 ÷ $315,000 = 0.78). This means that 78 percent of your total expenses are used to run programs.

Overall, you're better off with a high program spending ratio because donors want to fund programs, not the administrative and fundraising costs to operate your nonprofit. If the percentages in this example were the other way around, you probably wouldn't get too many donations if only 22 percent of the total expenses supported programs. Of course, sometimes there's room for exceptions. If you're renovating or upgrading your building, for example, you'll have something to show for the disparity.

Determining the fundraising efficiency ratio

The fundraising efficiency ratio tells what percentage of dollars were spent to raise another dollar. Nonprofit managers have a challenging job to raise capital while keeping costs down. This ratio is important because donors like their money to go directly to the programs they're supporting.

You divide fundraising costs by total contributions to get your fundraising efficiency ratio. (You need to refer to your statement of activities to get the total contributions for the year; see Chapter 17.) To calculate the fundraising efficiency ratio, consider the following hypothetical scenario.

If you received $425,000 in contributions and your fundraising costs were $13,500, your fundraising efficiency ratio would be 3 percent ($13,500 ÷ $425,000 = 0.03). It costs only 3 cents to raise a dollar.

A 3 percent fundraising efficiency ratio is considered a good ratio because it shows that you're keeping fundraising costs down. Larger organizations can have a higher ratio, but small nonprofits should strive to keep this number as low as possible.

IN THIS CHAPTER

» **Knowing why you need to close the books**

» **Completing year-end entries**

» **Including notes with your financial statements**

Chapter **21**

Closing the Nonprofit Books

A s you come to the end of your accounting year, you need to wrap up your books for the previous year and start the books for the next year. Your accounting period indicated the beginning and end of your reporting period, which can be 6, 12, or 18 months, depending on the needs of your non-profit. If you choose the most common reporting period of 12 months, this period can be a calendar year (January to December) or a fiscal year (using another 12-month period). No matter when your accounting year ends, you need to close your books and start a new accounting cycle or year.

When you close your books, you need to make sure all your temporary accounts, such as your revenue and expense accounts, return to having a zero balance so revenues and expenses in the next accounting cycle can properly record and close. To do so, you have to make some closing entries to certain accounts. Closing your books is an important process because you need to transfer the balance from statement of activities accounts to another account, so only statement of financial position accounts remains open.

This chapter discusses closing the temporary accounts (revenue, expense, gain, and loss), making some of the necessary notes to your financial statements, preparing adjusting and reversing entries, and reading your books for the next accounting period.

If you're using a manual system (see Chapter 8), closing the books may turn out to be a little more work than if you were using accounting software because computerized systems close the accounts for you (see Chapter 9 for information about using computerized accounting software). No matter which system you use, you need to understand the procedures to end one accounting period and begin another.

Understanding the Need to Close Your Nonprofit's Books

During the course of the year, you've had money coming in (revenues) and money going out (expenses). This is a continuous cycle taking place in your organization. At the end of your accounting year, you need to close your books.

You close the books to move your nonprofit's bottom line from the statement of activities (see Chapter 17) to the statement of financial position (see Chapter 18). Your accounting period has a beginning and ending date. If you operate on a calendar year, your beginning date is January 1 and your ending date is December 31. If you have a fiscal year end, your closing date is the last day of any other month of the year, such as May 31 or September 30. If you don't close your books, you have no ending to your accounting period and no new beginning.

However, keep in mind that you can't close your books until your books are adjusted. Start by reviewing your unadjusted trial balance to determine what accounts require adjusting journal entries. After making all adjusting journal entries, prepare the adjusted trial balance and then your financial statements. At this point, you can close your books and start a new accounting cycle. After your financial statements are done, you can turn your information over to a certified public accountant (CPA) if your nonprofit is required to secure an independent audit.

To understand how to close the books, you have to know the difference between temporary and permanent accounts:

>> **Temporary accounts:** Revenue, expense, gain, and loss accounts are considered temporary accounts and are the accounts you close out at the end of the accounting cycle. Temporary accounts report on the statement of activities. The closing process resets these accounts to zero so that only current accounting period transactions accumulate in the accounts.

>> **Permanent accounts:** These accounts report on the statement of financial position. They carry over from year to year, so you normally don't close these accounts. However, it's necessary to close your temporary accounts to a permanent account, which I cover later in this chapter in the section "Finalizing with closing entries."

When you close the books, you transfer the balances of your temporary accounts to the income summary account. The income summary account records the net effect of closing all temporary accounts for a given period. This will be 12 months if you're closing the books at the end of the calendar or fiscal year.

REMEMBER

The balances for all your accounts — revenues, expenses, gains, losses, assets, liabilities, and equity — are in your general ledger.

Think of the income summary account as a bucket holding the net effect of the difference between total revenues/gains and total expenses/losses. That net effect results in either an increase or decrease in net assets, which then is transferred to the statement of financial position. The net assets at the beginning of the year are added to the current period net asset increase (decrease), resulting in the total net assets at end of the year.

REMEMBER

All net assets must be allocated between those without donor restrictions and those with donor restrictions.

Closing entries accomplishes two things:

>> **It causes all revenue, expense, gain, and loss accounts to begin the new accounting period with zero balances.** Each accounting period shows performances taking place only during that period. Thus, revenue, expense, gain, and loss accounts are used only temporarily to store current period accounting activities. After the accounting period ends, you transfer the results of everything that transpired during that period to the income summary account.

>> **It transfers the net effect of the past period's revenue and expense transactions to your net assets account.** During your accounting cycle you made purchases, received support and revenue, and paid bills. Now that this accounting period has expired, you only need to reflect the net effect of the activities that happened in it. So, by closing revenue, expense, gain, and loss accounts to the income summary, the income summary reflects the net effects of those accounts. This net effect is transferred to net assets by closing the income summary to net assets.

The following section explains the steps in adjusting and closing the books and explains when reversing journal entries may come into play.

Adjusting, Closing, and Reversing Entries

During your year-end closing process, you'll probably need to adjust some of your accounts to correct some balances and make cash-to-accrual adjustments. After you make your adjusting entries, you can prepare an adjusted trial balance, which you use to prepare your financial statements. Then you need to make closing entries to close your temporary accounts to the income summary account, and close the income summary account to net assets. Finally, at the beginning of the next accounting period, you may want to reverse some of the cash-to-accrual adjustments you made at the end of the previous accounting period.

The following sections walk you through the closing process, including when you may have to reverse and adjust some entries at year-end.

Making year-end adjusting entries

Adjusting journal entries is an important part of preparing materially correct financial statements. For example, under the accrual method of accounting, when a transaction begins in one accounting period and ends in a later one, an adjusting entry matching expense to the revenue for the same reporting period is required.

Adjusting entries are also used to make corrections due to transposition and other errors made during the year. These types of adjusting entries are also called *correcting entries.* All adjusting entries are made in the general journal.

Certain accounts, such as prepaid expenses, require adjustments at the end of your accounting period due to their nature. *Prepaid expenses* are assets until they're used in the operation of your organization. Examples of prepaid expenses are the unused portion of subscriptions to journals and magazines, or insurance that was paid in full for a year and only four months of the policy period have elapsed prior to the end of the accounting year.

You may also have adjustments relating to the basis of accounting and time-period concepts. Using different bases of accounting may require adjustments if you've kept your books on the cash basis throughout the year and your financial statements must be presented on the accrual basis according to generally accepted accounting principles (GAAP).

The cash basis reports revenues and expenses when they're received or paid. GAAP requires assigning revenues to the periods in which they're earned and expenses to the period in which they're incurred. You use adjusting entries to make cash-to-accrual adjustments. (Chapter 2 walks you through the differences between the cash and accrual methods of accounting.)

One type of adjusting journal entry is made is when accounts like payroll overlap accounting periods. For example, suppose you get paid every two weeks, but the end of the year falls right in the middle of the two-week period. Wages for the first week were $2,000. Accrual accounting requires you to recognize the payroll expense when it was incurred, not when it's paid. Here's an example of a typical payroll-adjusting journal entry:

Date		Debit	Credit
20XX			
Dec 31	Wages expense	2,000	
	Wages payable		2,000

To accrue the last week's wages for 20XX

Here's an example of a correction of error adjusting journal entry: Let's say the mortgage payable balance in your general ledger is $4,900 and your interest expense is $900. However, your notice from the bank says your mortgage balance is $5,000 and the interest you paid for the year was $1,000. After you verify that the notice from the bank is correct, you make the following entry to correct (adjust) the balances in your general ledger (to increase an expense, you debit it; to increase a liability, you credit it):

Date		Debit	Credit
20XX			
Dec 31	Interest expense	100	
	Mortgage payable		100

To adjust mortgage payable and interest expense to bank's records

Finally, consider an example of a cash-to-accrual adjustment. Assume there is a zero balance in accounts payable at the end of the year. However, in early January, you receive a $50 telephone bill for the month of December, which you pay in January. The expense was incurred in December, so the accrual basis of accounting requires you to recognize the expense in December, not January. To do this you post the following entry:

Date		Debit	Credit
20XX			
Dec 31	Telephone expense	50	
	Accounts payable		50

To post accounts payable at 12/31/XX

When you record the payment in January, you either debit accounts payable in your cash disbursements journal or debit the telephone expense if you reversed the cash-to-accrual adjustment at the beginning of the year. I discuss reversing entries later in this chapter.

To make the adjustments at the end of each accounting period, prepare a worksheet called a Working Trial Balance. Figure 21-1 shows an abbreviated working trial balance. (I walk you through preparing this worksheet in Chapter 8.)

Work Sheet for Month Ending December 31, 20XX

Account	A) Unadjusted Trial Balance		B) Adjustments		C) Adjusted Trial Balance		4) Income Statement		5) Balance Sheet	
	Dr.	Cr.	Dr.	Cr.	Dr.	Cr.	Dr.	Cr.	Dr.	Cr.
Assets										
Liabilities										
Net Assets										
Revenue										
Expenses										

FIGURE 21-1: Abbreviated working trial balance.

Finalizing with closing entries

To close out your accounting period, you need to make three important closing entries: one for expenses, one for revenues, and a final one for the income summary. Here are the steps:

1. **Close expense accounts.**

   Your expense accounts are found in your general ledger; each one has to be reset to zero. To close an expense account, you need to decrease it or zero it out by doing a credit. (**Remember:** Expense accounts have a normal balance of a debit.) Expense accounts are closed by credits equal to the total account's debit balance.

   To close, you write a closing entry in the general journal listing all the expense accounts, like this:

Date		Debit	Credit
20XX			
Dec 31	Income summary	WW	
	Telephone expense		XX
	Supplies expense		YY
	(Keep listing expenses)		ZZ

   To close expense accounts to the income summary

Note in this example the total of all the credits to the expense accounts equals the debit to the income summary. So, for this example, XX + YY + ZZ = WW. Closing the expense accounts transfers the total of expenses to the income summary.

2. **Close revenue accounts.**

Your revenue accounts are also found in the general ledger, and you have to reset each one of them to zero. To close a revenue account, you need to decrease it or zero it out by doing a debit. Revenue accounts have a normal balance of a credit, so you close them out by making a debit equal to the account's credit balance. To close a revenue account, follow this example:

Date		Debit	Credit
20XX			
Dec 31	Contributions	WW	
	Program fee income	XX	
	(Keep listing revenues)	YY	
	Income summary		ZZ

To close revenue accounts to the income summary

In this example, the total of all the debits to the revenue accounts equals the credit to the income summary. So, for this example, WW + XX + YY = ZZ. Closing the revenue accounts transfers the total of revenues to the income summary.

3. **Close the income summary account.**

Your income summary account is a temporary account in the general ledger set up to close the revenue and expense accounts. The balance in the income summary equals the total expenses (debits) posted to the account in Step 1 netted against the total revenues (credits) posted to the account in Step 2. If the income summary has a credit balance, then you had a *surplus* (increase in net assets) for the year. If it has a debit balance, then you had a *deficit* (decrease in net assets) for the year. So, the last step is to transfer the balance from the income summary to net assets by closing the income summary to net assets. The entry looks something like this:

Date		Debit	Credit
20XX			
Dec 31	Income summary	XX	
	Net assets		XX

To close the income summary

Notice in this example there was a surplus for the year because I had to debit the income summary to close it. There would then be a credit balance in the income summary, which means revenues exceeded expenses. In this scenario, if the debits had exceeded the credits, a deficit would've resulted, showing that expenses were more than revenues.

The income summary account is closed to your net assets account on your statement of financial position.

Reversing entries to close temporary accounts

If you keep your books on the cash basis during the year and make cash-to-accrual adjustments at the end of the year for your financial statements, you need to reverse those cash-to-accrual adjustments at the beginning of the next year. If you don't, then you'll count the revenue or expenses twice: once in the period you made the cash-to-accrual adjustment, and again in the next period when you receive the accrued revenue or pay the accrued expenses. Reversing the accrual entry subtracts the revenue or expense that was accrued and recognized in the previous period, and it eliminates the amount accrued to the related asset or liability account on your statement of financial position.

Record reversing entries in the general journal. To prepare a reversing entry, you debit what was credited, and you credit what was debited in your year-end cash-to-accrual adjustment. Remember the example for an adjusting entry for December's $50 telephone bill received and paid for in January? I moved the expense from January into December by making the following adjusting entry:

Date		Debit	Credit
20XX			
Dec 31	Telephone expense	50	
	Accounts payable		50

To post accounts payable at 12/31/XX

If you continue keeping your books on the cash basis and don't make reversing entries at the beginning of the next year, you'll recognize the $50 of telephone expense twice — once in December and again in January. You'll also still show $50 in accounts payable even though the bill has been paid. That's because accounts payable is found on the statement of financial position and is a permanent account; it isn't reset to zero at year-end. So, to prevent all this from happening, you post a reversing entry:

Date		Debit	Credit
20XX			
Jan 1	Accounts payable	50	
	Telephone expense		50

To reverse previous year's telephone accrual

Looking at these two journal entries, December 31 shows an increase to accounts payable by crediting it for $50 and an increase to telephone expense by debiting it for $50. The effect of the December 31 journal is completely reversed with the January 1 journal entry by debiting accounts payable and crediting telephone expense. You would then proceed to reverse all of the previous year-end's cash-to-accrual adjustments in a similar fashion.

WARNING

It may not be necessary to reverse all your adjusting journal entries. Some adjustments correct balances and shouldn't be reversed. Some expenses, like depreciation, aren't paid with cash, and so those entries wouldn't be reversed. But entries that move income or expenses from one period to another need to be reversed if you keep your books on the cash basis and make year-end accrual adjustments for financial statement purposes.

Completing the Notes to the Financial Statements

The notes (also referred to as footnotes) to your financial statements provide additional valuable information about your financial picture that can influence the overall judgment about your organization's future. According to GAAP, all financial statements should contain notes of disclosure (see Figure 21-2 for an example).

Folks inside and outside your nonprofit review your financial statements to figure out how well your organization has done and is doing. However, many people consider the notes to financial statements just as important as the financial statements themselves because the notes explain things that the numbers can't.

The following sections give you a better idea of what to include in the notes to your nonprofit's financial statements. Some examples are organization and operation, significant accounting policies, and liquidity information.

Jay & Top Community Cat Project
Notes to Financial Statements
December 31, 20XX

Note 1 - Organization and operation

Jay & Top Community Cat Project is a nonprofit organization under Section 501(C) (3) of the Internal Revenue Code. Jay & Top's purpose is to provide veterinary care to community cats and provide support to community cat shelters in the local area.

Note 2 - Summary of significant accounting policies

Basis of presentation

The accompanying financial statements are presented on the accrual basis of accounting in accordance with accounting principles generally accepted in the United States of America.

Net assets and revenue, expenses, gains and losses are classified based on the existence or absence of donor-imposed restrictions.
Accordingly , net assets are classified as follow:

Net assets with donor restriction - subject to donor restrictions that may be or will be met by actions taken by Jay & Top in the passage of time.
Net assets without donor restrictions - available resources other than donor-restricted contributions.

Contributions

Classified as either conditional or unconditional. Conditional contributions are recognized when donor imposed hurdles are satisfied. Unconditional contributions are recognized as revenue and receivable at commitment.

Cash and cash equivalents

Jay & Top considers all cash on hand, checking accounts and short-term highly liquid investments available for current use with a maturity of three months or less when acquired to be cash and cash equivalents.

Liquidity Information

Assets list by nearness of cash conversion and liabilities list by nearness to resulting use of cash.

Note 3 - Contingencies

Jay & Top participates in grant programs assisted by various governmental agencies. These programs are subject to financial and compliance audits by the grantors or their representatives. Management does not deem any liability arising from such to be material.

Explaining changes in accounting methods

The note outlining the various accounting methods (also known as *significant accounting policies*) you use to prepare your financial records is usually contained in the first or second note written to your financial statements. Important disclosures for nonprofits are the method of accounting, classification of net assets, and any change in accounting methods.

The method of accounting is normally accrual in accordance with accounting principles generally accepted in the United States. The discussion about net assets explains the fact that net assets and changes therein are classified between net assets with donor restrictions and net assets without donor restrictions.

Occasionally, your nonprofit may have a changing accounting method that might bear a significant effect on your reported income or skew results when doing year-over-year trend analysis. Thus, any changes must be disclosed. Some common accounting methods disclosed in your notes are

>> **Inventory methods chosen to record value and cost:** Your chosen inventory method sets the price you use to value your inventory. You may have recorded it at the cost you paid for it, or its current market value. The inventory valuation method you use should be indicated in the notes to the financial statement. Also, you should disclose in the notes when you make changes, a topic that should always be discussed with your CPA.

>> **Depreciation method or writing off of assets:** Depreciation is the writing off as an expense the cost of an asset over its useful life. Because depreciation reduces net assets, changing your depreciation method affects your net income. Likewise, discuss a change in depreciation methods with your CPA.

If last year's statements were prepared using a different method, they'll most likely not be comparable with the current year's statements. Financial managers like to compare apples to apples and oranges to oranges, and changes to accounting methods will probably necessitate comparing apples to oranges. Even though they're both fruits, they're pretty different. You need to disclose any changes in your accounting methods and the financial impact of those changes in your footnotes.

For example, think of the relationship between your statement of activities and your statement of financial position. Your statement of activities records all revenue, expense, gain, and loss. Your statement of financial position records all assets, liabilities, and net assets. The difference between revenues, expenses, gains, and losses are closed out to the statement of financial position as an increase or decrease in net assets. So, if you change the accounting method for any account tied to an expense, the change in method makes a difference in your net assets.

Two principles shed some light on changes in accounting methods:

>> **The Full Disclosure Principle:** This principle states that users of financial statements have every right to information relevant to their decision making.

>> **The Consistency Principle:** This principle states that consistency should be used in the treatment of the same accounting events period after period.

Noting all lawsuits

Because lawsuits may have an adverse effect on your nonprofit's finances, you need to both disclose any lawsuit and fully describe the nature of the lawsuit in the notes of your financial statements. Why do you need to include this information? Your stakeholders need to know who may potentially want to sue you and why because they have a vested interest in your nonprofit's livelihood.

GAAP requires this information at least via a footnote. Based on the circumstances, you may have to prepare a journal entry to show the effect of the lawsuit as an actual part of the financial statements. See the next section, "Including all contingent liabilities," to learn the two criteria for reporting lawsuits as a part of the financial statements.

Wondering how a nonprofit might be a party in a lawsuit? A disgruntled employee may want to sue the nonprofit, seeking damages for injury or workers compensation, or someone may want to take you to court for wrongful death or negligence of someone entrusted in your care. For example, if you operate a nonprofit daycare facility and one of your employees leaves a child in a van, you could face a lawsuit from the child's parent or guardian.

Although you can't prevent lawsuits, you can protect your organization by purchasing liability insurance to offset the effects of someone winning a case against your organization.

Including all contingent liabilities

Based on the facts and circumstances of the contingent liability, you may have to report the effect of contingent liabilities on your financial statements. A *contingent liability* is a noncurrent liability that exists when your nonprofit has an existing circumstance as of the date of the financial statements that may cause a future loss, depending on events that have not yet happened (and, indeed, may never happen).

Examples of events that could be considered contingencies are

>> Pending litigation, which means the nonprofit is actively involved in a lawsuit that is not yet settled, such as a former employee's lawsuit for lost wages or wrongful termination

>> Not filing Form 990 and forgetting to file an extension that results in penalties

See FASB ASC 450-20-55 for more information about accruing losses due to pending or threatened litigation. (I show you how to find free access to FASB ASCs in Chapter 13.)

If a loss due to a contingent liability meets the following two criteria, it should be accrued and reported in the nonprofit's financial statements, which shows up as a charge against income:

>> **The chance of the loss event happening is probable,** which means that the future event will likely occur.

>> **The amount of the loss can be reasonably estimated,** which means you can come up with a highly accurate loss dollar amount. For example, if the nonprofit finds out it has to pay damages in a lawsuit, the cost is fixed and determinable.

Refer to Figure 21-2 for generic wording relating to contingent liabilities in the notes.

Noting conditions on assets and liabilities

Sometimes donors impose restriction on the assets they give your nonprofit, and these restrictions need to be included in the notes to your financial statements. Also, if you've pledged assets as collateral for loans, you should include this in the notes. If you have long-term liabilities, you should disclose the effective interest rate, maturity dates, repayment terms, and so on.

Before I close this section about the notes to the financial statements, I want to highlight a few additional disclosure requirements your nonprofit may encounter, including those relating to the statement of cash flows and functional and net asset reporting. The following list is not comprehensive, but it includes key examples:

>> **Statement of activities:** Report the amount of changes in each class of net assets and the changes in net assets as a whole.

>> **Statement of cash flows:** Provide the nonprofit's accounting policy for determining if an item is a cash or cash equivalent. Classify cash receipts and disbursements as operating, investing, or financing with investing and financing reporting shown separately.

>> **Net assets:** Follow the self-imposed limits set by the board of directors on use of net assets and detail the nonprofit's endowment spending policy.

>> **Functional reporting:** Furnish a description of major programs and report expenses by functional category via statement or notes. Disclose any payments to affiliated organizations.

Putting Last Year Behind You and Looking Forward

After you've closed the books, you can prepare your financial statements. When all of that number crunching is finished, make sure to store the journals, general ledger, and any supporting documentation someplace safe. You never know when you're going to need that info, and you definitely don't want to mix the old records with the new ones.

You also need to start a new set of books for the new fiscal year. Start by journaling. Maintain good records throughout the year, and you'll end with polished audited financial statements. When you end the year, you'll find yourself going over the same procedures for the next year. Think about how good you'll feel when it's over!

5

The Part of Tens

IN THIS PART . . .

Find tips on how to keep your organization in compliance with accounting standards and IRS rules.

Get pointers on keeping your books to ensure everything balances and is materially correct.

Find ways to remain solvent, such as finding new funding sources and writing grant proposals.

Make sure you can pass an audit and meet the federal guidelines that relate to your nonprofit organization.

Chapter 22

Ten Important Things to Know When Keeping a Nonprofit's Books

A s the executive director or manager of a nonprofit, your job is to make sure your organization's books are in order. You want to make sure your staff follows the guidelines set in the generally accepted accounting principles (GAAP). You also want to verify that you and your staff are following these guidelines through detailed documentation.

This chapter reviews the ten most important things you need to know when keeping your nonprofit's books. Ignoring any of these items can negatively impact your nonprofit's books and the success or future of your organization.

Monitoring Cash Contributions

Cash is the most liquid asset. Due to its nature, it is inherently risky and sometimes hard to track after you exchange or receive it. To prevent any potential problems, your organization needs to have an in-house policy that describes how to receive and handle cash.

Factoring in frequency of occurrence, you should deposit cash donations on a regular basis so that any time lags in deposit dates are obvious. For example, maybe your nonprofit makes a bank run every Monday, Wednesday, and Friday; if a bank run was not made on those days, find out why.

When you establish your policy, remember that the same person should never both receive the cash and pay the bills. Accountants refer to policies like this example of segregation of duties as *internal controls*. Ideally one person prepares the bank deposit slip, and another makes the bank run and has no access to any blank deposit slips. Lacking collusion among employees, this system of cash controls is very strong.

Another example of internal controls is that you can put up a sign on your clerk's desk reminding donors that they should receive receipts for all donations. Without this receipt policy (and sign), you increase the risk that the clerk may pocket the money because your nonprofit has no record of the transaction without physical documentation.

I also suggest you compare your cash-based deposits to bank statements against your budget entry for cash receipts. If your budgeted figure is off from actual, it makes sense to find out why. Could be you were too optimistic when preparing your budget, which may affect your budgeting process for the next year. If the figures don't reconcile due to misappropriation, it's best to find out as soon as possible.

Keeping a Donors List

Making a donors list and checking it twice pays off. A donors list is simply a complete and up-to-date list of all the people who have donated to your organization, including their names, phone numbers, and addresses, along with the dates they donated and the amounts they contributed. Updating this list is important because the Internal Revenue Service (IRS) or an independent certified public accountant (CPA) may need to verify a donor's list.

For example, when an individual deducts a charitable donation from their income taxes, the IRS sometimes tracks this donation back to the organization that received it to verify that person's donation. Your up-to-date donors list can provide the verification the IRS is looking for. When your CPA audits your books, they require a donors list. During the audit, your CPA performs a random test by contacting some of the people on your donors list to verify contributions.

Balancing Your Nonprofit's Checkbook

Your checkbook is a good place to start when you're trying to get a handle on your finances. When your checkbook is out of balance, you need to balance it as quickly as possible as you need to know how much money you have, how much you've spent, and how much you need to cover currently due costs.

Because banks make mistakes, you must keep an eye on your checking account to make sure you and the bank are on the same page at all times. All banks offer online banking, which makes it a simple task to review your account as often as daily. At the very least, you should balance your bank account monthly. (See Chapter 7 for step-by-step instructions on how to do this.)

Leaving a Paper Trail

Document and keep copies of everything that takes place in your organization (for example, services and programs offered, fundraising events conducted, and salaries paid). Keep copies of every receipt, invoice, and bill paid. It's not a bad idea to scan all paper checks your organization writes to justify and verify your expenses. Every transaction that occurs in your organization has to leave a clear path that explains when it happened, why it happened, and how it happened.

REMEMBER

When you have supporting documentation to justify every transaction that takes place in your nonprofit, you maintain your accountability. Plus, complete documentation allows you to clearly and accurately show why you did what you did, who gave you what, when things happened, and how you kept up with them. Your auditor will want to see invoices, receipts, and other documents to verify your financial activities.

Protecting Your Nonprofit from Employee Theft

Unfortunately, nonprofits face a similar problem that for-profits face — employees who steal from their own organizations. You can lessen the impact of employee theft by protecting yourself by taking the following simple actions to help protect your assets:

>> **Give your potential employees a standard test.** By having potential employees answer certain questions, you can gauge the likelihood that they

may steal. These tests are usually electronic and include multiple-choice questions that ask potential employees what they would do in certain scenarios. For example, one question may ask what you would do if you witnessed another employee stealing from the organization. Answers to questions like this one are good indicators of personal values, ethics, and attitudes.

>> **Segregate duties.** Segregating duties means not putting the same person in charge of making decisions about purchases, writing checks to pay for those purchases, receiving the purchases, and keeping up with inventory. When you don't segregate duties, you make yourself vulnerable to potential employee theft because if the same employee is in charge of all duties regarding a particular purchase, they could steal the purchase, and no one would know. After all, no one else may even know the purchase was made.

>> **Place security cameras in your building.** Security cameras protect you from outside threats, as well as internal threats, by recording what happens in your building at all times.

>> **Do background checks on potential employees.** In some states, employers have to do background checks on volunteers and employees who may work with children. Check with your attorney general's office or state department of public safety for information about how to get a background check of a potential employee. Always get prior signed approval from the potential employee before doing a background check. Do a little homework before you choose a company to do your background checks because fees vary.

>> **Reference a potential employee's credit reports.** Pulling a potential employee's credit history can help you gauge that person's character. Responsible individuals usually pay their bills on time. Make sure you get signed approval from the potential employee before running a credit history.

Talk to your auditor about other protective measures you can take to safeguard your assets. (Check out Chapter 2 for more about protecting your organization's assets.)

Considering Your Constituency

Your constituencies are your donors and the people you serve. In the nonprofit world, your constituencies are your stakeholders (individuals who have a vested interest in your outcome to make a positive difference in the lives of the people in your community). Your stakeholders are very important to the livelihood of your organization because your organization can't survive without the people who donate money or the people who use your services. Therefore, before making any major decision, always consider the impact it will have on your constituency.

Staying in Compliance

In exchange for your tax-exempt status, you have certain obligations to fulfill to the state and federal governments. You can stay within the guidelines the IRS gives you by filing all necessary paperwork in a timely fashion. You have to follow the IRS's rules regarding how you should operate and run your program on a daily basis to maintain your tax-exempt status. In addition, if your nonprofit receives federal grants, you should've received a list of policies that you need to follow to continue to receive your grant funds.

REMEMBER

Here are three of the most important rules you need to stay in compliance with:

>> **File your 990 on time.** If you forget to file Form 990 for three years in a row, you lose your nonprofit tax-exempt status.

>> **Avoid commercial activities.** If you start operating like a for-profit entity, you can lose your nonprofit status.

>> **Stay out of politics.** If you start campaigning and encouraging others who benefit from your services to vote a certain way, you can jeopardize your tax-exempt status with the IRS.

Limiting Nonprogram Income

Nonprogram income is any income generated by a nonprofit business that is *regularly* carried on and *unrelated* to the exempt function of your nonprofit. Engaging in excessive unrelated business transactions can change the status of your organization from a nonprofit to a for-profit, which means you lose your exempt status.

Unfortunately, Internal Revenue Code (IRC) and Treasury Regulations are somewhat lacking in clarity as to how much unrelated business income is permissible for nonprofits under IRC 501(c)(3). As a general rule, if you stay within the scope of the tax-exempt purpose of your nonprofit, you should be okay. However, this is a thorny topic and should be added to the list of questions you have for your accountant or tax return preparer.

TECHNICAL STUFF

There are court cases upholding the revocation of tax-exempt status because of a commercial activity that "exceeded the benchmark of insubstantiality." For one example, see `https://law.justia.com/cases/federal/appellate-courts/F2/893/529/268074`.

Keeping Charities and Politics Separate

REMEMBER

You can encourage the public to vote, but if you're not an advocacy group, don't rock the boat by rallying and campaigning for candidates. Also, never use your website, newsletters, or any other form of advertisement to persuade people to vote for a particular candidate.

You have only one vote — yours, not your organization's — and although you have the right to exercise that vote, you don't have the right to use your nonprofit organization to persuade other people how to exercise their votes. Using your organization to sway beneficiaries to vote for a specific candidate is something you can't do if you want to keep your tax-exempt status, not to mention maintain a positive image for both you and your organization.

Getting Free Support

Running a nonprofit definitely has its challenges. One way to make everything a tad easier is to rely on the free support available. I suggest you start with the following services first:

>> **IRS:** Although you may not realize it, the IRS actually *does* want to help you. The IRS offers many free classes to assist you with operating your nonprofit. For convenience, many courses are offered online, and conference calls can be scheduled to discuss issues that directly affect your organization.

For example, the IRS offers several free training courses to assist you with filling out and complying with Form 990. If you need help with your payroll or tax forms, or if you have other burning tax-related questions, you can contact the IRS for answers. For more information about training provided by the IRS, visit www.irs.gov.

>> **SCORE:** Assess your organization's weaknesses and search for ways to strengthen its capacity by taking advantage of the many free services offered by SCORE, a nonprofit association that counsels small businesses in the United States. If you need a little help with the overall operations of your nonprofit, contact SCORE online at www.score.org.

>> **National Council of Nonprofits:** This organization has many tools and resources to help you run your nonprofit more efficiently and effectively. Its website has a fantastic section on starting and running a nonprofit, fundraising, marketing, and a whole lot more! Find out more about the National Council of Nonprofits at www.councilofnonprofits.org/running-nonprofit.

>> **NonprofitReady.org:** This organization provides more than 500 course and certification programs that are completely free. Grant writing and keeping your nonprofits books are just two that you may be interested in. Find out more at www.nonprofitready.org.

Chapter **23**

Ten Tips for Keeping Your Nonprofit Viable

Accountability is more important than ever in the nonprofit sector. People think very hard about where to invest their hard-earned dollars. To maintain good standing in your books, you need people to see your organization as a solid investment option. Long gone are the days when a person's word was their bond. Today you have to prove that you're a good steward if you want to receive donations; after all, people aren't going to give money because of what you say but rather because of what you do and stand for.

Consider changing your mindset of doing business as usual. The fundraising method you've been using for years may not appeal to donors today. Every gift you receive is an investment in your programs and services, so letting donors know that you're valid and trustworthy is important.

Although your community programs and services are the reason behind your nonprofit, its daily operation depends on much more than just these programs to survive. Clearly, the organization can't flourish without finances; after all, money is the oil that keeps the wheels turning. This chapter gives you a few tips to help keep your head above water. It addresses the importance of balancing your books, maintaining a positive reputation, planning your future, and making the right connections.

Keeping Your Books Balanced

A good financial manager wants to evaluate how they're doing at the end of each month. To keep a good handle on your income and expenses, have your bookkeeper do monthly financial reports. If you opt to use computerized accounting software (see Chapter 9) you can pull figures more frequently because accounting software programs make updates across your books automatically. When you enter or change something in one field, your system should be able to show the results of that change in terms of your overall financial situation.

WARNING

Not keeping balanced books can cost you overdraft banking fees and cause you to lose your credibility with creditors and vendors. As a result, your organization may receive a bad credit rating, which can affect your organization's financial future. (See Chapter 7 for how to balance your organization's checkbook.)

Waiting until the end of the year to put your accounting in order isn't good financial management. Suppose you have an emergency situation to resolve (like an unexpected computer crash or a pipe that bursts), and you need to quickly evaluate how much money you have and compare that to how much money you need to correct your problem. Maintaining current accounting records with balanced books can save you a lot of time during an emergency, not to mention during tax season.

Filing Paperwork with the IRS

No matter the size of your nonprofit, you have to file the appropriate paperwork with the IRS to keep your nonprofit status active. I walk you through selecting the correct form (Form 990-N, Form 990-EZ, or Form 990), the deadline to file and requirement to file the return electronically in Chapter 16.

The decision about whether to file Form 990-N, Form 990-EZ, or Form 990 is based on the gross receipts your organization generates in a given year and your total assets for that year. The thresholds and limits that determine which version of Form 990 your organization files are subject to change, so make sure to check the IRS's website (www.irs.gov/charities-non-profits/annual-filing-and-forms) for the most up-to-date information.

Paying Bills on Time

Your organization has a reputation in your community. As a good steward, you actively take steps to maintain its good name. To keep a good reputation (and to keep your books accurate and up to date), pay your utilities, rent, employees, vendors, creditors, and all other bills on time.

Just as paying bills on time is important for your own personal credit score, paying bills is also important for your organization's credit score. If you find that you can't meet your obligations, approach your bank about taking out a short-term working capital loan or call your creditors. Many of them may be willing to work out some type of arrangement to keep you as a customer.

TIP

Use reminders on your phone and calendar, to help you remember to pay your bills on time. Nowadays, you have no excuse for forgetting to be on time.

Exploring New Fundraising Ideas

No matter how large or small your nonprofit is, you don't want your fundraising efforts to become stagnant. Without fundraising money coming in, your nonprofit's bottom line can suffer. To keep fundraising fresh, consider new ideas.

TIP

The best way to come up with new ideas is to brainstorm with your staff and board members to generate innovative ways to bring funding to your nonprofit. Forget about what everyone else is doing and figure out your own approach. Have your staff and board members list any ideas that come to mind. Remember that no idea is bad. You'd be surprised at the types of innovative ways you have to keep your head above water in terms of fundraising. After you finish brainstorming, break down the list and look at the ideas to determine which ones work best for your nonprofit.

Watching Your Nonprofit's Bottom Line

Keeping a close eye on your nonprofit's bottom line (see Chapter 17) is key to survival, as is review of a current statement of cash flows (see Chapter 19). You need money to run programs, to pay employees, and to keep the lights on. Make sure you know how much money your nonprofit has at all times by keeping a close eye on your checkbook balance.

Pay close attention to donation trends and track your nonprofit's budget on a monthly basis. Compare what happens to what you expected to happen and take note of the differences. By doing so, you can identify signs and signals that may indicate a problem — these signs can be very helpful in the future.

Looking for New Funding Streams

Believe it or not, your nonprofit is a business. Your board needs to have a clear vision about the future of your organization and how much money you need to get there. To get there, take the following steps:

>> **Analyze.** Assess where you are now and where you want your nonprofit to be in three to five years.

>> **Evaluate.** Look at where you are currently and project future funding needs.

>> **Plan.** Create a strategic funding plan that clearly sets the path for your future.

>> **Research.** Look at your current funding streams and research what untapped funding sources are out there that are new or that you failed to consider in the past. Visit https://donorbox.org/nonprofit-blog/find-grants-for-your-nonprofit for tips and sources to find grant opportunities for your nonprofit.

Getting Grant-Writing Training

Federal grants provide an important way for your nonprofit to receive money to pay for its programs. However, you can't receive federal grants if you don't know how to correctly apply for and request the grant money, so knowing how to write grants is to your advantage. Your nonprofit helps your community by supporting people through services, and because you qualified for nonprofit status, you're eligible for grant funding.

Find out where to find grants, how to apply for grants, and how the federal grant system works by getting some training. Contact your local university or United Way office to find out where training is available. If you prefer online classes, you can get quality online training through ed2go; find a list of online courses at www.ed2go.com. If you prefer books, take a look at *Nonprofit Management All-In-One For Dummies*, by Beverly A. Browning et al. (Wiley).

If you prefer more personal attention, consider hiring a grant consultant to mentor and coach you through the grant-writing process. A grant consultant can give insight about the process from the perspectives of both the granting agency and your organization. Knowing more about grant writing increases your chances of receiving grants and placing your nonprofit on the government's grant map.

TIP

Gain the knowledge you need to relieve some of your financial worries by getting some help. Put together a team within your organization to find out more about how corporations, foundations, and government agencies award grants. Take advantage of the information available to you at www.grants.gov. Read the information on that site about how to narrow your search for grants before you start going down the crowded grant highway. (Check out Chapter 11 for more about federal grants.)

Obtaining an Independent Audit Opinion

Getting an independent financial audit report is often a requirement if you plan to apply for grants. An independent auditor is a certified public accountant (CPA) who audits your organization's financial records and offers a professional opinion about whether your records are prepared in accordance with the required standards and free of material errors or fraud. Your independent auditor must be unbiased in the view and performance of professional services. (For more about selecting and hiring an independent auditor, see Chapter 14.)

Updating Communication Strategies

To operate in an effective fashion, your nonprofit must have a communication strategy that accurately reflects your mission statement to increase awareness in your community and raise funds. Key to this is reaching your target donor with an attractive support appeal.

To be successful, consider multiple outreach tactics. Don't limit yourself to just a mailer campaign or calling/texting past donors. Have a robust social media presence. This process can be very time consuming at the beginning, so research what social media platforms similar nonprofits in your area use and build from there. I also recommend the 16-page online PDF about "ePhilanthropy" at https://catalog images.wiley.com/images/db/pdf/0471691887.excerpt.pdf.

Attending Networking Activities

To have a viable and fluid nonprofit, you have to network with the important people and organizations in your community. In other words, you need to reach out to your city's chamber of commerce, United Way office, city council members, representatives, congresspeople, governor, and other key people and organizations.

The reason is simple. These organizations and people, such as the chamber of commerce and the governor, have a good understanding of the direction in which your city is moving, in terms of new industries and other forms of growth. You need to know which new companies are coming to your city so you can present your cause to them and, hopefully, solicit their support. Furthermore, other organizations, such as United Way, usually know most of the other nonprofits in your state. Using their resources, you can find out more about your competition. However, don't think of this as a turf war of us against them; instead, think of your competition as your allies.

Index

donor payments, in cash receipts journal, 119

donor restrictions

about, 280, 283

net assets and, 82

recording, 124

donor tools, in Aplos, 146

Donor type (QuickBooks), 138

donors lists, maintaining, 342

double-declining balance depreciation, 38–39

double-entry accounting, 29

drawdowns

federal grants, 194–198

requesting, 198

due diligence, 218

dues and subscriptions account, 86

duplicate checks, 103

E

economic entity principle, 216

Electronic Federal Tax Payment System (EFTPS)

about, 248

paying quarterly payroll taxes with, 260

electronic funds transfer

paying quarterly payroll taxes with, 256–260

tracking for federal funds, 197

Electronic Handbooks (EHBs), 195

embezzlement, 40

employees

bonding, 41–42

contract, 263–264

exempt, 252

insuring, 41–42

nonexempt, 252

receiving Form W-4, Employee's Withholding Allowance Certificate from, 248–249

segregation of duties, 41

setting up payroll accounts for, 246–247

theft by, 343–344

training accounts for, 86

employers, use of Form W-4, Employee's Withholding Allowance Certificate by, 249–251

employment relationships, 219

end-of-year forms

about, 261

Form W-2, Wage and Tax Statement, 261–262, 263

Form W-3, Transmittal of Wage and Tax Statements, 262–263

engagement letter, 219

entries

adjusting, 96–97

adjusting prior, 126–128

ePhilanthropy, 322, 353

equipment account, 95

errors

in audit findings, 242

correcting, 97–100

finding and addressing in checkbook, 115–116

establishing

chart of accounts, 19

checks and balances, 40–41

evaluating

data on statement of activities, 285–290

numbers on statement of financial position, 301–303

risk factor of audits, 236

executive directors, as internal users, 46

executive managers, as internal users, 46

exempt employees, 252

expenses

about, 14–15, 30–31

account for, 95

allocating, 319–322

identifying common, 109–111

recording, 124–125

recording in ACCOUNTS, 148–150

on statement of activities, 284, 286–287

subtracting, 108–111

external auditors, 224–225

external users, of financial statements, 46–47

F

FAF (Financial Accounting Foundation), 53

Fair Labor Standards Act, 247, 252

fair market value, 36

insurance and bonding account, 86

intangible assets, as a long-term asset, 297

interest income, in cash receipts journal, 119

internal auditors, 218, 224–225

internal controls

about, 225, 236, 342

segregation of duties through, 240–241

setting, 40–42

Internal Revenue Code (IRC), 174, 209, 243, 345

Internal Revenue Manual (IRM), 243

Internal Revenue Service (IRS)

on charitable contributions, 108

examination by, 243–244

filing paperwork for, 350

free support from, 346

income rules of, 106

IRS 990 series, Return of Organization Exempt from Income Tax, 212

IRS Publication 15-T, *Federal Income Tax Withholding Methods,* 249–251, 254, 255

letter of determination, 237

Online Ordering For Information Returns and Employer Returns, 263

statute of limitations for, 62

statutes, 212

Tax Exempt and Government Entities (TE/GE) division of, 243

internal users, of financial statements, 46

Intuit. *See* QuickBooks

inventory account, 94

inventory methods, 335

investing activities, cash flows from, 309, 311–312

Investing section, of cash flow statement, 55

investment income account, 84

investments, as a long-term asset, 297

irregularities, in audit findings, 242

J

journals

about, 118

cash, 118–121

as components of manual systems, 63

correcting entries, 99

defined, 31

examples of entries, 124–129

general, 123–124

maintaining, 15

purchases, 121–123

in QuickBooks, 139–140

recording entries, 93–94

sales, 121–123

L

labels, in spreadsheets, 65

land account, 80, 95

lawsuits, on notes to financial statements, 335–336

leasehold improvements account, 80

ledger paper, as component of manual systems, 63

ledgers

correcting entries in, 99–100

defined, 31

in QuickBooks, 141

legal services account, 85

letter of determination, audit reviews and, 237

liabilities

about, 13–14, 30

in chart of accounts, 80–82

contingent, 336–337

on notes to financial statements, 337

on statement of financial position, 295, 298–299, 301

liability insurance, 50

licenses and permits, as a common expense, 109

Listing Reports (ACCOUNTS), 151

Little Green Light, 152

long-term assets, on statement of financial position, 297

long-term debt account, 82

long-term liabilities

about, 81

on statement of financial position, 299

losses, on statement of activities, 284–285

loyalty, to your organization, 290

M

maintaining

accrual-based books, 34–35

compliance, 20, 210–212, 345

data integrity, 70–71

donors lists, 342

operating budgets
  about, 153
  balancing cash flow with, 153–167
  creating, 155–166
  identifying, 31
  importance of having, 154–155
  performance of, 166–167
operating cash flow (OCF) ratio, calculating, 313
operating income, 30
Operating section, of cash flow statement, 55
operational audit, 18
organization
  federal grants and, 20
  maintaining, 160–162
organization operating budget, audit reviews and, 237
organizational bylaws, audit reviews and, 237
organizational goals, 158–159
original cost, 36, 215
other assets
  about, 79
  as a long-term asset, 297
other expenses account, 86
Other Matters section, 225
other unpaid expenses, as a current liability, 298
outstanding checks, 114–115
overdraft fees, 106
oversight audits, 233–235
overtime, adding to payroll, 252–253
owners' equity. See net assets

P

paper trails, maintaining, 18, 343
paying
  bills, 351
  federal taxes, 22–23
  quarterly payroll taxes, 256–260
payments, in cash disbursements journal, 120
Payroll (QuickBooks), 136–137
payroll journal, in QuickBooks, 140
payroll tax expense account, 85
payroll taxes payable
  account for, 81
  as a current liability, 298
payroll/payroll taxes
  about, 245–246
  accounting for contract employees, 263–264

calculating FICA taxes and deductions, 254–256
  as a common expense, 109
  completing end-of-year forms, 261–263
  deducting taxes, 247–254
  paying quarterly taxes, 256–260
  setting up accounts for employees, 246–247
performance
  of desk audits, 231–232
  of operating budgets, 166–167
performance audit. See operational audit
Performance Progress Report (PPR), 184
permanent accounts, 327
petty cash account, 80
physical assets, 39–40
planning independent audits, 227
plant, property, or equipment (PPE), 35
pledges receivable, 290
politics, separating from charities, 346
posting to general ledger, 94–96, 125–126
prepaid expenses
  account for, 97
  as a current asset, 296
prepaid insurance account, 94
preparing financial status reports, 199–203
printing and binding account, 85
prioritizing goals, 157–160
private donations, 103
private donors, as external users, 46
private gifts and grants account, 84
private grants, 188
professional help, hiring, 212
profit-and-loss statement. See statement of activities
program expenses, on statement of functional expense, 320
program income, 185
program spending ratio, calculating, 323–324
Program Support Center (PSC), 194
progress reporting, 204–206
prohibited relationships, 219
public donors, as external users, 46
public grants, 188
public watchdog groups, as external users, 47
publicly held company, 211
purchases, in cash disbursements journal, 120
purchases journal, 121, 122–123

Q

qualified report opinion, 229

quarterly payroll taxes, paying, 256–260

QuickBooks

  about, 68–69, 135

  customizing, 136–138

  pros and cons of, 135–136

R

ratios, calculating using statement of functional expense, 323–324

reading, federal grants and, 20

realized gains and losses, on statement of activities, 284–285

reasonable cost, 180

receiving grant audit findings, 226

recording

  accounting transactions, 89–100

  assets, 36

  automatic bank drafts, 111

  in cash journals, 118–121

  costs in chart of accounts, 84–86

  debits and credits, 16

  direct bank drafts, 111

  donor restrictions, 124

  expenditures, 124–125

  expenses in ACCOUNTS, 148–150

  income in ACCOUNTS, 148–150

  journal entries, 93–94

  process of, 89–93

recordkeeping

  about, 59

  creating manual systems, 61–63

  manual system compared with computer software, 60–61

  software programs, 68–70

  spreadsheet programs, 63–68

  system security, 70–73

references, for employees, 344

reigstering, with state authorities, 211

reliability principle, 216

Remember icon, 3

rent, as a common expense, 109

repair and maintenance account, 86

reporting

  audit findings, 241–243

  financial position, 291–303

  layers in Aplos, 143–146

  progress, 204–206

  in QuickBooks, 141–142

  requirements for, 198–206

Reports, Backup, and Help action (ACCOUNTS), 149

requesting drawdowns, 198

Research Performance Progress Report (RPPR), 199, 203

restricted fund, 35

restricted net assets, on statement of financial position, 300–301

restrictions, 181

retained earnings. *See* net assets

revenue

  about, 14–15, 30–31

  account for, 95

  in chart of accounts, 83–84

  on statement of activities, 283, 286–287

revenue recognition principle, 216–217

reversing entries, 332–333

risk, of audit, 228

risk factor, assessing for audits, 236

rows, in spreadsheets, 65, 129

rules, for federal grants, 21–22

S

salary and wages payable

  account for, 81, 85, 95

  considerations for payroll, 251–252

  as a current liability, 298

sales discounts, 119–120

sales journal, 121–122

sales tax payable, 120

salvage value, 36

SAM.gov, 175

sanctions, 181

Sarbanes-Oxley Act (SOX) Act, 20, 217–220

savings accounts, 80

SCORE, free support from, 346

Section 501(c)(3), 271

Securities and Exchange Commission (SEC), 53, 211

security, of systems, 70–73

supplies and materials account, 85

support, free, 346–347

suspension, 181

system security, 70–73

T

tags
  budgeting by, in Aplos, 146
  configuring in QuickBooks, 138–139

tangible assets, as a long-term asset, 297

Tax Exempt and Government Entities (TE/GE) division, of IRS, 243

taxes
  deducting from payroll, 247–254
  thresholds for Form 990, 266

Taxes (QuickBooks), 136–137

Technical Stuff icon, 3

TeleCheck, 104

templates, setting up for financial reporting, 130–131

temporary accounts, 326

temporary services account, 85

ten-key adding machine, with tape, 62

terminology, 12–16

terms, in purchases journal, 122

third-party software, for backup, 73

time, tracking, 317–319

time and attendance (T&A) reports, 317–319

time sheets, 317

timeliness, for filing Form 990, 267

Tip icon, 3

total assets, on statement of financial position, 297

total liabilities, on statement of financial position, 301

tracing donations, 48–49

tracking
  cash, 34
  cash with statement of cash flows, 306–307
  electronic transfer of federal funds, 197
  fund balances in ACCOUNTS, 150–151
  grant expenses, 238–239
  nonprofit donations, 103–108
  time, 317–319
  transactions, 19

trading securities, 36

transaction fees, as a common expense, 110

transactions
  about, 89
  accounting cycle, 93–100
  classifying, 12–15
  debits and credits, 92–93
  methodology of, 15
  process of recording, 89–93
  recording, 89–100
  tracking, 19

transferring grant money, 195–197

transposition error, 98

travel account, 85

travel expenses, as a common expense, 109

trial balance
  defined, 91
  finding, 96

U

unallowable cost, 180

uncollectible accounts, 290

unconditional contributions, 11

undeposited receipts account, 80

unearned revenue account, 81, 97

unemployment insurance contribution account, 85

Uniform CPA Examination, 10

Uniform Grant Guidance (UGC), 222

Uniform Guidance (UG), 178

United Way, 268

unqualified report option, 229

unrealized gains and losses, on statement of activities, 284–285

Unrelated Business Income Tax (UBIT), 106

unrelated business taxable income (UBTI), 256

unrestricted net assets, on statement of financial position, 301

updating communication strategies, 353

U.S. Department of Labor, 181, 247, 264

USASpending.gov, 184

USB drive, for backup, 73

user privileges, limiting, 72

utilities
  account for, 85
  as a common expense, 109

V

W

Y

About the Author

Maire Loughran is a certified public accountant and small business owner. Her professional experience includes four years of internal auditing for a publicly traded company in the aerospace industry, two years as an auditor in the not-for-profit sector, and even some experience as a U.S. federal agent! Her public accounting experience includes financial reporting and analysis, audits of private companies, and forensic accounting.

A full adjunct university professor for 20 years, she has written *Auditing For Dummies*, *Financial Accounting For Dummies*, and *Intermediate Accounting For Dummies*, and is a contributing author for *Accounting All-in-One For Dummies* and *Nonprofit Management All-in-One For Dummies* (all published by Wiley).

Dedication

To my much-loved son, Joey, who served his country aboard the U.S.S. *Harry S. Truman*. I am prouder of you than mere words can ever describe. And to my late husband, Jeff, so long gone from our lives but never absent from our hearts.

Author's Acknowledgments

To the Ursuline nuns and Jesuit priests who provided me with a stellar education, and to my parents, who selflessly footed the bill.

To Barb Doyen, the literary agent who started me on this adventure.

And to Elissavet Topalidou and Elizabeth Kuball for all their fantastic advice, editing, and follow-through.

Publisher's Acknowledgments

Executive Editor: Lindsay Lefevere

Editorial Manager: Murari Mukundan

Editor: Elizabeth Kuball

Technical Editor: Elissavet Topalidou

Production Editor: Saikarthick Kumarasamy

Cover Image: © nd3000/Getty Images